D1297000

JOE HUMPHREYS'S
TROUT TACTICS

JOE HUMPHREYS'S
TROUT TACTICS

Joseph B. Humphreys

Foreword by George W. Harvey
Illustrated by George Lavanish

STACKPOLE
BOOKS

Published by
STACKPOLE BOOKS
5067 Ritter Road
Mechanicsburg, PA 17055
First published in paperback in 1981
First published in hardcover in 1993

Printed in the United States of America

10 9 8 7 6 5 4 3 2 1

Portions of this book first appeared in slightly different form in *Fly Rod & Reel*.

Library of Congress Cataloging-in-Publication Data

Humphreys, Joseph B., 1929–
    [Trout tactics]
    Joe Humphreys's trout tactics / Joseph B. Humphreys : foreword by
George W. Harvey : illustrated by George Lavanish. — Rev. ed.
        p.   cm.
    Includes index.
    ISBN 0-8117-0874-8
    1. Trout fishing. 2. Fly fishing. I. Title. II. Title: Trout
tactics.
SH687.H774   1993
799.1'755 – dc20   93-8106
                                                               CIP

CONTENTS

Foreword 7

Acknowledgments 10

Preface to the Second Edition 12

Preface to the First Edition 14

Part One

1 Finding Trout 19

2 Nymph Fishing 48

3 Wet Flies 84

4 Streamers 105

5 Dry Flies 118

6 Brush Fishing 143

7 Night Fishing 163

Part Two
1 Water Temperatures 187
2 Nymphing 191
3 Wet Flies 209
4 Streamers 213
5 Dry Flies 218
6 Night Fishing 240
Index 254

Foreword

During the past three decades I have had the opportunity to meet and the chance to fish with many of the great anglers and outdoor writers and flytiers of our day. Some were excellent all-around fishermen with the long rod. Many wrote a lot better than they could fish, and much of what they wrote was passed down over the years by others or by fly anglers who were not adept with the pen. Even today, with all the current literature available, competent all-around fly anglers are few and far between—just about as scarce as fly-caught twenty-pound brown trout.

Since I started teaching angling courses in 1934 at Pennsylvania State University, I have had many students who were excellent fly tiers and fly fishermen. To the best of my knowledge, none has ever progressed to the extent that the author of this book has.

I have known Joe Humphreys for the past twenty-five years and have spent many enjoyable days astream with him. He has been an avid fisherman from the time he was a youngster, and spent most of his early years prospecting on Pennsylvania's internationally famous Spring Creek. This was a great laboratory for a beginner because of its stock of stream-bred brown trout. Anyone who could learn to fish the long, placid, meadow pools successfully with their conflicting currents could take trout from any stream in the world.

In addition to this great limestoner there were dozens of beautiful and productive freestone and mountain streams available within a short drive of his home in State College, Pennsylvania. He spent many hundreds of hours fishing these small, brushy streams and became so proficient that few could compete with him on any type of water.

During his college days, Joe enrolled in the course "Techniques of Fly-Tying and Trout Fishing" that I was teaching, and he was so far ahead of the other students that I asked him to assist the other students who were having difficulties with the techniques of fly-tying.

From that time to the present day we have been fishing together. During those formative years Joe was eager to learn; no one ever had a more inquisitive mind! He would follow me on the stream or we would fish side by side; soon all the techniques I had learned over the years by trial and error he acquired in a very short time. We discussed water temperature and its effects on the feeding and movement of trout and its importance to the trout fisherman, the techniques and methods of fishing wet flies, dry flies, streamers, nymphs, and terrestrials, and yes—night fishing for big browns, too!

During Joe's college years he was an excellent athlete and afterward became a very successful wrestling coach in the secondary school system. While teaching physical education and coaching in the Bald Eagle, Pennsylvania, school system he organized and taught the first angling and casting course at the secondary school level in the United States.

During the late sixties I began to think about retiring, and I wanted to see the angling course I had initiated and taught at the university continue. There was no one on the staff who had the knowledge or expertise to carry on the angling and casting courses, so I had to look to the outside.

Of all the people I knew, only one could fill the job, and that was Joe. I hired him two years before I retired and he worked with me as an assistant for one semester and then he handled all classes by himself. Today, in my estimation, he is one of the best fly-tying and casting instructors in the nation. He has held numerous angling clinics, had numerous articles published in sporting magazines, lectured to many sportsman's and angling clubs, and received the Order of the Hat award from the Harrisburg Fly Fisher's Club.

So you see it is both a privilege and a pleasure for me to write the foreword to this book. Joe is my friend. There is no finer trout angler I know of. I have said many times that if I was ever to compete against any two-man team in a fly-fishing contest and had to pick my partner, it would be Joe. Of course,

I would never be a part of such a contest and I merely mention this to illustrate my confidence in Joe's abilities.

Fly-fishing for trout is the most enjoyable, challenging, exciting and exasperating individual sport in the world today. One can spend a lifetime with the sport and never master all the techniques—there is always something new to master. Every stream you fish is different. Every time you take a step up or down a stream conditions change. This is why we must learn to read the water and be versatile enough to change tactics as each situation demands. To really enjoy the sport to its fullest you must be able to fish throughout the season under all types of water conditions. In other words, you must be a complete angler.

Joe Humphreys *is* a complete angler. What he has written in this book should be invaluable not only to the neophyte but the seasoned angler as well. I recommend it highly to all who want to learn more about this great sport.

GEORGE W. HARVEY

Acknowledgments

To acknowledge my wife Gloria would seem a commonplace, but she is uncommonly patient and supportive both as a professional helper and companion. Her continued understanding over the course of twenty-three years has been a real fisherman's blessing.

Among all the people I could acknowledge for their contribution to this book, none is owed more, or more willingly given, than to George Harvey. George, a legendary fisherman in his own right, has been my professional mentor and more: a friend. He was responsible for sponsoring my present position as an assistant professor at the Pennsylvania State University, and for much of my personal growth as an angler. I look forward to many more years of his companionship and advice on the stream.

I acknowledge the influence of my father, still the finest man I have ever known, who took time to introduce me to fishing. His affection, understanding, and encouragement have been a constant in my life through over fifty years. At this writing, he's ninety-one, still sharp, wry, and wise, and I enjoy his company as much as that first trip on Spring Creek.

I also thank the editors of this book, Jerry Hoffnagle and Craig Woods. Their aid and editorial talents often made the difference.

George Lavanish, a generous talent and a friend, whose own work decorates and enhances this book.

Sharon Bernard, who first said, "Why don't you write a book?" — and never stopped until I did. Her photographs also appear herein.

Tom Miller, another believer, and a fine fishing friend.

Paul Blankenhorn, whose photography and encouragement saw me through the project.

To my sister Helen Daniels, who traveled from California to Pennsylvania and traded visiting time for typing time on this manuscript.

Daryl Awarjo, Vance McCullough, and Bruce Bronsdon, my associates, for their assistance in the underwater research on nymphs.

Bernard "Lefty" Kreh for his advice and encouragement.

Dr. Richard Parizack, for his contributions to the geological research.

The dean of the Physical Education Department, Karl Stoedefalke, for his professional support and assistance.

Ralph Dougherty, friend and fishing companion, for his advice and casting help — when I needed it.

Lee Hartman, friend and believer.

Dr. Bob Butler, for his help and advice.

The Cortland Line Company, Dick Jennings and Leon Chandler, for their kind assistance in my ideas.

The Fenwick-Woodstream Company and Lloyd Riss, for their encouragement contributions.

Finally, many thanks to Tom and Martha Greenlee, Mardy Gentry, Ed Shenk, Katharine Holsworth, Jim Butler, and Chet Fish.

Joe Humphreys

PREFACE TO THE SECOND EDITION

I was a teacher for thirty-two years and a wrestling coach for fifteen of those years. My experience includes nineteen years teaching such angling rudiments as fly fishing tactics, casting, and fly tying.

My teaching and coaching philosophy has had three key elements:

• Know your material. Be an expert. You owe it to your students.

• Drill students until the material becomes second nature. We learn by doing things over and over.

• Be fair, be compassionate, and have a sense of humor.

The streams I've fished most for over half a century can be challenging and unforgiving. They're the hard-fished limestone and freestone waters of central Pennsylvania. You either adjust to their changeable conditions or you fail. It's mainly a mental game.

I love the challenge of finding creative approaches to catching "uncatchable" fish. By necessity, I've become an explorer and pioneer along various avenues to fishing success.

For instance, in what some younger readers will think of as "the old days," I at first found myself stumped in my desire to roll the bottom with nymphs in the deep, fast, and heavy runs of Penns Creek. The substantial diameter of fly line (and its consequent resistance to currents) made it impossible for me to get nymphs to the bottom and control a timely roll. Eventually I found success with monofilament and its small diameter, using weight on the business end. Back then, at the end of the 1940s, monofilament was just coming into being and was basically unknown, still a mystery to the multitudes who later invaded the streams with spinning gear.

Volumes have been written on float time and how to mend a fly line. Much of it is misinformation that can reinforce mistakes and take away the angler's joy—catching fish. Within these pages, I pass along insight and technique on these aspects of fly fishing. I'm not aware that anyone else has ever covered some of these points.

Bill Koll, a three-time NCAA wrestling champ, was one of the greatest ever to walk onto a mat. I had the privilege of working with him when he was head coach of wrestling at Penn State. I'll always remember something he once told me: "The most primary and basic moves, refined and done to perfection, become the most advanced moves."

So within the pages of Part Two of this book, I don't just pass along to you new and useful ideas and tactics, I also take some of the sound basics and repeatedly aim to instill upon you their importance. In casting, for instance:

- Shock the forward stroke.
- Now drop your elbow and the rod tip.
- Look for that 90-degree angle between rod tip and line.
- Adjust the leader for the immediate conditions you face.
- Lead the nymph through the drift with the rod tip.
- Adjust the amount of weight on the leader and within the flies for the depth and speed of the water you're about to fish.

My hope is that this approach will help you refine your basics into advanced tactics that will help you enjoy trout fishing even more.

PREFACE TO THE FIRST EDITION

I was fly-fishing a stretch of a big eastern limestone stream. The hatches were shifting gears and I was caught in the middle, grasping for answers and flies. To make things worse, another angler moved in above me and caught three trout. Then he slipped in below me and landed two more. He stopped briefly to chat and said, "You're Joe Humphreys, aren't you?"

"Yes," I replied, although I would gladly have been someone else just then.

"Heard you speak in Williamsport, Pennsylvania, at a Trout Unlimited seminar. It looks like the expert is having trouble today," he said.

"Expert I'm not, having trouble I am," I replied with a laugh.

This encounter reminded me that the heart of my fascination with fly-fishing is its unpredictability—the way in which even a familiar situation can suddenly turn into a completely new challenge.

I suppose that's why I've always resisted the worn formulas and rules that are handed down from angler to angler and in many fly-fishing books. I think the best teacher is the stream, the best way to learn is again and again.

Following set rules and formulas only limits the flexibility of the angler. He stops thinking for himself. He relies on what someone else has said instead

of the stream itself for the answers to angling problems. Fly-fishing is a thinking man's sport and, in our day, a constantly changing one. Yet I often hear well-meaning anglers and angling teachers make hard, generalized statements that just *ain't* so. These statements may be based on a one-shot observation or a good-sounding idea or what someone else has said. They are not formulated by personal experience or tested by time and common sense.

When my friend George Harvey was retiring from Pennsylvania State University as angling professor, I kidded him about all the fish he'd catch now that he had more free time. George looked at me and made this comment, "After sixty-five years of fishing and thirty-eight years of teaching fishing, now maybe I'll have some time to learn something about this game!"

Another friend of mine, Lefty Kreh, who is also a fine fly fisherman, once told me that there are two words you remove from your vocabulary when fishing: "always" and "never." The stream before you is constantly changing. If you are not flexible and confident enough to adapt to changing conditions on the stream, you are sure to fail.

One season, just before Memorial Day, my friend Lewie Weaver and I were fishing a large Pennsylvania limestoner. Lewie was a confirmed and talented live-minnow fisherman. That evening he was casting his minnows well and on the retrieve he was teaching them to do the Charleston. The minnows performed admirably, but the fish were not impressed.

A few Green Drakes were coming off, and I had nymphed up a couple of decent brown trout. Darkness was edging daylight when the hatching began in profusion: previously inactive trout now were boiling on the surface.

I quickly changed to a deer-hair drake pattern and immediately took a trout. Below me was Lewie. The air around him was filled with flies and bad language. Lewie had practically thrown his arm off casting minnows, to no avail, and now was vainly trying to throw a dry fly with soft level, monofilament. The fly and the monofilament line kept collapsing in a pile directly in front of him while trout were doing their own Charleston all around him. Lewie was silent as we walked the railroad tracks back to the car that night.

"Lew," I said, "You ought to try this fly-fishing." He nodded, stopped, lit a cigar, and puffed a cloud of smoke into the air just as the old Pennsy had done for years.

I relate this story not to argue for the superiority of fly-fishing as an angling method, but to emphasize the fundamental importance of flexibility to successful trout fishing. I learned a lot about fly-fishing from bait fishermen like Lewie, and it is important for today's angler to take his lessons wherever they can be found—not just in books (even this one) or from "experts," but from hard work on the stream.

My purpose here is to help you shorten the time it takes to solve fly-fishing problems on the stream by introducing tactics that have been proven by my test of years astream. Some of these tactics may seem familiar; some may startle at first; some may seem irrelevant to the real end product of fishing fun. But they all have one thing in common: they work consistently. They help take fish. But above all, I want to demonstrate why it is important to approach trout fishing with an open mind—to help you become flexible when fishing. I hope that when I describe tactics that have been effective for me that these tactics will not become set rules or formulas for you. They are the result of my forty-five years fly-fishing on trout streams, but they are most valuable to you if you can combine them with your own techniques and observations.

If fishing without formulas sounds like work, I promise it also has rewards in more fish hooked and more opportunities to take trout. For me, there's more to fishing than the display of equipment and discussing nifty theories and knowing the Latin names of the insects our flies imitate—there's the sudden tug on the line that says you've found the answer to a particular angling problem.

PART ONE

1

FINDING TROUT:

A Matter of Degrees

A Pennsylvania farmer went into the general store and was sold a thermometer, which he took home and hung on a bush.

The next morning was the beginning of a cold snap that sent the mercury plunging. The first time he looked at the thermometer, the farmer counted ten frosty degrees above zero. The second morning the temperature had dipped to one above zero. The third morning there was a five-degree drop, and by the end of the week the thermometer recorded a frigid ten degrees below zero.

The following week the farmer went back to the store for supplies and the proprietor asked him how he liked the thermometer. "I had to smash the darn thing," was his reply.

"What on earth for?" asked the storekeeper.

"Well if I wouldn't have, we'd have all froze to death!"

The farmer, like the great majority of trout fishermen, didn't understand how a thermometer can be helpful. To most anglers, the very idea of using a thermometer on the stream seems to take the fun out of going trout fishing. A thermometer seems like just another piece of excess baggage, a part of the work-a-day world fishermen want to escape.

If we look more closely, these anglers who shun the idea of the thermometer break down into two groups. One group is the legions of anglers who fish the stocking-truck odds. Early in the season in stocked streams most of the available cover holds unselective hatchery fish—at least until June. After June, when the fish disappear, these fishermen hang'up the rod. These anglers seldom, if ever, ask *why* the fish take, but simply *where* the truck has been, a question the thermometer can't answer.

The second group is comprised of ambitious anglers who fish the same streams regularly year after year and have learned what spots produce fish on what patterns throughout the season. But they've acquired this knowledge of local streams by rote. Like the anglers who follow the stocking truck, they don't necessarily understand *why* a certain hole or undercut always holds a fish or two, or why most of the fish seem to disappear after the middle of June. "It just works that way," they say, "—or at least it did last year."

What both groups of anglers have in common is that they are following a routine, a superficial pattern. They are not responding to the stream's changing signals, the most important of which is water temperature. For both groups of anglers, theirs may be a pleasant enough way to fish, but it is not the best and most accurate way to find fish consistently throughout the season.

A thermometer is actually the modern angler's geiger counter, a way to locate fishing water throughout the whole season (although as we will see it accomplishes this in different ways in the early season than in the middle and late part of the season). Even many thorough anglers shy away from a thermometer almost as if it were going to tell them something they didn't want to know. But a five-dollar stream thermometer can make more fishermen better fishermen than any other single piece of equipment available today. The best angler using a two-hundred-dollar fly rod to cast a super-realistic mayfly imitation on an 8X tippet over a five-pounder holding under a flowering bough won't have a chance of taking that trout if the water temperature is eighty degrees Fahrenheit. In fact, there probably aren't *any* feeding fish in the entire stream at that temperature!

Where trout hold and how and when they feed, both on a daily basis and throughout the season, can be plotted by water temperature. I'm talking about a temperature range of about twenty degrees that determines trout feeding patterns and angling success.

A trout's metabolism increases with the rise in water temperature. When its metabolism increases, the trout's demand for food is greater. Optimum temperatures for fishing are in the sixties, because at these temperatures a trout's demand for food is greatest. On the other hand, as the water temperatures rise into the seventies, the fish's body chemistry dictates a change to a higher oxygen level and a lower temperature – and the requirement for food lessens.

Each species of trout is active within a narrow temperature range that is biologically most suitable for it. Though the following temperatures will hold true for most trout, wherever they are found, one may find exceptions.

The native brown trout usually feeds at temperatures from forty-five degrees to seventy degrees. The best range is normally from fifty-six degrees to sixty-five degrees. A single best temperature for feeding browns, if you wanted to put your finger on one such temperature, would be sixty-one degrees.

Rainbows have nearly the same feeding range, forty-five degrees to seventy-five degrees, but their range is more flexible. Native or holdover rainbows might feed readily at forty-three degrees to forty-five degrees, the optimum temperature again being sixty-one degrees. Brook trout are adapted to colder water and are active at temperatures ranging from forty-five degrees to sixty-five degrees. The optimum temperature is fifty-eight degrees.

"Optimum feeding temperature" does not mean in the case of brook trout, for example, that fifty-eight degrees is the only temperature a brookie will take an emerging mayfly. It simply means that the closer the actual water temperature is to this reading, higher or lower, the more actively the fish is likely to be feeding and moving from cover. Its metabolism is in high gear at this temperature. For all trout species, fifty-eight degrees, fifty-nine degrees, sixty degrees and up to sixty-five degrees are the up-and-at-em trout-stream temperatures.

These temperatures have been confirmed by readings taken on thousands of fishing trips on streams across the country by myself and by my friend George Harvey. The result is that we can now fish "by the degrees" all season long and especially in the midseason and late season, when success on the stream becomes a matter of one or two degrees.

I must stress, however, that these temperature ranges are *general* guidelines for the angler, and exceptions occur. For example, each individual fish, like a human being, has its own critical point. One person might face heat prostration at a temperature of one hundred degrees while another may not notice especial discomfort at the same temperature. I've caught rainbow trout in water that was seventy-eight degrees, yet have been unable to raise browns at a temperature of seventy degrees. It is also important to note that at the higher end of the trout's tolerance, if a fish is played too long and then released, it's chances of survival are affected. A chemical change takes place in the fish's system during the struggle that may cause irreversible damage.

Several years ago I was fishing the Pere Marquette in Michigan with Buff Smith for wild rainbows using big nymphs and imitation spawn. We were having fair success even though it was late in the season. There had been some rain the day before and the warmer precipitation had raised the water temperature from forty-two to forty-four degrees—close to the lower end of the rainbow's feeding range. We were catching fall-run steelhead, some as large as ten pounds, and small, first-year wild fish as well as ten-inch to fourteen-inch brown trout. The entire population of fish was working as if each fish knew the season was drawing to a close and it was the last chance to store up reserves for winter.

The next day a cold front moved in; it snowed five inches and the water temperature dropped to forty degrees. For the following two days we fished the very same riffs and pockets with the same patterns, plus dozens of others, and could not take a good fish. The temperature change of four degrees put those trout on the inactive list.

In that situation, of course, the thermometer offered no solution, only a demonstration of how critical water temperature is. But as we'll see, the thermometer can help the early- or late-season angler find active fish—perhaps by locating warm spring water entering a snow-fed stream. It will help him know *when* and *where* to fish.

Besides its relationship to the trout's metabolism, the temperature of the stream gives the angler a general reading of other essentials, especially oxygen level and the activity of the food chain itself. The food chain—including insects, plants, and microscopic stream life—also responds to water temperature. At low temperatures the trout's activity is determined by the activity of the food chain. At high temperatures it is limited by the availability of oxygen. When an active food chain and a suitable oxygen level are present, as they usually are at sixty-one degrees, peak conditions for feeding and fishing occur. Knowing where and when these conditions are likely to be found is the problem that the thermometer can solve.

Temperature is a catalyst for the food chain, from algae to plankton, nymphs, dace, and trout. But because we tend to limit our observation and our fishing strategy to what we see, we often miss the real cause-and-effect relationship. In practice, most fishermen depend on insect activity to give them a visible clue about where and when to fish. Even the regularity of the hatches, however, obscures the important fact that it is the water temperature (resulting from a combination of sunlight intensity, water volume, air temperature, altitude, and some geological factors) that sets the trout's feeding alarm off.

The Green Drake hatch in Pennsylvania limestone streams, according to local lore, "always occurs on the last weekend in May." This schedule probably has as much to do with the fact that anglers have a long holiday weekend to fish as it does with the actual record of past hatches, which is also why I call it the "Memorial Day Classic." In any case, it is certain the flies do not emerge in honor of America's war dead. In fact, I have had success fishing Green Drake patterns as early as May 22.

The emergence timetables in books are so generalized because of all the variables involved. An unseasonably cold spring, for example, can throw a hatch back by two weeks, leaving the weekend anglers saying, "The Such-and-Such hatch didn't come off this year." Like heck it didn't.

Conditioning

It is easy to understand how low temperatures affect the metabolism of the trout, but the oxygen factor is a less obvious one. Generally speaking, the higher the temperature, the less oxygen remains in flowing water. In kitchen-chemistry terms, the dissolved oxygen steams off as water temperatures rise, though we can't see it until it literally reaches the boiling point. Actually, oxygen can be depleted by a combination of factors, including temperature, acidity, weed growth, pollution, and chemical spills. Most fish kills are the result of the loss of oxygen due to one or more of these factors—not high water temperature per se. But mortality for trout will occur around eighty degrees for rainbows and browns and at seventy-six degrees for brookies if the oxygen is removed.

To illustrate this temperature-oxygen relationship, let me relate a story told to me by a friend of mine, Daryl Arawjo. Daryl was working at a summer camp in Connecticut, which included a swimming impoundment created from a small stream. At the outlet of the dam, the stream dropped down a shaded chasm. The water coming off the top of the dam was eighty degrees, but as it tumbled through the chasm it became so heavily oxygenated that Daryl caught brook trout in the seventy-five-degree water at the bottom of the falls. Even though this temperature is just short of a temperature that could cause mortality, those brookies had enough oxygen to compensate for the higher temperature.

Daryl's brook trout also survived the high temperatures in their stream because of another important survival principle: conditioning. Conditioned trout can often provide exceptions to the activity and water-temperature ranges. As we have seen, water temperature is the trigger for feeding activity. In most parts of trout country, different streams reach optimum feeding temperatures at different times each day. The trout will respond best when the optimum temperature range is present. But under some conditions there is very little temperature fluctuation throughout the season, and fish become adapted to extreme temperatures. In the Rocky Mountains, for example, trout live and feed in some streams and ponds fed by snow runoff in water that never rises above forty-five degrees. These fish are conditioned to the lower and narrower water-temperature range and feed actively in water that would turn their lowland cousins into underwater zombies.

I fished Avalanche Lake in Glacier National Park one summer several years ago. The snow runoff in the warmest part of the day was feeding water into the head of the lake, and the water was so cold that I could barely stand in it for longer than a minute or two. Yet fish moved actively to wet flies fished a foot or so under the surface. I took thirty or forty trout that afternoon, sometimes doubles on two wet flies. Had I been fishng Pennsylvania's Penns Creek at the same temperature, I would have been lucky to snag a fish!

Native trout can also be conditioned to feeding temperatures at the other extreme, up to temperatures in the high seventies, as Daryl's fish were. Bob Brown, who supervised Pennsylvania's cooperative fishery program for many years told me of one fish nursery at Clarks Creek near Harrisburg in which trout grew in races where high temperatures reached eighty degrees plus— well above usual mortality temperatures. But the rate of water exchange in the races was so high (up to five times an hour) that these trout survived and fed actively. Like Daryl's fish, they had enough oxygen coming in to survive the high temperatures and to feed actively.

Conditioning can take other forms, too. In the case of hatchery trout, fish become conditioned to feeding overhead. From the time the little fish are fed in jars on starter food until they reach the size of an inch and a quarter or more and are put in raceways, they are fed from overhead. In the raceways they are fed pellets from overhead by machines. What happens to these fish when they are put in the stream?

I was fishing a stocked stream early in the season with plenty of company. None of the anglers were having any luck. Then one fisherman picked up a handful of stones and threw them across the pool. Almost immediately everyone began catching fish. The hatchery trout were so conditioned that the overhead activity triggered their feeding response to flies, cheese, spinners, and gravel in spite of the fact that the water temperature was forty degrees. The conditioned feeding instinct overwhelmed the natural feeding temperature range. If you examine the contents of a stocked trout's stomach, you often find hemlock needles, seeds, corn, or water beetles—whatever happened to be at the right level when the feeding response was triggered.

Early-Season Temperature Strategy

Unless fish have been conditioned to another feeding trigger, their feeding activity is determined by the fluctuation of temperature in the stream. When it enters their feeding temperature range, the lunch whistle blows. Most streams fluctuate throughout the year, cold temperatures being prevalent in the early spring due to snow runoff. The warming trend begins as early as June, followed by extended periods of warm air temperature and low water. In most parts of trout country, the stream temperature changes significantly throughout the day, the warmest temperatures being registered in the early afternoon. The range of temperatures also changes throughout the season so that the feeding alarm may go off at a different time of day in April than it does in June. By August, the peak daytime temperature may be thirty degrees higher than the peak temperature in April.

The characteristic we are keying on is *fluctuation* in temperature, something that is not as crucial on most limestone creeks and spring creeks, such as the Letort in Pennsylvania or Armstrong Spring Creek in Montana. Some big western and midwestern freestoners maintain a fairly constant water temperature by a combination of snow runoff and springs at lower elevations, or geologic character that has the same constant-cooling effect as springs do.

Locate tributaries that flow into a trout stream in the early season, such as this one to the right and left of the tree in the middle of the photograph. They'll come in handy in midseason.

This photograph shows the same scene as in the previous photograph in late season when the tributary no longer flows overground. But it still contributes cold water to the main stream by flowing underground. *Photo by the author.*

Even so, as these streams spread out in the valleys, temperature fluctuation becomes a factor in late summer. The principle is what's important. Learning to interpret water-temperature information on your streams is the key. The flexibility a thermometer gives you can be translated into changing tactics as the temperature pattern changes across the season.

The early-season scenario that follows is very generalized, but this pattern fits many eastern and midwestern freestone streams as well as spring creeks exposed to high temperatures over their course.

April traditionally opens the trout season in the East and Midwest. In northern latitudes it may mean ice and snow and water temperatures of forty degrees in the morning. At temperatures that cold, native and holdover fish are still in low gear. You could bounce a nymph off their noses without a strike. It is possible to catch trout in slower water, especially hatchery fish, with overhead flies, spinners, or bait. When I am fishing for native trout, I work the slicks and backwaters where I can get a fly down to the bottom and move it slowly and naturally. Rather than getting out on the stream at sunrise to beat the other anglers, I wait until 9 or 10 A.M., when the water temperature may have risen to forty-five degrees, perhaps even forty-eight degrees. At these temperatures the food chain has been activated; the warming trend has started nymph movement, and the trout are starting to become a little more interested in feeding. By noon the water temperature may be forty-eight degrees and the native fish are starting to move a little bit; I may pick up a fish or two on wet flies.

By 1 P.M., the water temperature may be up to fifty degrees. The other anglers have been fishing streamers or live bait, but have been moving them too fast. Some may have started fishing with wet flies without results because they also have not allowed a slow, natural drift. But as it approaches the warmest part of the day the water temperature reaches fifty-one degrees, the threshold of trout feeding activity. From noon until 2 P.M., many anglers are taking an extended lunch break — exactly when they should be fishing. At 1 or 2 P.M. in the afternoon, I test the water at fifty-one degrees, perhaps even fifty-two degrees, and the fish have started to put it into second gear. The warming trend of the water has further activated the food chain, including the trout. I've started to take fish on nymphs and wet flies drifted from bottom to top.

By 3 P.M., other anglers are ready to fish again; they've had their siesta. They pull out some new patterns they tied last winter, and get excited again. They may get some action yet. The optimum water temperature for the day is still present, but it starts to drop rapidly; by 4 or 5 P.M. it's two or perhaps three degrees lower than it was at noon. The fish go off their feed as quickly as they went on. Lunch is over. It was a short feeding period, but with the help of the thermometer I could tell when I was most likely to pick up fish.

As we go on through the end of April into May, water temperatures are rising and water levels are dropping. The optimum feeding temperature extends through a greater and greater part of the day. Let's go fishing on a typical day in early May.

I get up at 6 A.M. and test the water temperature. It reads forty-seven degrees; right away I put on nymphs and start to work the bottom — where the action is. By 8 or 9 A.M., the water temperature may already be up to fifty-two degrees, or at least fifty degrees. Nymphs are becoming more effective as the food chain moves into low gear. By noon the water temperature is up to perhaps fifty-eight or sixty degrees, and the food chain has moved itself into second gear. Flies are starting to hatch, nymphs are struggling to the top. Wet flies take fish from 10 A.M. until about 1 P.M., and perhaps throughout the afternoon.

At the warmest time of the day, about 2 P.M., the water temperature reading is sixty-two degrees. I know this is optimum feeding temperature; flies are hatching, trout begin to break, and I begin to fish on the surface. But the early-season sun doesn't have the staying power that it will have in June, and

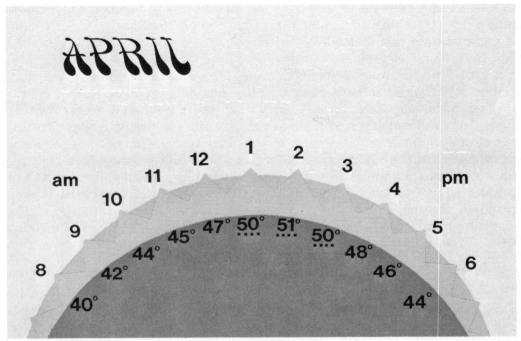

This illustration shows typical water-temperature fluctuation during a twelve-hour period in April.

by 4 or 4:30 P.M., temperatures drop back into the lower fifties again and the trout become inactive.

Later in May the water temperatures may rise to fifty-eight degrees, even sixty degrees in the evening, so the prime fishing time is late afternoon and evening. By the end of May the water temperature has begun to reach the optimum feeding range by 11 A.M., and I have my choice of fishing nymphs or dry flies.

As we can see, the feeding temperature range has begun to last longer during the day, and also the peak temperature in late afternoon becomes higher and higher. On our typical variable-temperature stream, that means that soon the peak water temperature will be higher than the upper end of the trout's feeding temperature range. Then the pattern of temperature response will shift, and the trout will wait for lower temperatures to begin feeding.

The regularity of the major early-season hatches masks the fact that through June, at least, it is the water temperature that is the catalyst for all this fishing activity. Over more and more of the early-spring days the water has remained within the fifty-degree to sixty-five-degree range of activity for trout.

Now all that will change. As we move into June, by 10 A.M. the water temperature may be seventy degrees or higher on an open, lowland, freestone stream, and it is likely that this temperature will rise another eight degrees — well beyond the trout's comfortable feeding range:

Then one day in late June, when the air temperature is eighty-five degrees, anglers may return to their favorite stretch of a broad, open, freestone stream with the same flies that killed them last week. It's about the same time of day, say 10 A.M., and they cast to the same pool where they brought up good fish last weekend. They cast upstream and downstream with nymphs, wets, terrestrials, and streamers. All they get are a few chubs. This is the stream they have been fishing all season with greater success each trip. Now it almost seems as if the fish have packed up and left.

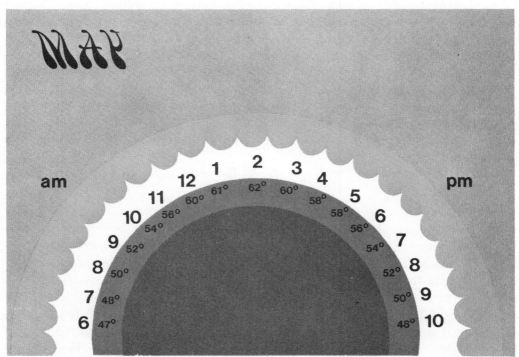

Typical water-temperature fluctuation during a sixteen-hour period in May.

Midseason and Late-Season Temperature Strategy

My father and I were fishing the Loyalsock, a freestone stream in northern Pennsylvania. It was the second week in June, and we had gone up for the weekend. We fished all the first day, and we caught chubs, fallfish, and rock bass, but no trout. We had fished apart and I was tired and discouraged. Toward evening I stopped fishing to pull the camp gear together.

Just then I saw a man wander down to the stream and prepare to fish. I decided to spend the time waiting for my father to return chatting with this fellow. He mentioned to me that he had done extremely well the night before and had taken his limit of nice trout. I didn't know whether to believe him or not. He assured me that the trout were still there and suggested that I wade out below him in the riffs and wait. I did.

By 9 P.M., the temperature had already dropped noticeably, and a few flies had started to hatch. I saw a fish break in front of me. And then another. I reached for my fly box and opened it and was about to select a fly when I noticed trout were milling at my feet. It was like a hatchery pool—I couldn't believe what I was seeing! I put a weighted nymph on and dropped it in front of me. A trout came up and grabbed it even before the nymph had a chance to settle. I played him in without much ado, and then promptly caught several more. My father came up below me and I told him to move out into the riffles, and though he had difficulty seeing to put a fly on, he did raise a few fish. That was an exciting discovery. The fish were there all the time, waiting for the right combination of temperature and oxygen before they came out of the pools and began feeding in the super-oxygenated riffles. This was the key!

The next weekend, the third weekend in June, Dad and I were so confident in this discovery we didn't even fish before sunset. When we finally gave up at 1 A.M., we had caught nothing.

It seemed as though the fish had left the stream completely.

By midseason, the question the angler should ask with the thermometer shifts from "When should I go fishing?" to "Where are the trout?" or actually, "Where is the cool water?" The answer may look more obvious than it is.

The low water of midseason exposes more and more pocket water and pools. But by June 1, most pools and runs on most eastern freestone streams, and parts of some limestone and spring creeks, have warmed considerably by midday, and may be marginal for trout throughout the day. So the angler's first task is not directly to find fish, but to find water temperatures that fish can survive in. Even freshly stocked fish seem to disappear. They're still around, of course, but they've been forced into smaller and smaller zones of

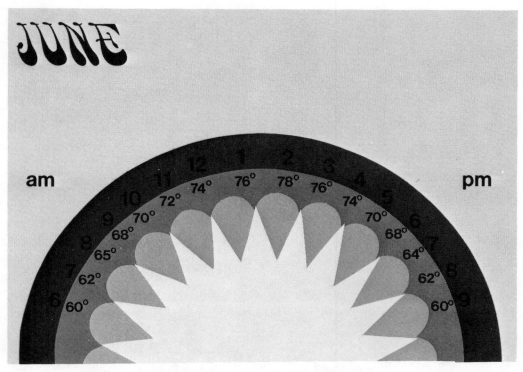

Typical water-temperature fluctuation during a fifteen-hour period in June.

cool water, sometimes out of the main stream entirely. Unless they are trapped by dams or otherwise conditioned to high temperatures, the fish migrate to find this water. This migration is very much like a synchronized group movement, such as a salmon run. But the driving instinct is not reproduction; it is the need to find comfortable temperatures. Although there is no set pattern or travel route, the fish seek that combination of optimum water temperature and oxygen level almost as keenly as the salmon seeks its home stream. You can follow the fish using the thermometer.

The starting gun seems to be a drop in oxygen content in the main streams. Your thermometer won't read oxygen content, but when the water on a free-stoner is seventy degrees or higher, you can bet the oxygen level has dropped. The best cast you can make is to your car to look for cool water. If you start catching rock bass or chubs, as my father and I did on the Loyalsock, or you are sure there are brook trout in the stream but you can't raise one, those are signs that the migration has begun.

Typical water-temperature fluctuation during an eighteen-hour period in July and August.

The migration actually breaks down into two stages. When the water temperature reaches seventy to seventy-four degrees and upwards and holds there for four to eight hours, the trout begin to move. Seeking oxygen and cooler temperatures, they congregate at the head of the pool, where aerated water comes in from broken water above. Some fish may move deeper into the pool where they have a balance of lower temperature and oxygen. The water temperature at night or early morning may still drop as low as sixty-five degrees, so the fish can move out of the pools and into the riffles to feed. During the day, they return to the deepest part of the pool or pocket water or heavy riffs and hold.

This pattern will continue as long as nighttime temperatures dip into the feeding range. Now night fishing comes into its own, though the exact schedule for the feeding impulse can be as variable as it is during the day in early season. As the season progresses, the conditions for feeding activity become more and more restricted on streams that are subject to temperature fluctuations, which form a great majority of the streams we fish.

The Second Stage

The reason Dad and I didn't find fish in the riffles *or* in the pools on our last trip to the Loyalsock was because of the second phase of migration, triggered by higher temperatures. The second stage of the migration usually results in the fish moving a greater distance from their early-season holding water—and perhaps out of the main stream entirely. Trout move to the mouths of tributaries and feeder streams or they move over spring holes where there is colder water coming from underground. Sometimes the fish are blocked by low water at the mouths of tributaries. The trout are likely to be concentrated wherever cold water sources come in, and for the night fisherman it can be like catching fish in a barrel.

When a good rain pulls the water levels up, the trout will move up the tributaries or up the main stream above what I call the "cutoff point." The cutoff point simply means that point above which trout can find optimum tem-

Early Morning 65° Late Evening

Temp. + O₂

In the first stage of the migration, trout move into the riffs at the head and tail of a pool for cooler, oxygenated water or they will seek the proper combination of temperature and oxygen content in the deeper parts of the pool. In early morning and late evening when the water temperature is sixty-five degrees, they will move out to feed.

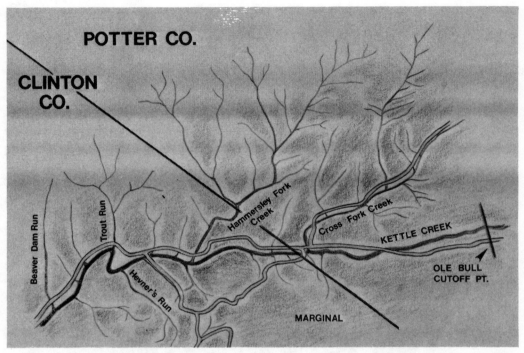

Locating cutoff points and cold-water tributaries helps insure that you spend your fishing time in the most productive spots.

peratures in the stream. This cutoff point is a boundary line that can be found on any marginal waters. The point to remember is that the trout will seek it like spawning salmon seek their home waters—and so must the successful midseason and late-season angler.

It's also important to remember when fishing in tributaries that the tributary itself may have a cutoff point. I once had a fisherman say to me, "Well you told me to move up into the tributaries if I couldn't find fish in the main stream. Well I went up a tributary and didn't catch a fish."

"How far up the tributary did you go?", I asked. "Did you take a thermometer and check the temperature?" The lower portions of tributaries can also be marginal in late season.

The best illustration I can offer of how water temperature zones literally define fishing opportunities in midseason and late season, both in the time and the place, is an experience I had on the upper Delaware. Tom Miller and I had fished for three straight days at the confluence of the East Branch and the West Branch of the Delaware. The East Branch came in at eighty degrees.

The West Branch averaged between fifty-seven degrees and fifty-eight degrees during those three days, which is acceptable feeding temperature.

We fished the West Branch mostly at night, and raised exactly three trout there during our whole stay. We tried nymphs on the bottom, we worked drys, streamers, everything. The only time those fish fed was during a brief time slot from 8 P.M. to 8:30 or 8:45 P.M. It was almost as if they were conditioned to a half-hour-long hatch that we couldn't see. Before and after that time we couldn't raise a fish.

We knew that the East Branch was far too warm but we didn't know where the spring holes might be found, and we didn't have the time to look. We continued to concentrate on the West Branch. Finally on the fourth night, at 2:30 A.M., we found sixty-three-degree water below the confluence of the two branches. It was in one straight alley of water. That lane was no more than ten feet wide, a long "pool" of cool temperature in the middle of the river. When I threw my flies out and swung them across that sixty-three-degree lane, I picked up a fish every time. Once we found the right spot, I hooked a sixteen-inch brown, lost another fine fish, and hooked a third good one within ten minutes. This is a graphic illustration of trout finding a comfortable temperature zone and staying in it.

This is also an example of natural water-temperature patterns. But man-made conditions can also shape the temperature pattern. On many western and southern rivers, such as the South Fork of the American River, and the Sacramento, in California, a series of dams feed cold water from the bottom of impoundments, keeping the water below the dams a constant sixty-one or sixty-two degrees. Below the dams, for a stretch of perhaps a half-mile, the water is almost sterile in terms of insect life. But if you go down the stream another mile, there is increasing insect life and fish, and the temperatures are good feeding temperatures: a constant sixty-one to sixty-five degrees year-round.

In the two examples above, there are obvious clues that suggest the shape of the temperature zones and where to prospect with the thermometer: the confluence of cold water with warm water of the branches of the Delaware and a three-hundred-foot high dam.

In midseason and late season, the feeding alarm goes off in increasingly smaller sections of the stream where cool water and oxygen come together to create acceptable feeding conditions. By mid-June on eastern freestone streams, these occasions are becoming more and more limited, both in time and space.

In midseason, I like to explore the upper reaches of my favorite early-season stream and begin prospecting for the cutoff point, and if it's keepers

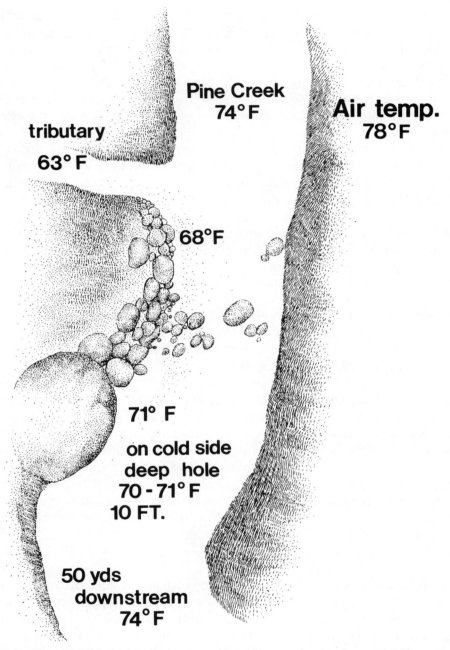

Pine Creek
74°F

Air temp.
78°F

tributary

63°F

68°F

71° F

on cold side
deep hole
70 - 71°F
10 FT.

50 yds
downstream
74°F

Tributaries that may be cooler than the main stream will mix with the water of the
main stream and affect the water temperature.

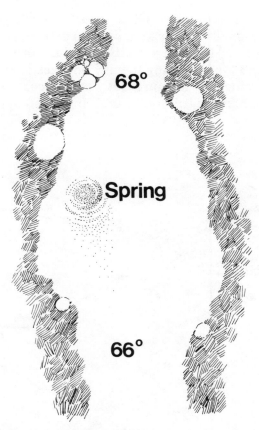

Entering springs can affect the water temperature of a stream below the point where they mix with the water of the stream.

I'm after, up the tributaries I go with terrestrials. And I know where the spring holes are on the main stream, so I can jump from "cold spot" to "cold spot" on my way.

Actually, by late June or July I prefer to limit my fishing to night forays. Often as I come on the stream at 10 or 11 P.M., most anglers are just leaving. At night, the cool mountain air drops down into the valleys, lowering the water temperature the critical two or three degrees into feeding range. In August I've had to wait sometimes until 3 or 5 A.M. for the air to mix with water and oxygen in the pools and riffles. Many a night I've gone home and had a cup of coffee, watched the late movie, and then gone out to find the temperatures I know will turn the fish to feeding.

Limestone and spring-fed streams, of course, hold temperatures more consistently, and it's usually there I'll see most other anglers by August and September for some good terrestrial and nymph fishing. By the end of September, the optimum feeding range starts to occur during the daytime again, and it lasts longer and longer during the day on freestoners with a good water supply and active springs. By season's close, the process is complete, although many fish will remain in the tributaries until high water comes in the fall.

In the midseason and late-season periods you can locate the cool-water

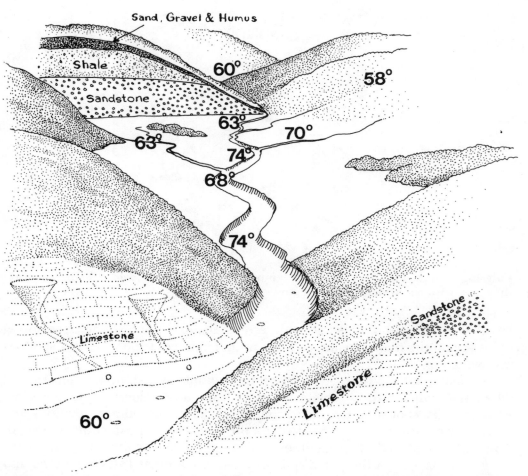

Profile of a freestone stream and its tributaries: from mountains to meadow note that as it enters limestone country, limestone springs and outcroppings contribute colder water.

areas that may hold trout by finding spring holes, cold-water tributaries and feeder streams, and rock outcroppings.

Spring holes often reveal themselves by patches of white sand on the bottom. You can also scout for spring holes in the early part of the year when frost is still on the ground. The warmer spring water, perhaps fifty degrees, plus the warming trend of the sun will foster aquatic-weed growth early in the season. Deep cuts in mountain ranges may funnel cold water from the water table to adjacent springs that emerge in a stream as a spring hole, so such formations and contour nearby to the stream are good places to check for spring holes. In the summer you can prospect for spring holes by wet wading in a pair of sneakers, swimming, or drifting down a stream until you feel a sudden change in water temperature. Also, if you suspect that there is a spring hole in a large pool, take the water temperature at the head and tail of the pool. If, for example, at the head of the pool the temperature is sixty-eight degrees and at the tail of the pool the temperature is sixty-six degrees, you can be sure there is a significant spring entering the stream in that pool. Finally, you can locate spring holes on a cold winter day because the warmer spring water will steam in the area above it.

It is important to remember that when a spring or a small tributary enters a larger stream, its water mixes very rapidly with the water of the main stream. Even a large spring entering a deep pool may only change the water temperature three to five degrees. The mixing action of the larger stream prevents a radical change, but sometimes that is enough to make a difference in a trout's feeding response, especially if it's a large cold-water source.

The importance of feeder streams to late-season angling is obvious, but even if the tributary seems to have dried up in late summer, chances are that the same little stream is still flowing underground and creating a cold spot in the main stream where it enters.

In limestone country, water collects in underground caverns and emerges through limestone outcrops. In freestone shale areas, the water will run along the contour of the rock formation (unlike limestone, shale is impervious, i.e. it doesn't absorb water) and emerge where the stream bisects the formation, which is usually marked by a ledge or rough outcrop of rock. Trout will be lying close to these ledges in a suitable temperature zone.

Limestone Trout Streams

Limestone streams are basically spring-fed streams. They usually start at the base of a mountain and gather water throughout the valley floor from a

A limestone outcropping from which cold water may emerge and join a trout stream. *Photo by Paul Blankenhorn.*

Stream bisecting a shale outcropping. Spring water seeps along the contour of the rock formation and joins the stream. *Photo by the author.*

Cold-water spring holes often reveal themselves as patches of white, bubbly sand. *Photo by the author.*

In the early season the combination of warming air temperatures and warm spring water often fosters growth of aquatic weeds, as shown on far edge of this stream. *Photo by Irv Swope.*

Where the main stream bisects deep cuts in mountain ranges you are likely to find cold-water spring holes entering the main stream. *Photo by the author.*

Sink holes in limestone country can hold water for extended periods of time before releasing it to the underground water table. *Photo by the author.*

myriad of sink holes that feed underground water to the stream. Some of these sink holes hold water on the surface for extended periods of time, sometimes for weeks, because their outlets are small or restricted. The water slowly filters down into the underground table, cooling all the while, and eventually it returns to the surface via springs. I like to compare the mechanics of this process to a giant coffee percolator where the water filters down through a myriad of sink holes to the coffee pot below and then comes out through the stem as cold water springs.

Underground limestone pockets hold water in varying amounts and release this water very slowly into the underground water table. The practical point for anglers is that the process is a continuous one and that the water is

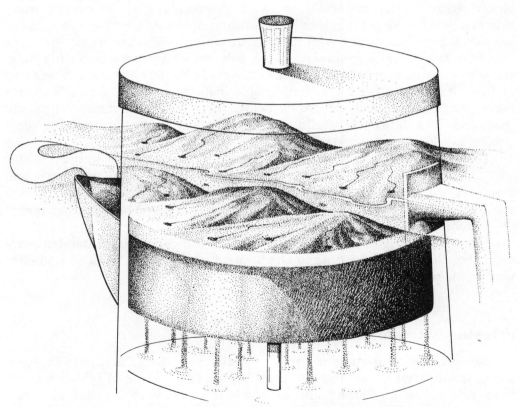

The dynamics of water release to limestone streams can be likened to the working of a coffee percolator. Water seeps into the "pot" and is released through the "spout" as cold, enriched water.

constantly being cooled. The result is a constant volume of water being released at a constant temperature.

Limestone streams are always valley streams, even though they may flow through mountain ranges (as Penns Creek in Pennsylvania does) and cross sandstone, granite, and shale areas. Although they may be warmed by impoundments, channelized sections, or flow considerable distances between cooling springs, these streams with intermittant springs maintain the unique limestone quality of more constant temperatures as long as the mean annual *air temperature* falls within the temperature requirement for trout. It's not likely that a limestone stream in the desert country of Israel will support trout, but it is highly probable that a limestone stream in Pennsylvania with springs along its course will have a good trout population.

Where a large cold water tributary enters the parent stream, even if the parent stream is marginal water, the water temperature, on the cold tributary side can be a few degrees colder for a considerable distance below the confluence of the streams, even with the mixing action of the waters.

Tom Miller and I frequently night fish one of Pennsylvania's big limestone streams together, I'd always take the cold tributary side which was two or three degrees colder for a considerable distance downstream. We always fished one big hole a quarter mile below the junction. Invariably I caught trout and Tom didn't. He would say to me, "I just don't understand it, am I fishing my flies too fast, too slow?"

I'd say, "Tom, I don't know, are you giving them a touch with the rod tip?"

"Yes, I'm doing that," he'd reply. "Are you fishing them very slow and deep?" I'd ask. He'd answer that he was. I'd say, "Well, I don't know, I can't take the rod in my hand and fish for you." I knew that 2 or 3 degrees meant the difference between catching and not catching.

Tom was a beginning fisherman then—he knew about water temperatures, but didn't take the time to check them, and I could think of no better way to make a point.

Freestone Streams

Eastern freestone streams of the Appalachian Range originate in sandstone, granite, shale, or sand and gravel formations, some of which are less porous than limestone strata, and so tend to fluctuate with the amount of surface water available. Sand and gravel areas on the top of eastern mountains hold water like a blotter and release it gradually into the underground water table, much as limestone does. However, as opposed to the percolating effect

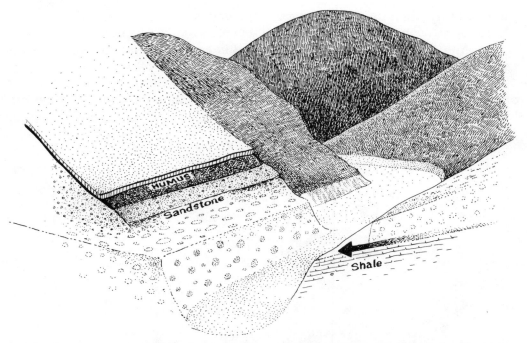

Profile of a typical freestone mountain stream. The sandstone strata can be likened to a giant sponge, seeping water from the water table. The shale outcropping also contributes runoff water from underground.

of sink holes, gravity creates a funneling effect in freestone country. In the mountains, the water channels naturally down through the draws and gaps. The sandstone layers of the mountain ranges go deep under the mountains, they are the roots, but are porous and act like a sponge collecting the water to replenish and restore the underground water table. Where the rivers and streams cut through the gaps and bisect the water table, springs drain the system and pump life into the mountain streams.

But due to the porous nature of sandstone the underground formations release water rapidly and unless supplied by a good amount of precipitation, the water table drops rapidly. When it drops below the level of the stream that bisects it, the stream drops in level. So because of its geologic base, there is a greater fluctuation in water level, greater than the limestone streams that originate in the valleys.

If freestone mountain streams spread out in the valley floor below, and there is a decrease in water level and an increase in air temperature in mid-

June and July, then the main stream in the valley becomes marginal and temperatures, as we have seen, rise into the seventies and the trout move for colder water. Any fisherman who understands this knows where to look for fish, and when.

Sand and gravel areas of the Midwest drain the rolling woodland contour of upper Michigan and Wisconsin in a constant underground water system that feeds the streams with intermittent springs that bubble and seep from

Mountain freestone streams drain an area in a fashion similar to a funnel.

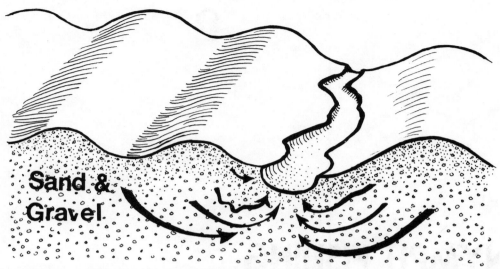

Sand and gravel areas drain and release water to freestone streams via springs on some midwestern streams. Examples of such streams are the Manistee and Au Sable in Michigan.

underneath and along the course of the rivers. The springs keep the levels and temperatures from fluctuating radically. The Au Sable, Manistee, Pere Marquette, and Betsey rivers in Michigan hold trout year-round.

Western freestone streams that drain the high-altitude ranges depend on the snowpack and rainfall to maintain the levels and temperatures suitable for trout. Without the snowfall and other precipitation, many western freestoners become marginal. Like eastern freestoners, the funneling effect of the western ranges induces fluctuating levels. The snowpack maintains the temperature.

I'd never take a trip without knowing first if it's freestone or limestone water I'm fishing. If it's freestone water, I want to know something about the topography and the geology of the area. In July in the Appalachians, from Georgia to Maine, where the streams broaden in the valleys below, you might be hard pressed to find a trout in freestone waters. And the same goes for many far western streams in years when there is very little snowfall. A fisherman who knows what to expect in a given geological area already has a basic plan of attack. The more he knows about the geology of the stream, the better he can formulate a strategy through the season.

2

NYMPH FISHING:
Getting to the Bottom

George Harvey and I were invited to fish a private stream near Williamsport, Penn-sylvania. Our host, John Youngman, sent us to a beautiful stretch of pocket water that tumbled along hemlock-lined banks at a mountain's edge. George, my fishing mentor and frequent on-stream companion, and I engage in friendly competition whenever we fish together. That day, George laid the ground rules. "We'll fish nymphs upstream and alternate pockets and pools," he said. "You take the first one."

I nodded and waded into the pool, stripped twenty feet of line off the reel, and flipped a cast up and across the glide. It was rather a deep, swift glide, so I thought a short cast with a tight line and quick retrieve would be the answer. But even with the weighted fly I was using, I had trouble getting the nymph deep enough in the strong current.

No strikes. Fifteen minutes later I noticed that George was growing impatient. I waded to shore without saying a word, thinking that the fish just weren't there.

George took the next pool. He stood far back from the tail and shot a cast to the head. He stopped his rod sharply at the 10:30 position, and the weighted nymph bounced back in the air, under the line, and dropped into the water. Then, holding the rod tip high, George stripped in the loose line as it drifted back to him. He continued to lift his rod tip as the nymph drifted closer. I noted that this technique kept the line straight and tight between his hand, the rod tip, and the fly all the way—but the drift was never completed. The line twitched and a highly colored, fourteen-inch, native brown trout soon succumbed to the pressure of George's fly rod.

But I was still determined to do things my way. "So George found a taker and I didn't," I thought, "so what?" I'd show him that my tried-and-true techniques of fishing nymphs on a short line could also produce. My next cast was to a perfect pocket behind a midstream boulder. I moved off to the side of the pocket and laid a short, upstream cast tight to the boulder. I extended my arm and led my nymph through the pocket—again and again.

Nothing. Tired of waiting, George slipped around me and poked another cast into a pocket similar to the one I was fishing. Out of the corner of my eye I saw his rod arc and vibrate. "Another one! Damn the lucky . . ." I thought to myself. But after George had released the fifth and then the sixth trout, I knew luck had little to do with it.

That afternoon, after lunch, George laid it out for me. "You see," he said, "to use your short-line cast you had to get too close to the trout. You scared them before you ever made a cast. That water is low and clear. Even more important, your nymph never reached them in the deeper glides and pockets."

He went on to explain to me the mechanics of his cast. "Shoot to the top of the pool or the pocket, then check your cast high so that the weighted nymph actually tucks back under the leader and hits the water and gets to the bottom before the drag of the floating line has a chance to begin lifting it. When you complete your cast, keep your rod tip up. That way you can further eliminate drag by keeping as much line as possible off the water. And, of course, you must keep the line between you and the nymph as tight as possible. As the nymph comes back to you, make a steady retrieve of the line as you raise the rod tip. That keeps you in touch with where the nymph and the trout really are.

"Also, when you shoot to the top of the pool or pocket, your nymph covers the bottom of the pool from one end to the other. Covering that distance you have a better chance for a fish than merely working the tail, and you also have less chance of spooking the fish. It's just good common sense that the nymph enter the water first.

"Here, wade down below that pocket water at the breast of the dam and cast up behind that farthest boulder." Following his instructions, I used a short, sharp stroke that gave me the "tuck"—and the cast did exactly what he said it would. "Now keep that tip up!" instructed George.

His instructions stopped there and so did my line: a beautiful fifteen-inch brown interrupted the drift.

The tuck cast has produced for me a thousand times since, and from it I have developed other casts and nymphing techniques to form a complete system of fishing with weighted nymphs that works admirably under almost any stream condition. Four elements are critical to nymphing success: proper depth of presentation, natural drift of the fly, line control and a good imitation. The right combination of fly, tackle, and technique allows the angler to fish nymphs with consistent success, and the tuck cast is an integral part of successful nymphing.

Getting the fly to move naturally underwater is perhaps the most important aspect of nymph fishing, and ninety percent of the time the fly must be on the stream bottom, where the naturals and the trout are. That sounds so simple, but few of us think of techniques for doing this other than adding weight to the fly or leader or using sinking lines—all of which techniques sacrifice natural drift and line control for fishing depth.

The tuck-cast system is designed to allow the angler to maintain contact with the fly, to let the fly move naturally, and to get maximum drift of the fly on the stream bottom. The most important characteristic of this cast is that it gets the nymph down to the bottom quickly because the fly enters the water first, with the full momentum of the cast. The energy of the cast is translated from the horizontal movement of the line into hard, vertical movement of the fly.

All of the tuck casts and other casts with weighted nymphs require that the knuckles and thumb of the casting hand move in a horizontal plane, other-

Making a tuck cast, shooting the nymph to the top of the pocket to cover the entire bottom of the pool. *Photo by Sharon Bernard.*

On a tuck cast the wrist must be straight as the power stroke is made. The cast should come straight overhead.

wise the cast will cowtail. That is it will cant off to the side, losing much of the momentum and line control. The execution of the forward power stroke is critical. The thumb *must be on the top of the rod handle* during the casting stroke, and you should end up with the thumb and knuckles pointing directly at the spot you want to hit. The cast comes straight overhead and your wrist must be straight in line with your thumb. If the rod cants off at an angle to the wrist, the nymph will curve out to the side — and the result will be too much slack line between the rod tip and the nymph.

Remember, a trout can pick up the nymph and drop it before you can get any indication of the strike if there is too much slack line between rod tip and fly. And even if the strike is made apparent by line movement there will probably be too much slack to pick up to set the hook. Line contact can be maintained only if the cast is executed properly.

In the balance of this chapter, I will describe how to make the basic tuck cast and the variations of the tuck cast that make up my tuck-cast system of fishing nymphs for trout. Later sections of this chapter deal with retrieving the fly after the cast, lines for nymphing, and tying effective nymph patterns.

The Basic Tuck Cast

The basic tuck cast is designed to get your fly to the bottom as quickly as possible and to keep it on the bottom throughout the drift. It is useful whenever you need to fish on the bottom.

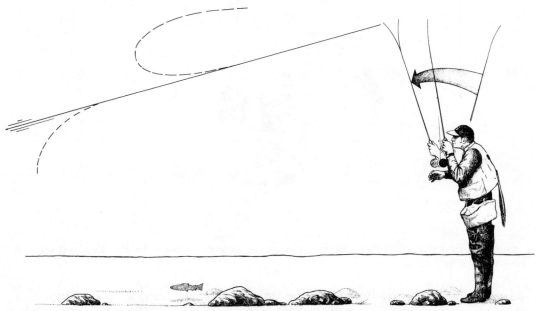

To make the tuck cast the rod is drifted forward to the 10:30 position and then stopped sharply with the last two fingers of the casting hand pulling and the thumb pushing. It's a quick, squeezing action.

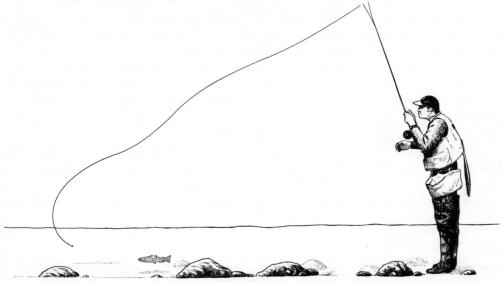

The weighted nymph tucks back under the leader and drops to the bottom before the drag of the water through the line has a chance to lift the nymph off the bottom.

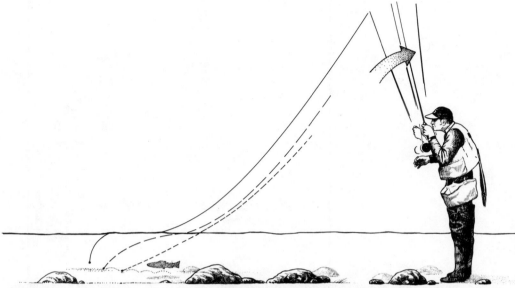

When you complete the tuck cast keep the rod tip up to further eliminate drag and keep the line tight between the tip and the nymph while the nymph covers the bottom.

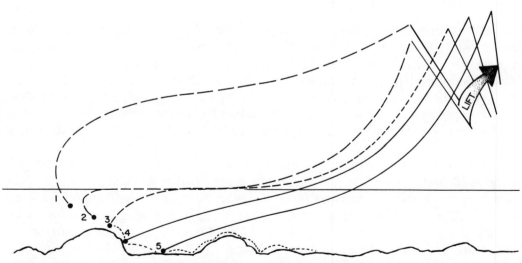

A steady retrieve of line combined with a continuous elevation of the rod tip throughout the drift gives you line control and keeps the nymph down on the bottom. You're in touch with the nymph throughout the drift.

The tuck cast can be made from any position. Here is an example of a tuck cast made with rod hand and forearm across the chest in order to avoid obstructions that would impair the basic tuck cast.

The Downer-and-Upper Tuck Cast

For casting short distances, or in situations where a long upstream cast is not possible because of obstructions, I use a compact version of the tuck cast called the "downer-and-upper." The name describes the dynamics of the cast. This cast is used when the angler is unable to position himself for a full back-cast or an upstream cast—whenever a short drift is the only option available. It accomplishes the same thing as the basic tuck cast: getting the fly to the bottom fast by transmitting the momentum of the cast from the line to the fly itself.

The downer-and-upper is really a variation of the short-line technique I employed that day on the private stream near Williamsport with George. But it is also more than a simple short-line technique, since the dynamics of the cast result in the fly entering the water at a steep (ninety-degree or less) angle, as opposed to actually tucking under the line. The casting stroke is very short: the thumb of the casting hand pops forward and down as the loop unfolds (the downer), and a quick, short thrust of the rod upward (the upper), and finishes with the thumb pointing straight up. This sends the weighted nymph into the water first, bending back slightly under the leader but not as sharply

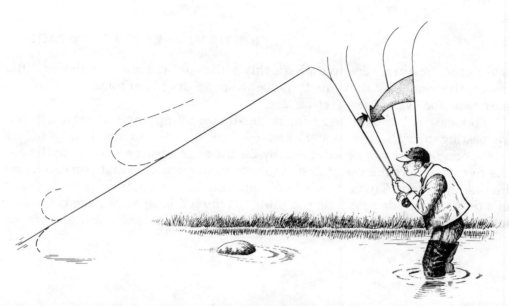

To make the downer and upper tuck cast, the thumb and knuckles on the rod point in the direction of the cast. The casting stroke is short and the thumb of the casting hand pops forward and down. As the loop unfolds on the nymph end, a quick, short, upward lift of the rod hand and forearm is employed with the thumb now pointing up; this sends the weighted nymph into the water first, forcibly. The nymph doesn't have the pronounced tuck as in the basic tuck cast, but drops directly in at a shorter angle.

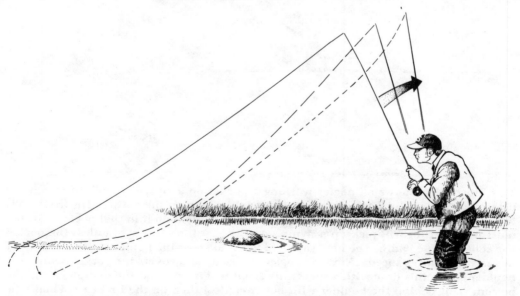

It is important that the rod tip is held up at the termination of the cast and continues to lift throughout the cast. There is very little line on the water from start to finish, thus little or no drag and excellent control of the nymph.

as with the tuck cast. The nymph quickly settles to the bottom with very little line on the water, so that ninety percent of the drag is eliminated. This is a *short* cast, for casting ten feet or less.

This cast is basically used for an upstream nymphing technique. If you are casting to riffs, fast water, and pockets directly in front of you, the downer-and-upper can be extended by means of an upstream mend in the air. The nymph enters the water first, and acts as an anchor so that you can mend the line upstream. This extended cast allows you line control for more depth on a downstream drift. A long rod (nine to ten feet) is an advantage because it helps keep the majority of the line off the water for a long, natural drift. Be

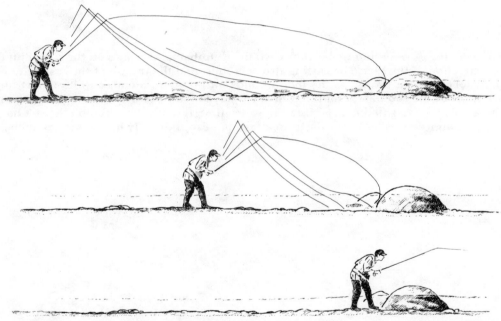

This illustration shows an angler working a pocket on a typical stretch of stream by using an upstream tuck cast and weighted nymphs to cover the bottom. His first cast is to the top of the pocket behind the boulder. One cast will do it in that pocket. For the most part, a trout will pick up a nymph on the first time through, unless the pocket has considerable width. The next casts are to the sides of the boulder where the water mixes and changes speeds. Next the angler moves up and covers the pocket behind the boulder again, this time with a shorter line that will insure that the nymph gets to the bottom right behind the boulder with better control than on the first cast. Finally he moves farther up and covers the broken water of the riffs feeding the top of the pool and the pocket behind the log. Depending on the distance, he uses a short tuck cast or the downer and upper.

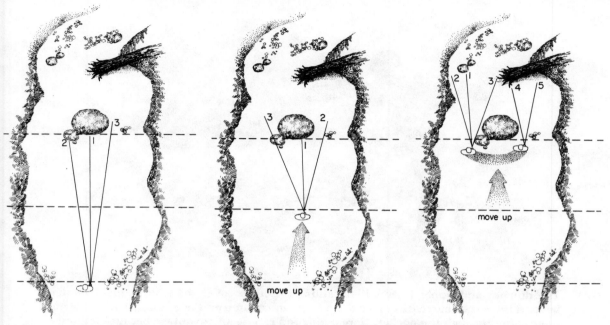

These illustrations show the tactics shown in the preceding illustration viewed from above.

sure to lead the nymph with the rod tip through the entire drift, keeping as much line off the water as possible.

The Rolling Tuck Cast

The rolling tuck cast is essential when you are nymphing where obstructions limit the backcast, although it can also be used on open water effectively. The weighted nymph enters the water directly, and you might call it a modified tuck because the nymph doesn't pull back under the leader as much as the tuck cast. But the nymph reaches the bottom quickly and the end result is the same. The fly covers the bottom throughout the cast.

The Tuck and Mend Cast

The tuck with a mend has the advantage of giving your nymph even more time than the regular tuck to get to the bottom because it sends a loop of line upstream. A mend can be used with the regular tuck cast as illustrated on page 63, or it can be combined with the rolling tuck cast. In either case, the angler

The downer and upper in this illustration is used to cover the slower pocket water beyond the heavy currents to give the nymph more time on the bottom. The rod leads the nymph through the pocket. Here a long rod can be an advantage because it allows you to lift the line over faster currents.

makes the upstream mend just as the nymph tucks under the cast on the forward stroke. The mend is made by simply lifting the line in an upstream direction while the nymph is tucking downward.

The advantage of the straight tuck and mend cast is that it allows the angler more time to get deeper than the regular tuck, which makes the cast desirable when fishing very fast or high water.

Lines for Nymphing

For most streams, my first and, with one exception, only choice for a nymphing line is a weight-forward or double-taper floating line. You can follow the drift of a nymph easily with a floating line, and these lines telegraph the trout's take more readily than the heavier lead-core or sinking lines.

Floating strike indicators at the end of the fly line can be helpful within reason. Cortland's fluorescent Nymph Tip has a dual advantage: it floats well and is highly visible in riffs and broken water. The additional weight of the Nymph Tip line also helps add momentum to the tuck cast. Most floating strike indicators, however, impair nymphing techniques. In this class, I include cork cylinders, bobbers, rolled styrofoam, and so on, mostly because the extra drag in the air inhibits the tuck cast at the critical time when the line kicks.

Sinking lines are the least desirable solution next to using an anchor. They are difficult to control, and they belly underwater, which allows for little sensitivity. You must retrieve the whole line before you can make another cast. Sinking-tip lines on a stream are, in my experience, the worst of both worlds. Using the proper leader and weight system is the best solution, together with the tuck cast for maintaining that critical balance among fishing depth, line sensitivity, and control.

Actually, my ace line system for deep nymphing and line sensitivity is monofilament. You can cast monofilament with a fly rod? How can that be? Monofilament has no weight, there's no resistance. True, but when the weight is on the nymph end, nymphing with monofilament becomes a very effective way of fishing deep, fast water—about the most effective there is. When you want to shoot for distance *and* get your nymph down to the bottom, I feel monofilament is the answer, not a sinking-tip line or a sinking line or a lead-core shooting-taper and short leader. All of these lines, because of their weight and diameter, tend to belly underwater—often the fatal flaw in nymph presentation, especially in longer casts. As the current pushes through the line, it creates a belly and drags the fly. The greater the belly, the less communication the angler has with the actual movement of the fly. These other lines can do the job; a 30-foot lead core shooting head will cover deep, fast water effectively, but I feel monofilament with the weight on the business end is even better. Cortland's Cobra flat monofilament is my choice.

To cast monofilament, you simply have to wait until you feel the pull of the weighted nymph behind you before you drift the rod forward into the power stroke. Any technique employed for nymphing with a fly line can be aptly accomplished with flat monofilament. The tuck cast, the tuck and mend, and the conventional cast can all be done with monofilament. Only the roll cast is difficult. But by letting your line and nymph drift below you, then turning and facing upstream, using the pull of the current as your resistance in lifting the nymph to the surface, you can shoot a distance cast upstream or up and across—a sort of roll cast using the stream to create line tension.

The advantages of monofilament for nymphing (and for fishing streamers) are many. But, above all, the diameter of the line is small and so there is minimal air and water resistance, which means less drag. And that means better sensitivity to the fly.

Level, flat monofilament with a tapered leader suitable to the waters the angler wants to fish will do the job of a fly line with considerably less confu-

To begin the rolling tuck cast, pick up the line in front of you. To do this drop the rod tip and point it at the line in the water, pull in the slack line in front of you, and lift the rod tip gradually at a vertical angle until there is maximum line resistance. As you lift the rod your thumb is on top of the rod handle and knuckles are pointing forward. Drift the casting hand to ear level and wait until the line coming off the rod tip is behind you (at the 1:30 position) and has completely stopped. The rod is fully loaded and ready for the forward stroke.

Bring the rod sharply forward, and when your thumb is in sight make a short, sharp power stroke.

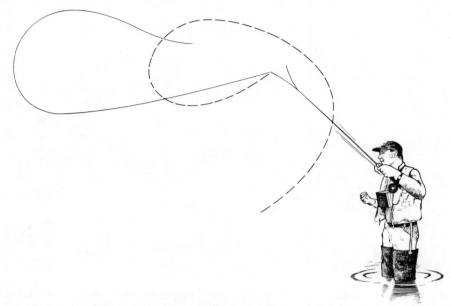

With the thumb snapping forward and upward and the back two fingers applying a prying pressure on the base of the rod handle, the loop rolls forward.

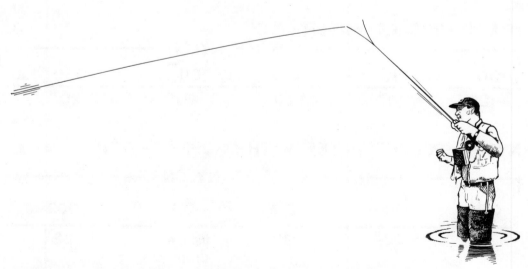

When the loop straightens out, the casting hand is lifted up and back sharply.

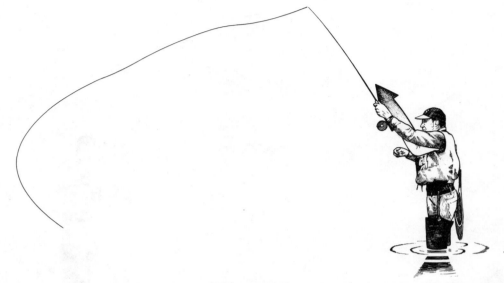

With the rod moving skyward, the weighted nymph dives forward and down. The nymph enters the water first, and the rod is held high, keeping the line tight between rod tip and nymph.

NYMPH - POCKET WATER - 7' 6"

STIFF NYLON				
.017	.015	.013	.011	.009
12"	20"	20"	20"	20"

NYMPH - POCKET WATER WITH DROPPER - 7'4"

STIFF NYLON				
.017	.015	.013	.011	.009
12"	20"	20"	16"+ 4" dropper	22"

Leader designs for nymphing.

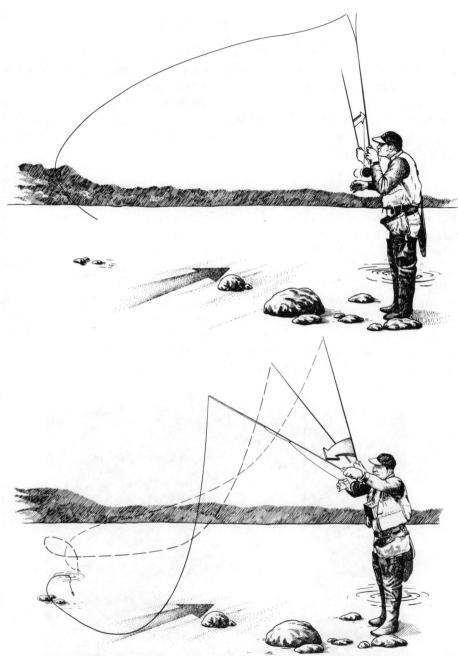

To make the tuck and mend cast, begin by making a basic tuck cast. As the loop unfolds and the weighted nymph heads into the water the line is lifted upstream by fully extending the casting arm and the rod upstream. A unique cast in the nymphing game, the nymph tucks downward while the line is drifting upstream.

sion than using a complex formula that calls for monofilament backing plus level fly line plus high-density shooting-taper plus leader. When weighted nymphs or additional weight is adjusted properly on the leader, and the line is tight from rod tip to fly, you can feel almost every rock and pebble on the stream bottom through the monofilament, even at distances beyond thirty feet. For shorter casts, it's possible to use a simple underhand-flip cast and still enjoy the sensitivity of a fly rod.

Retrieves

No matter what line the angler is using, any cast is only as good as the contact the angler has with the fly. My cardinal rule about retrieves is: don't trap the line against the fly rod during the retrieve. I extend the index finger of my rod hand away from the rod and curl it gently over the line as I retrieve with my free hand.

Nymphing retrieves should be done in conjunction with the elevation of the rod tip. Keeping the rod tip up will help keep unwanted slack out of the line. The two retrieves that I use are the hand-twist retrieve and the strip retrieve.

I prefer to use the hand-twist retrieve when the current is slow and I'm working pockets and riffs directly in front of me with a short line. To work

The basic strip-line retrieve: note the line is not trapped against the rod. *Photo by Sharon Bernard.*

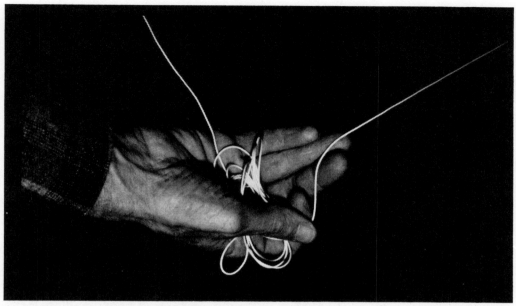

The basic hand-twist retrieve: alternate forefinger and two middle fingers gathering line. *Photo by Sharon Bernard.*

deeper, faster water, I use the hand-twist retrieve with an occasional line strip. But if the water is so deep and fast that a quick retrieve of line is necessary to keep slack out and to maintain contact with the nymph, a line-strip retrieve is what I use. Again, these retrieves are used in conjunction with the elevation of the rod tip for best results.

Nymph Design and Construction

Now we are down to the end of the leader, to the place where the tackle meets the trout: the nymph. It's an imitation—but what should it imitate? A mayfly nymph? If so, what kind? A burrowing mayfly nymph? A swimmer? A clinger? In limestone streams, maybe it's a freshwater shrimp or a cress bug. Regardless of what form of underwater life we are trying to imitate, they all have a common denominator to the trout: movement.

If you ever have the chance to see a nymph hatch in an aquarium, it'll be a sight you'll never forget. It struggles to get to the top to hatch. The nymph's movements prior to the big life from the bottom are undulating, pulsating, surging, gill-waving movements—almost perpetual motion that turns trout on.

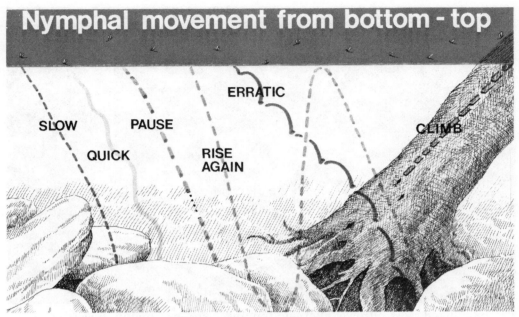

Different nymphs show different actions prior to emergence.

Tying perfectly lifelike imitations of nymphs with vinyls, plastics, and Space Age dubbing materials is often at cross purposes. It's the nymphal movement that stimulates the trout's feeding response, and most super-realistic nymphs I've seen lack this movement. I'd file most of these imitations under arts and crafts. It's how the nymph looks to the trout, not the angler, that counts.

For years I have fished scraggly fur and hair nymphs based on early, crude ties, but they far outcaught the realistic flies I've tried. An in-depth, anatomical study of nymphs, and proper identification of naturals can be important, but it is useless information without the proper tying technique, fishing tactics, knowledge of the stream, and casting ability. My friend Craig Woods best summed up my attitude toward "bugology" and fishing by a story related to him by Phil Wright, Jr., of Wise River, Montana. Several highly sophisticated fishermen were sitting around a tackle store in Idaho "Latinizing" when a fisherman came in off the stream. They interrupted their discussion long enough to ask how he did and he said that he had taken many fish. Amazed at this success, the Latinizers quizzed him about what fly did the trick. To which the fisherman replied, "I caught them on this little gray bastard."

The accompanying illustrations show basic nymph and crustacean designs that I have found effective.

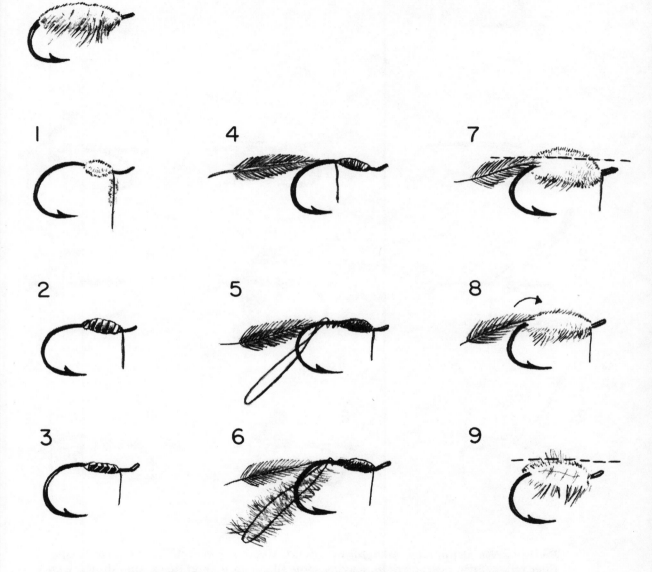

Cress Bug (imitates crustaceans). 1. Begin by dubbing hook as shown. 2. Wrap flat lead strip over dubbing. 3. Cover with thread and flatten with needle-nose pliers. 4. Tie in grizzly hackle, tip first. 5. Loop thread for dubbing loop. 6. Pack loop with beaver or muskrat fur. 7. Wrap dubbing forward and trim as shown. 8. Wrap hackle forward. 9. Trim hackle as shown and whip-finish.

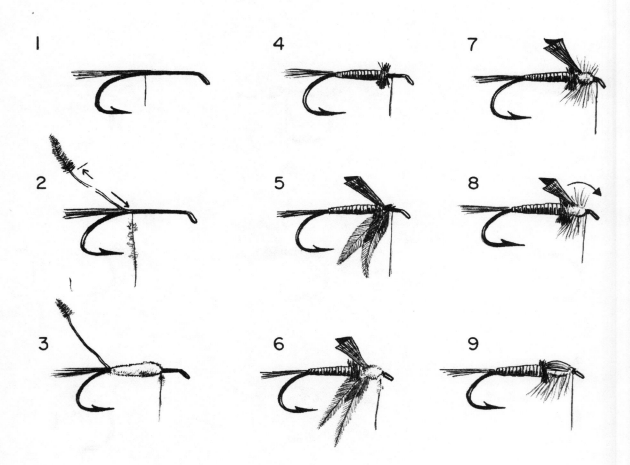

Emerging Nymph (imitates emerging mayfly). 1. Wrap thread on hook and tie in hackle-fiber tail. 2. Strip peacock quill, leaving some fibers on tip and tie in. Spin dubbing on thread. 3. Wrap dubbing as shown. 4. Wrap quill forward so fibers of quill tip spread where shown. 5. Tie in duck quill for wingcase and two hackles facing opposite direction, butts first. 6. Dub from wingcase to eye. 7. Wrap hackles separately, intermixing them. 8. Come forward with wingcase and tie off. 9. Whip-finish to complete fly. Colors of hackle, dubbing, and tail can be varied according to hatches.

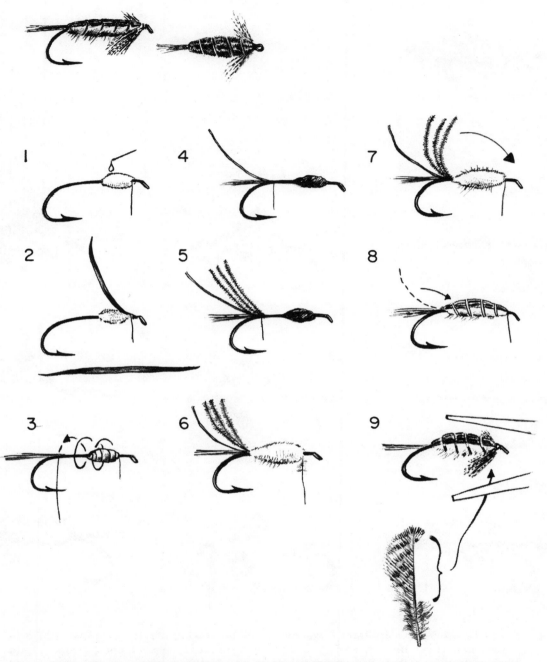

Harvey's Stonefly Nymph. 1. Dub front third of hook shank and apply a coating of quick-drying cement. 2. Tie in flat lead strip trimmed to taper as shown. 3. Wrap thread over lead and add tail of partridge fibers. 4. Tie in medium-gauge brass wire to be used for rib. 5. Tie in three lengths of dark brown or black chenille. 6. Dub body. 7. Bring chenille forward (all three lengths at the same time) and tie off. 8. Rib with brass wire. 9. Strip fibers from partridge feather and tie in as two separate bunches. The fibers should extend out from eye of hook on either side as shown. Whip-finish.

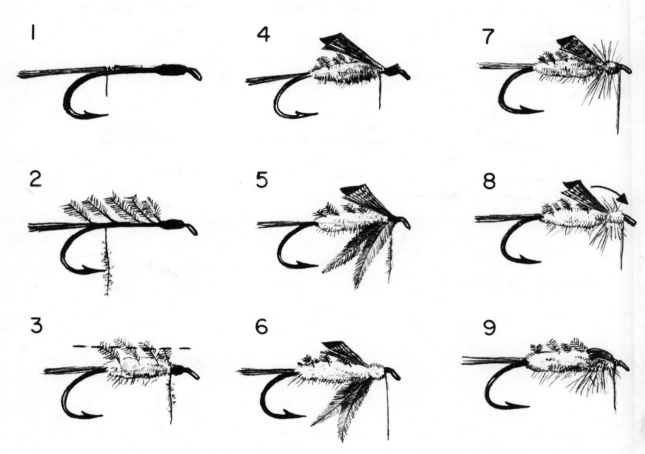

Green Drake Nymph (imitates large species of burrowing mayfly nymphs). 1. Tie in thread and cover hook shank. Add lead strip on front third of hook shank. Tie in hackle fibers for tail. 2. Add short sections of emu feather tips as shown. 3. Dub thread and wrap dubbing forward between emu feather tips to front third of hook. Trim emu as shown. 4. Tie in section of turkey quill for wingcase. 5. Tie in hackles butt first and facing opposite directions. 6. Dub head. 7. Wrap hackles forward, intermixing them. 8. Bring wingcase forward and tie off. 9. Whip-finish to complete fly.

Weighting Nymphs

Getting the fly and leader down to the stream bottom when nymph fishing is important, but what about the action of the nymph when it's on the bottom? In order to observe the effect of nymph designs and the addition of weight on the action of a fly, I decided to observe the fly in the water first-hand. The following data is based on many hours in a cold limestone stream with scuba gear observing the action of my nymphs on the bottom.

The area of observation was downstream of broken water, where two major currents joined below a stone. The pocket was an ideal spot for observing nymphs at a variety of water depths and in different current speeds. At the head of the riff the depth was several inches, but it dropped rapidly to twenty-four inches and then to forty inches within the first twelve feet.

In water that was several inches deep to forty inches deep, a weighted nymph alone was most effective in staying on the bottom *and* maintaining the right action. Lead attached to the leader was unnecessary and impaired the natural drift of the fly.

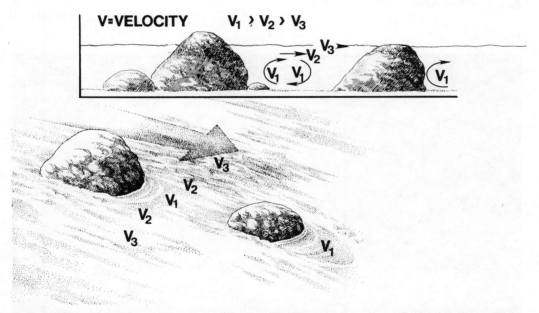

Being able to read the water and understand different current velocities is important to getting your nymph to the bottom. The water at V1 is significantly slower than V2, and V3 is the fastest. The cutaway view of the pocket shows how the velocity varies from top to bottom.

The bubbles in this photograph mark the different current velocities in a pocket. *Photo by Bruce Bronsdon.*

Trout will hold and feed at the line of current-velocity change shown in previous photograph. *Photo by Bruce Bronsdon.*

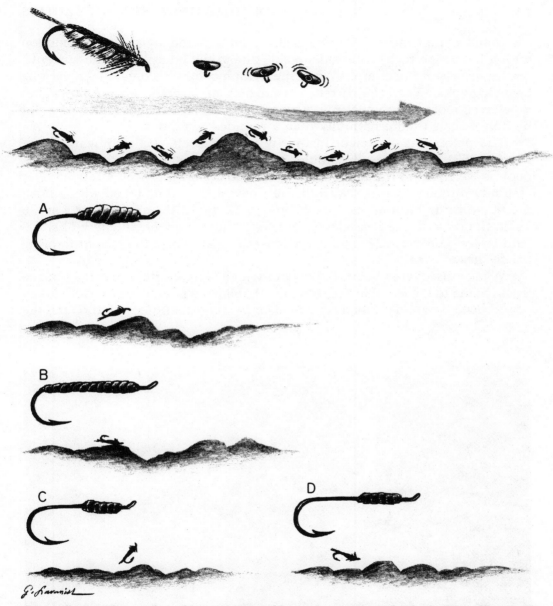

Top: a flattened nymph and its rocking and bouncing motion: this is the best all-around nymph shape. Nymph A is weighted on front half of hook shank but the shape is not flattened; it rides upside-down and head up. Nymph B is wrapped with lead the full length of shank and not flattened; it rides upside-down and planes along the bottom. Nymph C is wrapped with lead strip on front third and flattened; it rides hook down and head-up. Nymph D is same as Nymph C but the longer shank provides leverage for it to ride head-down.

A flat nymph drifts more naturally than a round nymph. An imitation with a flat shape rocks from side to side due to the interplay of the currents, on the surface of the nymph. When the nymph comes in contact with varying changing velocities of the current, on the bottom, it jerked up and down and it behaved more like the natural. Regardless of the speed of the current, a flat nymph behaved more naturally than a rounded nymph.

The placement of weight in the fly pattern itself was significant. I use Mustad 9671 hooks, sizes 6 through 12, 2XL, for most of my nymphs. If this hook is weighted in the front third of the hook (a strip of lead wrapped over cotton or dubbing, covered with thread, cemented, and flattened with pliers), the fly will ride head-up in sizes 8 through 12. But if the angler uses a size 6 hook, the fly will ride head-down. This is because the greater length of size 6 (and larger) hooks creates additional leverage that allows the weight to bring the fly head-down.

What I discovered about the way in which weight affects the float of the fly leads me to believe that it doesn't much matter whether the fly rides head-up or head-down. For many years, before my experiment, I thought the

Flat-bodied nymph weighted in front third of hook shank rides head up. *Photo by Bruce Bronsdon.*

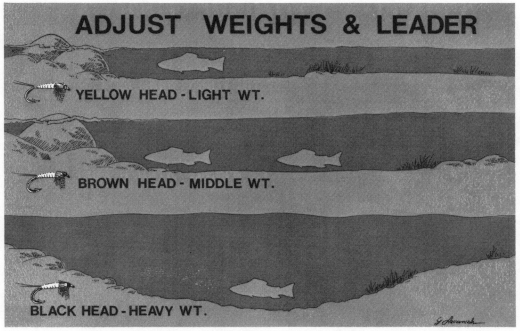

You can color-code your nymphs according to how heavily they are weighted; this allows for quick-change selection in water of varying velocity and depth.

smaller flies were riding head-down. Actually, I think the head-up float might be better because it looks more like a natural, active nymph. But the head-down float is not a bad compromise in itself because it probably results in less hangups on the stream bottom. One further thing I discovered is that if the nymph is tied with a round body, it rides upside-down (hook bend on top).

Since there are times when trout will take nymphs at any depth in the stream, I use several different weights of nymphs. I color-code these weights by using different colors of tying thread on the heads of the flies. The different weights allow me to change nymphs quickly to meet different stream situations as I encounter them. The different weights I use are:

Surface nymph. This fly has no weight, and it is tied with a dubbing body that is spun on or looped on. It is fished on the surface and just below the surface.

No-weight nymph. I use this fly for fishing to depths of about one foot. The only weight is in a medium-gauge brass wire used as ribbing. The greater the diameter of the wire, the deeper the nymph will ride in the water. The wire

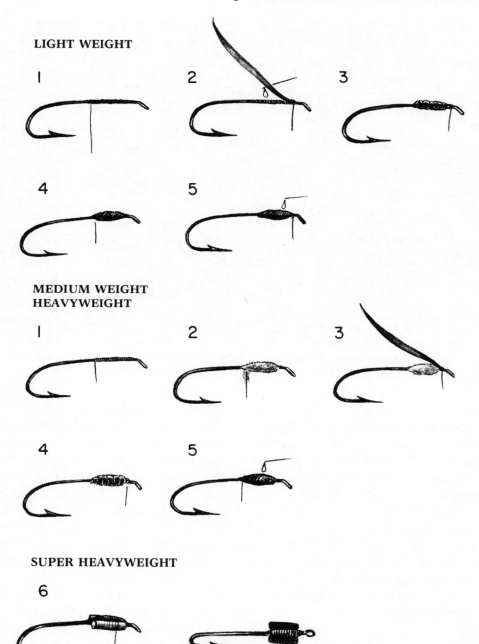

LIGHT WEIGHT

1

2

3

4

5

MEDIUM WEIGHT
HEAVYWEIGHT

1

2

3

4

5

SUPER HEAVYWEIGHT

6

A   B

Different styles of weighting to produce nymphs of varying weights.

will also hold a flattened shape. If the tier applies floatant such as Mucilin to the dubbing, the nymph will bob up and down in the surface film in faster water, which is a very effective action.

Lightweight nymph. Tie a strip of tapered, lightweight (.003-inch-diameter) lead foil over the first third or one half of the hook and cover with tying thread. Dental X-ray plates are excellent for the lead foil. Tie in the body fur and rib well with wire and flatten with pliers. I use this nymph and the following patterns to fish deeper than one foot, choosing the correct weight according to feeding level of the trout and stream conditions.

Middle-weight nymph. Spin a layer of cotton or dubbing over the front portion of the hook shank and cover with .030-inch-diameter wire.

Heavyweight nymph. This is tied the same as the middle-weight nymph, except .040-inch diameter wire is used. This fly is good for fast runs or pocket water.

Super-heavyweight nymph. This is tied the same as the heavyweight nymph, except before dubbing the body of the fly. Add two strips of lead wire to either side of the leaded portion of the hook, holding them in place with wraps of tying thread.

This weighted-nymph system allows for maximum flexibility on the stream. My underwater observations showed that weighted nymphs have several distinct advantages over unweighted nymphs with lead weight on the leader: a more uniform natural drift, fewer hangup problems, easier control of speed and level of drift. These advantages may come as a surprise: *"Weighted nymphs do that"* you ask? The general feeling among anglers has been that underwater flies tied without weight in them have more natural action than do weighted flies, that the weight built into a fly impairs the fly's action. Indeed, unweighted nymphs would have better action than weighted nymphs *if* they could get to the bottom by themselves.

With unweighted flies fished on the bottom it is necessary to add weight in the form of split-shot or wrap-around lead strips. When you add such weight, however, it creates a dead spot on the leader between the rod tip and the fly. The nymph travels underwater faster than the lead weight and the angler feels the weight bouncing along the bottom, not the fly. When a trout picks up the nymph, the angler may not be able to feel the strike. But even when the angler detects a strike, chances are that by the time he lifts the line and takes up the slack created by the lead weight, the fish will have dropped the fly. Trout can pick up a nymph and spit it out again in less than a second. The other alternative for getting unweighted nymphs to the bottom is a sinking-line system. But here again is the line-belly problem that impairs the angler's

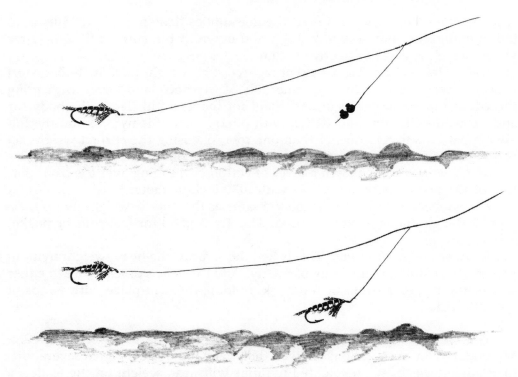

It is a common technique to add weight by placing split-shot on a dropper; if a nymph of the same weight as the split-shot is used instead, you double your chances of taking fish.

sensitivity to the fly bouncing along the bottom. When fishing nymphs, a fly with weight built into it and a tuck cast is the way to get to the bottom. In situations that require more weight, however, split-shot or wrap-around lead strips attached to the leader are preferable to a sinking-line system.

The only situation in which I use an unweighted nymph with split-shot attached is when fishing visible trout that are holding or feeding in less than a foot of water. One idea is to place a split-shot about four inches above a shrimp or other small nymph pattern and cast above a visible trout. The shot will sink to the bottom and anchor the nymph. The nymph will ride above the shot and move back and forth in the current. Usually it is only a matter of time before the trout will move up and take the fly. This is an exciting tactic to employ, and sometimes you have to wait a long time before the trout takes.

Finally, because in some situations it is necessary to use additional weight on the leader to get the fly down, I made a study of the effect of adding such weight. My results are shown in the accompanying illustrations. These illustrations should help you choose the proper amount of weight and combinations of weight, weighted nymphs, and nymphs on droppers for most trout-stream situations. It is also very important to experiment with the depth at which you are fishing your nymphs in order to find the depth at which the trout are feeding. Many anglers neglect to experiment in this way—trying out different amounts of weight and combinations of weight and weighted nymphs—because it seems like too much trouble. But if you take the time to experiment, you will often be rewarded for your efforts.

To illustrate the point: Daryl Arawjo and I fished a small limestone stream on an unseasonable, warm, sunny, late November day. The air temperature was in the high sixties. We were both fishing nymphs.

At the end of the afternoon we compared notes. I had taken a surprising number of trout; Daryl had taken a couple. On the way home I questioned him. "Did you change weights?"

No he hadn't; he had pinched a split shot on a foot above the nymph and stayed with it all afternoon. Was he fishing a weighted nymph?

No. Did he at anytime stop and adjust the leader tippet?

No, he hadn't.

"Daryl, I constantly changed weights today with varying depth and speeds of water." There was no way you could effectively get a natural drift at the proper level by staying with a fixed weight on either the leader or the nymph, and besides, one split shot was too heavy for nine-tenths of that water—the stream was small and the water level low. It's imperative that you get a natural drift at the proper level, and on this day that meant the bottom. It is also im-

The closer the weight on the leader is placed to the nymph, the closer to the bottom the nymph rides.

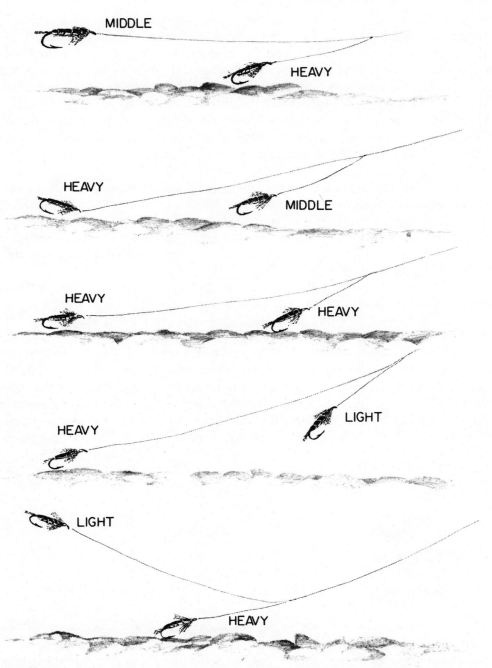

Combinations of weighted flies on droppers results in different drift levels in the water.

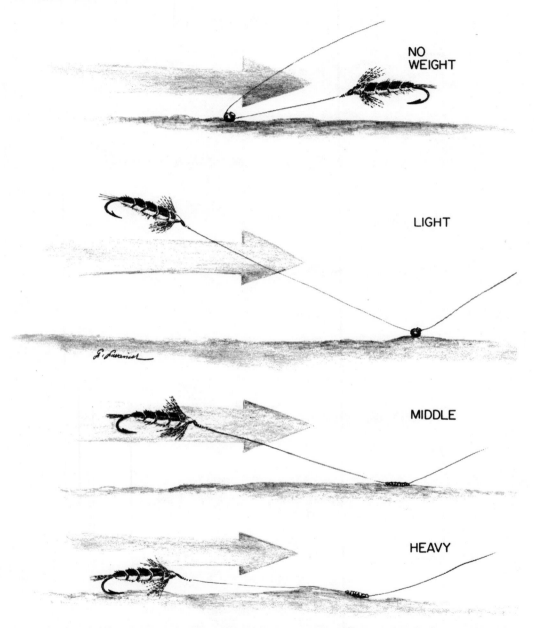

NO WEIGHT

LIGHT

MIDDLE

HEAVY

Nymphs in varying weight combinations with weight added to the leader: using line weight in combination with weighted nymphs increases the possibilities of drift levels and action. Note that an unweighted nymph actually drifts *ahead* of the point of contact with the bottom, which makes it somewhat harder to detect a strike.

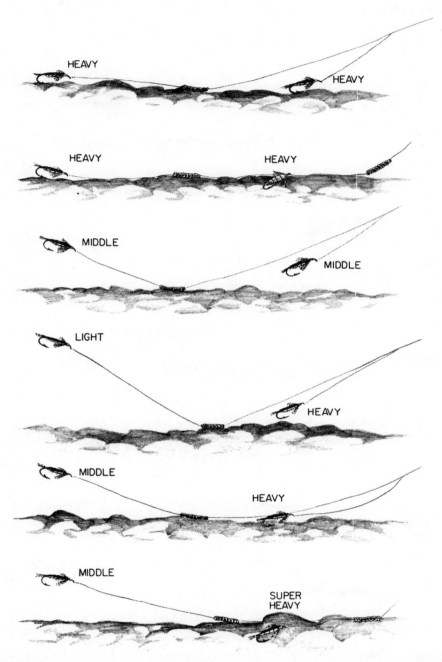

Adding weight on the leader between dropper flies makes still *more* possibilities by providing a sort of fulcrum for two flies of different weights. The second figure from top is the heaviest system I use.

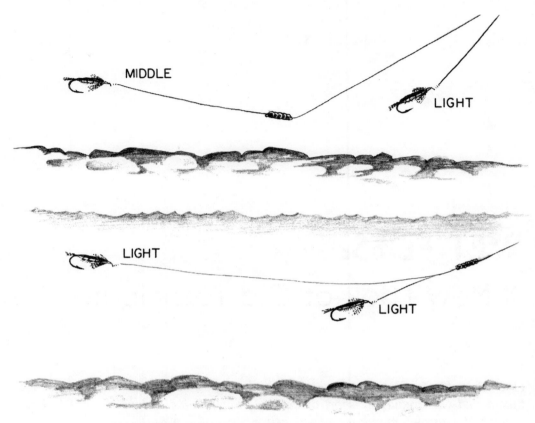

Putting the weight above both flies results in a natural drift.

perative that you control the drift, not allowing varying currents and the speed of the water to make for uncontrollable slack from rod tip to nymph. And furthermore you've got to adjust the length of the *tippet* for depth and drift.

Then he admitted, "I know better, but it seems like so much trouble to change; at times I'm dragging the bottom and the nymph is covered with algae or I'm hung up half the time."

I knew exactly what Daryl was saying. I had on many occasions done the same thing—stuck a split shot or two ten inches above the nymph and stayed with the same system all day. Sure I caught trout—but by hit and miss, only when I happened to hit pockets where the particular weight was right for that particular pocket or riff. What about the rest of the water? Had I been using some common sense I could have taken two or three times as many fish.

3

WET FLIES:

A New Look at Old Techniques

Clyde Schreffler was up in years and not in the best of health. He wheezed when he talked and was frequently short of breath, probably due at least in part to those damn roll-your-own cigarettes he smoked incessantly.

I was fascinated watching those gnarled, tobacco-stained fingers fashion a nearly tailor-made smoke, tobacco spilling down Clyde's shirt, as he related how he took a seventeen-inch brown from the Railroad Trestle hole on upper Spring Creek near Oak Hall. It wasn't the first time I'd heard the story, yet I was always anxious to hear it and if Clyde didn't start it, I'd prod him into doing so. I'd put myself in his place, imagine myself straining to bring the big fish to the net, visualizing the rolling strike and the throbbing rod tip.

Clyde knew I was a trout-bitten kid, obsessed with fishing, and that I fished every day. He'd watch me and give a knowing nod and smile as I pedalled by on my bicycle, fly rod across the handle bars, fly box and peanut-butter sandwiches piled in the wire basket. Perhaps he began to feel an obligation to introduce me to wet-fly fishing.

One late-spring evening, sitting on Clyde's porch swing and listening to how wet flies were best fished, he stopped suddenly, looked at me, and said, "How'd you like to go fishing with me?"

I shook with excitement and stammered, "Thank you."

"Get your rod," he said, "I'll see you in a few minutes."

Clyde's antiquated auto wheezed almost as bad as Clyde. The trip to the stream was an adventure in itself. Clyde was steering with both hands riveted to the wheel, leaning into the turns, and staring straight ahead as though we were traveling a hundred miles an hour instead of thirty-five.

Clyde had two Dark Cahills tied on a leader. The top fly was snelled and a heavy loop extended from the leader three feet above the tail fly. The wood-duck wings were faded and a bit yellow with age. The leader was a gut leader that had to be soaked to straighten out, and his pet bamboo, nine-foot, three-piece rod showed the effects of age and use.

His basic method was a downstream-and-across cast, letting the flies finish the arc with little or no movement, followed by a slow hand-twist retrieve. I was standing below him and saw a trout drift up under the fly and follow it, then stop, turn, and disappear. I can still see vividly the spots on that fish. "Come back here with me," cautioned Clyde, "you're too close to the bank. That trout saw you."

The fishing methods and tactics I learned on that trip never left me: follow with the rod tip the line you see in the water so you know where your flies are and keep that rod tip up. I never questioned why. You don't question expert advice when you're nine or ten years old.

The rest of the evening I followed old Clyde and thrilled as he hooked and landed four fish and missed as many. This was Spring Creek in 1938 or 1939, a limestone stream loaded with wild browns that had relatively little fishing pressure compared to today. The last trout, a foot-long wild beauty, he killed and laid on the grass for me. "For your breakfast," he said.

It was getting late. Clyde took his leader off and placed it in a tin box, took his rod apart, and carefully wiped it off. Clyde was thorough.

There were trips after that one, each a learning experience, but Clyde's heart gave him trouble and eventually he had to give it up. But still he would call me over to sit with him on the porch swing and quiz me about my fishing ventures, relate stories, and advise me.

Thanks Clyde, I never forgot.

The fishing methods and tactics I learned on that trip never left me: "Follow with the rod tip the line you see in the water so you know where your flies are." "Keep that rod tip up!"

Why, I never questioned. You don't question expert advice when you're nine or ten years old.

Even after forty plus years of questions on the trout stream, Clyde's advice is still good. In that time, I evolved a series of wet fly tactics, combining casting approach, drift, levels speed, and presentation. Wet flies are work-horse patterns, the ones I many times go to when the stuff that should work—doesn't. I think in many ways they are the flexible fisherman's best friend.

Wet Fly Fundamentals

Regardless of technique, there are some wet fly fundamentals that one must learn and follow to be successful:

The cast: This is one time you want to straighten the line out. You've got to be in touch with those flies with the rod tip, whether it be a straight cast, a mend in the air off a straight cast, or a roll cast.

You've got to eliminate the belly in the line throughout the drift. If the cast is out-and-across the stream, follow the line in the water with your rod tip completely through the drift until the line straightens below you.

A belly in the line has distinct disadvantages: It is difficult to pick up a belly and set the hook at the same time. It is impossible to be in touch with the flies when the currents are pushing through the line under or on the water. It is most difficult to effectively impart the action to the flies through a belly.

When fishing wet flies follow the line you see in the water with the rod tip completely through the drift. This keeps the belly out of the line. The shaded arrow shows movement of the rod through the drift, indicated by the outline arrow.

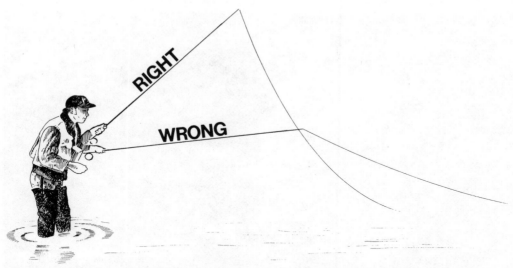

When fishing wet flies keep the rod at a ninety-degree angle to the line.

And if you want to fish your flies at a lower level, the currents pushing through the fly line lift the flies up and off of the fish's level.

A 90° angle of line from rod tip to the line in the water is a necessity. Trout don't grab, they inhale. There is enough slack in the 90° angle for the trout to hook itself. Those who point the rod downstream and at the water on a downstream presentation miss a goodly portion of their hits. The line is so straight and tight between the rod tip and the fly that there is no give, and little chance for a hookup. The old phrase "they're hittin' short" is a coverup: change the rod angle and they won't be hittin' short—you'll be hooking a far greater percentage.

With these fundamentals firmly in mind, the wet fly fisherman can adapt until he finds the solution. It is work, but it pays off.

The Problem-Solving Approach

Spring Creek in central Pennsylvania has been my training ground since youth. It has been good to me, presenting ever-changing conditions that tax my imagination, and force my thought process to work overtime—ofttimes in frustration. But, something can be gained with each experience, successful or not.

So it was on a late May evening that my mind and patience were put to

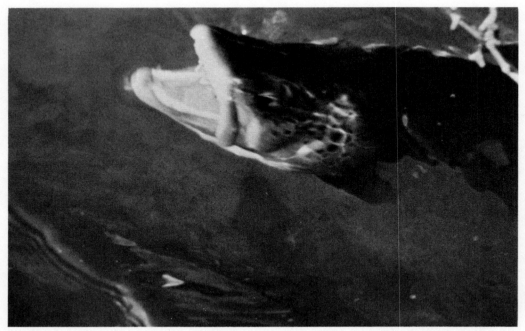

Remember! Trout don't grab, they inhale. The ninety-degree angle between rod tip and fly line allows the trout to hook himself when fishing wet flies (and streamers) downstream. *Photo by the author.*

the test. Earlier that afternoon I had good success fishing weighted nymphs in riffs and pockets. A sulphur hatch was in progress: by evening trout were breaking both in the riffs and in the flat water below. I was working a short-shank sulphur dun dryfly imitation over rising fish – working, but not catching.

I replaced the dry with a sulphur nymph, went below the fish, and began working upstream. I cast a greased fur nymph imitation upstream: the fish at the tail wasn't having any. I replaced the floating nymph with a no-weight fur-dubbed sinking nymph, one that floated just beneath the surface. The trout at the tail fell for it, but the next two didn't. I switched from nymphs to wets and continued the upstream approach, using a natural drift.

I continued the same approach but used rod tip action to impart movement on the drift, then greased and floated the wet fly, which can be deadly. It *can* be, but it wasn't. Then I reasoned that wets downstream might best imitate the nymph struggling to the surface.

The downstream, tip-action approach began to pay off in the broken water. I could get closer to the feeding fish, shorten and control my cast, and when a fish broke water, I could hold the fly in his feeding area. In a matter of minutes, three fish were hooked and released; others followed. I hooked fish that weren't feeding on top; they picked the fly up on the drift. The change of pattern made the difference. On this particular experience, six different techniques were used:

1. A floating wet fly on an upstream casting approach with a natural drift.
2. The same upstream approach with a spun-fur nymph that floated in the surface film.
3. The same approach with a spun-fur nymph sunk just under the surface.
4. A pair of wet flies fished upstream on a natural drift.
5. The upstream wet fly technique with movement imparted to the flies as they drifted.
6. Wet flies fished down across with rod tip action to impart movement.

Take note! I worked upstream systems until I exhausted the possibilities and *only then* went to a different position and worked the downstream approach. True, had I switched earlier to the down-and-across approach, I might have had action much earlier. But what I want to emphasize is that flexibility is important. This type of problem-solving approach will give you a plan of attack. The "either they take my dry fly or the hell with them" philosophy drastically limits the action on a hatch.

To many anglers, wet fly fishing itself means one technique: a downstream-and-across approach. They limit themselves by not working different approaches. At times, it's obvious how limiting the traditional techniques are. Tom Miller, a fishing companion and long-time friend, lived on the banks of the Yellow Breeches directly across from the Allenberry resort in Pennsylvania. It is a "fish for fun" fly area. That particular Sunday at the end of April we watched a parade of fishermen on the stream. As Tom and I chatted on the porch, we could not help but observe that every fisherman working through the broken water directly in front of the house was fishing wet flies, all using the same techniques. Down and across. Down and across. None of them catching trout, because not one was willing to change flies or techniques. They looked like robots.

Don't assume anything. When trout begin to break on top on major hatches, the logical shift is to dry fly. In most cases that's the right strategy. But don't lock yourself into them! If the fish are breaking, as in the sulphur hatch described earlier, I immediately go to wets if drys are refused. One test is to watch individual naturals float over a feeding trout. If they don't disappear, that's a clue that the trout are probably feeding underneath, even if they appear to be breaking the surface. I know some fishermen, Jack Scheffler of State College for one, who often fishes wets through the hatches with results that often humiliate the dry fly fisherman. But let's look at all the possibilities for wet flies in detail, first as a top water fly, then as a bottom. Remember, those are the two places the fish are likely to be holding—not in the middle of the current.

Wet Flies on Top

Probably the least used technique for wets, and yet one of the most productive, is the upstream cast with a natural drift. This system is the same as the upstream nymphing technique except for the tuck. You simply want to straighten the cast out so your flies, leader, line and rod tip are in a straight line for good control throughout the drift. No cowtails, loops, or curves on the terminal end. This means keeping the wrist absolutely straight on the forward cast, with the line passing straight overhead.

As your flies drift back to you, keep elevating the rod tip, take in the slack line—and watch the line for movement. Remember: with an unweighted fly

Bouncing wet flies on the surface close to shore: short-line technique with wets, used during hatches to imitate the action of the naturals.

when you see the line stop, nine chances out of ten it's a fish. Strike! This is especially true when fishing deep and faster water where the flies will ride near the surface. Any pause in the drift is probably caused by a trout, not the stream bottom. I find short casts in this upstream approach most effective in riffs, broken water and pocket water. The less line, the more control, and in broken water you can get close enough to the fish to use this method.

Paul Blankenhorn, my photographer friend, and I made our way to the bank for a high level pow-pow. The trout were there feeding but the cool waters of the Bald Eagle Creek that April evening weren't offering any sacrifices. What made it more difficult was my big mouth. I told Paul that if he went with me after work that evening I'd show him how to catch trout on a wet fly. I reasoned that since I had been successful with a pair of quill Gordon wets on a down-and-across approach the evening before I'd have little trouble. Nothing was farther from the truth. The trout were acting differently, periodically ripping the surface. The down-and-across system wasn't in their program. "They're on top!" Sure, that's it! But they weren't, and a dry fly didn't produce any better.

Darkness came early! It was time to motor home. I apologized to Paul but asked him to give me a reprieve; "Come back with me tomorrow and maybe we can figure them out." He agreed.

The following late afternoon trout were still breaking on top. Again, I persistently went down over them with wets; again they refused. Why not turn around and work upstream? It worked in the past. Why hadn't I thought of it?

I positioned myself below the last fish that broke in the pool. They weren't steady risers, but surfaced often enough to get a fix on them. The rest of that day is etched in my memory. With a pair of quill Gordon wets on the upstream approach and natural drift, I caught trout consistently. If I got a decent cast up and over a feeding trout, it took it. Those fish didn't want a fly dragging over them: it had to be a natural drift. That's the way their food was coming to them. On the natural drift upstream, it is critical that the flies move *the same speed as the current* — the way the naturals are moving. Getting that natural drift can be harder than you might think as I found one day in early May in the forties.

Up to this time all my fly-rod work had been with hand-twist retrieves and tip action. I had never thought about natural drifts; consequently, I was missing out on an exciting area of wet-fly fishing. It was early May, here and there a trout broke the flat water. My down and across, hand-twist tip action method simply would not produce. I couldn't raise those fish, and if I couldn't, who could?

I looked upstream, and saw another fly fisherman—there weren't many then—and I noticed that where I had fished over a trout, he was now playing one. I was incensed. I felt that here was a man invading my privacy and that fish should have been mine.

I continued to watch him as he worked his way down to me, and before he reached me, he landed another fish. Anger gave way to curiosity, and as he walked around me, I asked him, "Sir, what are you fishing?"

"Wet flies," was his reply.

"How are you fishing your flies?"

"Just drifting them," he said and walked away. He gave me the secret, though it wasn't until years later that I understood the concept. I then threw my flies across those fish and "drifted them," but there was still drag enough so that the fish refused to come up. I never did take those fish, but the seed of an idea was planted in my mind: you don't always have to move wet flies, you can let them drift naturally.

But it has to be *very* natural to be effective: Up-and-across casts, or straight across—or down and across all allow the currents to push through the line, and in doing so, move the flies at a faster speed. Even though this extra pull is imperceptible to the angler, it's not a natural drift and the trout know it. Casting *directly* upstream (or downstream with slack) is the best way to get a natural drift.

In order to imitate this natural level of drift, you can also prepare your flies in such a way that they will ride on the surface, in the film, or just under it. Live nymphs struggling or floating in the surface film, or those about to reach the surface are the easiest prey to trout. Sometimes the fish key on these crippled flies exclusively, and you must experiment to find what they prefer. Greasing a leader all but the last couple of inches can hold that wet fly just under the surface at a pre-determined depth. Or, go one step higher and dub the wet fly with muclin or a floatant and float it in a surface film. Don't ask questions—try it. You may surprise yourself.

Remember, as nymphs finally free themselves and attempt to become airborne Mother Nature doesn't always lend a helping hand. Cold air or water temperatures make them sluggish and wind makes it difficult for takeoff. In many cases, the trout end the struggle. To imitate these struggling flies I use a skittering technique I first learned as a boy.

When I was about twelve or thirteen years old, I spent considerable time fishing a section of Spring Creek called Rock, where a giant outcropping of limestone towered above the water. This stretch of water included riffs, pools, pocket water, and a dam that created flat water. This stretch also held springs and spring holes that fed the stream as well as a great wild-trout population. I learned much about trout fishing at Rock.

One morning, I think it was in May, I met a man on this stretch named George Close. George was a smallish man, late in years, and bent in stature. I remember few names from so long ago, but I remember his because it was significant. George Close fished close.

He took the time to show me, a mere lad, a wet-fly technique which I have used since to good advantage many times. Although well back from the bank and down on one knee, his casts were short and tight to the bank. He fished three, big-winged, size 10 or 12 wet flies on a seven or seven-and-a-half-foot leader. His approach was slow and cautious. With a short cast, he would flip those wets slightly upstream, hold his rod tip high, and dance that tip as he moved it in the direction of the flies as they swung downstream. The cast covered the area tight to the bank – where a sizable spring entered, its water flowing tight to the bank. That cold water promoted heavy weed growth and a big trout population. George used the wind to his advantage, letting it help dance the flies on the surface as they swung around.

This is a very effective technique; as a youngster I was amazed at the results. Fish splashed at those flies and George caught several brook trout as I watched. He told me that he used this technique most effectively during a hatch, when the bouncing flies would imitate emerging, flopping duns as they came off the water.

At the time I had a poor selection of flies (mostly mail-order flies from the Spiegel Company), but I did have a size 10, heavy-winged Beaverkill wet fly and a gray-hackled, yellow body fly – to which George contributed an additional fly. Following his instructions, using the wind and fighting for control all the while, I managed to bounce the flies on the water by dancing my rod tip, and I flipped a fat, eight-inch brookie onto the bank in all his red-spotted beauty. Ray Bergman was my hero at the time, and I had read his book, "Just Fishing," from cover to cover. The sections on trout fishing, worms, and wet flies were my favorites. With my heart beating in my ears with the excitement of this new discovery, I remember imagining that I was right up there with Ray Bergman as a fisherman! Well, almost.

Skittering wets to imitate the struggling nymphs and flies is also best done with a short line system. I work wet flies in this fashion by keeping a low profile on the bank, staying well back from the water's edge.

As soon as the forward cast is made, I push the rod skyward with an extended arm. I fish three flies on the leader: the top fly is the business fly. The other two flies move under the surface as emergers.

On a five-inch dropper, I tie on a size larger than what you might expect would do the job: a #10 instead of a #12. A larger fly gives more surface disturbance. The five-inch dropper is about an inch longer than the second dropper below, longer than I normally use. The extra leader material allows a trout enough slack to pull the fly as it dangles off the leader. Ordinarily I'd say a five-inch dropper is too long, since it would twist; but since some of the dropper is actually out of the water, you won't have that problem, and the fly has that much more free movement and action on the surface.

Once the cast is made and the rod lifted into position, I bounce the top fly on the surface. I keep the flies coming toward me with a steady lift, then pop another short cast. The strikes on that top fly are usually slashes, and the other flies produce just as often. If the winds are gusty, simply extend your rod then wind work the flies on the water. It's tough to control but the wind provides good fly action.

A natural drift can be accomplished on a straight downstream approach where it is impossible to wade or cast into a good position. You can use a slack cast to float the flies down to the fish. Let's say a heavy stand of Alders overhangs the glide below you. The currents in time have cut a deep gut at their roots—too deep to wade.

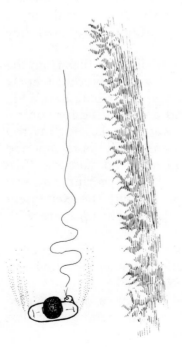

Vertical view of a downstream drift cast.

You take your time and position yourself upstream from the glide and back from the bank, within view of the water you want to fish. You strip enough line from the reel to cover the distance from the top of the glide to its tail. Then with a false cast shoot all the line on a forward cast. Check the rod high and as the loop unfolds, pull the rod backward and upward depositing slack line at the base of the cast, where line meets the water under the rod tip. Now drop your elbow and watch the line and leader drift, taking up the slack on the water in front of you. As the currents pull the fly to the dark water at the base of the Alders, watch the leader at the point where it disappears in the water! A hesitation, a twitch, or subtle drag tells you a fish has taken it. This is one occasion when I do have slack between the rod and the fly, which is a slight disadvantage. If the physical characteristics of the stream rule out an upstream approach, floating a slack line downstream is a good compromise; using a trained eye, you can still pick up fish.

Wet Flies Downstream

There are occasions when heavily-dressed flies in a straight downstream presentation can work: Early in Chapter 1, I talked about conditioned hatchery trout and overhead feeding. Because of this conditioned response, flies that hang in the riffs, pockets, or the slower water in tight to the bank are often good producers. Cast straight downstream into those areas and let your fly swing in the currents; slowly retrieve, release, and retrieve again. Move your rod tip to one side, then the other from time to time, to cover all the holding water. Hold the fly in there! Stock trout seeking overhead food might take awhile to find those flies in broken water. Give them time, especially in cold water. When caddis hatches are heavy in April or early May, try this: fish only heavy, broken pocket water – forget the flats. Use a short line and work downstream and fish only the pockets in behind boulders and breaks. Use a well-dressed palmered #10 or #8 wet fly, and bounce the flies in the pockets. A long rod of nine feet or better can be an advantage when trying to hold wet flies in one specific area. Heavy riffs or currents push through the middle of a line and drag your flies out of the productive water at edges of the currents. The trout never get a good look at your fly or refuse them as they drag; a longer rod can hold them there, since there's less line on the water.

Here's a simple casting technique which will also help hold the flies in a pocket without drag: just a mend in the air off a downstream cast. Mend the line up over the water you want to cover. At the completion of the mend, keep your arm and rod extended and hold the line in the specific area you want the flies to cover. Now impart movement to the flies if you wish. This is a good tactic to use covering the opposite bank of the stream where the fish hold in areas of lesser velocity.

As previously mentioned, the top dropper fly can be used effectively in skittering; it can also be used as an exciter. In early season when the water is green or high and off-color, a bright fly such as the Silver Doctor or Coachman type on a #10 or #12 can get you into a good fish. Most streams have an abundance of small fish: red fins, dace, small trout—that flash and turn in the currents. Wets with white wings or mylar bodies imitate the flash action of these small fish well. Over the years I have taken good native trout with flashy wets under these conditions.

Stock trout conditioned to overhead feeding patterns are also attracted to these highly-visible flies. I would highly recommend a Royal Coachman on the top dropper at the bridge hole where they always dump a few buckets of trout for the opening day.

Wet Flies on the Bottom

A fully-weighted fly allows you to leave the immediate surface and sub-surface to probe the bottom with wets which can be highly productive. One wet fly system I use is as follows: A weighted nymph or wet is the tail fly; two droppers are placed at two-foot intervals above it. If the water isn't too deep

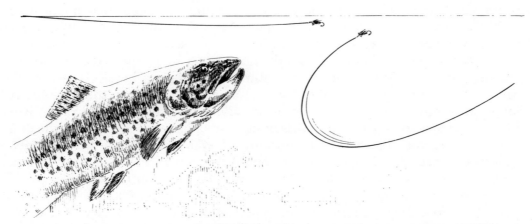

A upstream cast-natural drift (at left) with wet flies can be more effective at times than the down-and-across method (right), which drags the fly across the water.

The short-line, pocket-water, downstream technique with heavily dressed, palmer-hackled wets is often effective during a caddisfly hatch.

or fast a moderately-weighted fly will suffice. If the pockets are deep and turbulent, a heavily weighted fly is in order. (See diagram on weighted nymphs).

When hatches begin, the emerging flies can be found at various levels. With this chain of flies you've got three different levels and imitations to cover the stages on one leader. Chances are three times as good you'll find the level of feeding activity.

Here are some approaches using this system:

1. *A straight upstream cast,* tucking the nymph or weighted wet using a natural drift and no movement: let the flies sink and cover the bottom.

2. *If there is a deep gut or pocket in front of you, tuck the cast up and across,* elevate the rod to control the slack until the flies have gained the depth of the pocket. Then slowly lift them with action in the rod tip and a slow hand and twist retrieve.

3. *Let the fly settle and begin to drag on the bottom,* then lift the rod tip slowly and handtwist—no tip action. Repeat the process and add action to the tip.

4. *Let the flies settle on the drift.* As soon as the flies make contact with the bottom, lift the rod tip and let the fly settle again. Repeat this action completely through the drift: lift, drop, lift, drop.

5. Remember, weight isn't always necessary to achieve a bottom drift in slow water. The count-and-retrieve system works this way: cast and let the flies settle to a count of five — then begin the retrieve. Repeat the process with a ten count, then fifteen, then twenty. This is a way to prospect for feeding levels.

If the water moving is with any degree of velocity, the trout are either positioned on the bottom or just under the surface — both areas of lesser velocity — not hanging half way between where they have to fight the currents. Depending on the depth of the water and the speed of the currents, trout will move up off the bottom to intercept nymphs or your wet flies. The count system simply is a way calibrating your casting so that when you do get a hit, you can find the same level again. Remember that the count may be different in water of different velocity and depth. If they hit on a count of eight in a glide, they may hit on six in a slower pool.

To illustrate the effectiveness of the count system: my friend Miles Milliron, a good fly-rod man and a great muskelunge fisherman, were in Nova Scotia together.

We had fished in the Margaree for Atlantic salmon and were on our way home when we heard there was a good run of sea-run brook trout (coasters) in Trout River. When we arrived, sure enough there was a heavy concentration of trout in the pool at the bridge.

There was also a heavy concentration of fishermen, too; we watched at least a dozen, all using the same technique. Each one shot a line across the pool and stripped their wet flies back as fast as possible. Every fisherman that fished that pool used the same retrieve. They didn't change speed, they didn't change delivery, they didn't change anything. Not one fisherman caught a fish.

Miles and I cast our wet flies across the pool and let them sink. We began our retrieve after about a count of fifteen. We gradually lifted them, sometimes with a rod-tip motion, sometimes on a gradual straight lift — and had no trouble taking a trout. The fishermen around us observed our success, but never once stopped to ask what method we employed and never stopped to watch our technique. They continued to fish the same way.

Experimenting with counts and retrieves will often yield surprising results. Don't be afraid to try unusual combinations.

One day in 1946 I was fishing the Rock area of Spring Creek with no results. I sat down on a rock to rest and contemplate, and haplessly flipped my wet flies upstream. The flies sank and held on the bottom; it was deep, slow water. I picked my fly rod up to see if the flies were fast on the bottom, but they weren't. I set my rod back down and continued to daydream. Again I picked up my rod. But this time as I did so a decent fish stopped the flies on the lift. Not knowing whether this was an accident or not (I felt sure it was) I repeated the process. I threw my wets upstream, let them sink, lifted them up, let them settle again, and when they were well settled, lifted them slowly, and again connected with a fish. Thus a new tactic was learned by accident.

At the age of twelve or thirteen, as a knobby-kneed, freckle faced, pain-in-the tail boy scout, camping in the wilds of the Seven Mountain Range in Pennsylvania, I had a chance to discover another sinking-lifting tactic that worked on brook trout in a mountain pool.

Don Krumrine, a cohort, was equally as unmanageable, and encouraged me to duck out of a well-organized educational field trip. I grabbed my fly rod and headed for the stream. Lying on our stomachs in an off-limits area we watched half a dozen brookies placidly finning in a gem of a mountain pool — a couple of them ten-inchers. Excitedly Don directed my cast. It fell short, but I let it be and watched my wet fly slowly sink. The trout seemed mildly disturbed and moved out of the way of the fly as it drifted by them and settled on the bottom. Moments later I slowly lifted the wet off the bottom. It traveled but a few inches before a legal trout grabbed it. It never knew what hit him. The fish was air born and then flopping in the grass behind me. I killed the fish and we both admired it and then went back to fishing. The process was repeated. But, this time after the fly hit the water the trout milled around and it took considerable time before they settled. During this time the fly was resting on the bottom and once again the lift was employed. It was interrupted by a ten-incher. I jumped to my feet to play it, and that ended the lesson. I do remember vaguely as I strutted around the camp with my trout the scout master saying something about sending me home if the next time I ------.

As we have seen, wet fly techniques can vary both fishing level and speed, in fact, they should. Don't be afraid to tie a weighted nymph below wet flies, or place a split shot above a wet fly. If you are working wets over trout that won't cooperate, prospect for them on a different level. That usually means deeper. Lightly-weighted wets will drop the flies a tad deeper and if your wets aren't weighted, a pinch of wrap around a few inches above the tail fly and a pinch three inches above each dropper can do the trick.

Wet Fly Imitation: Speed, Movement, and Levels

The reason of course, all these techniques work at different times — is that different emerging naturals behave differently. Watching nymphal movement can give one insight not only in relation to the real action of the insects, but speed of that action as well. Most of us don't take the opportunity or enough time to simply observe at streamside. We are more interested in fishing than observing.

Daryl Awarjo and I monitored an aquarium loaded with a variety of mayfly nymphs through two fishing seasons. As the hatches progressed, we had the opportunity to watch the action. The different patterns of movement and the various speeds at which the nymphs surfaced and hatched gave me an understanding why over the years some of my wet fly techniques were successful.

The action imparted to the fly and the speed of retrieve are critical. The short lift of the rod tip throughout the drift I unconsciously used often was simply a habit. Now I know that you need to constantly adjust the speed of retrieve and tip action, or lack of it, till you find a fish-provoking combination. Many times I've slowed the hand and twist retrieve down to one retrieve per eight seconds with a slight, almost imperceptible, rod tip movement. Most of the time our retrieves are too fast, and we cover too much water, too fast. Just slowing down can help. Yet, there are times when a series of quick, extended lifts will make it happen, as in the case of mayflies as they push and sputter for takeoff.

On one occasion that comes to memory is a cold April day in 1945 on one of the Pennsylvania limestone streams I had been fishing the usual down across technique, mechanically bouncing the rod tip. Once in awhile a trout would break the surface, but I couldn't raise one. Then, more out of anger or impatience, I would throw directly over the rise and employ three or four exaggerated lifts. Then I'd lift the flies and make another cast not fishing the cast out. Which particular mayfly behavior I imitated could only be guessed, but it worked! Then, rather than working over rising trout, I covered the water off the far bank using the same technique and had excellent action the rest of the afternoon.

Patterns

But which patterns to use? Here is a tip that can help you prospect for feeding fish. In early season, the basic mayfly hatches are either dun, black, dark brown or a combination of the latter. Wets in these colors and shades tied in five different sizes—number 18 through 10—can keep you in the game. Many times a beginning fly fisherman is in a dilemma over the myriad of choices or suggested patterns. Size is important if the blue quill is hatching, a small dun mayfly on a #18 hook will work for you. If a large dark caddis is coming off, you might best imitate it with a #10 or #12 black-bodied palmered fly with a mottled turkey wing. Stick with those five sizes and five different shades: it narrows the field.

Wet flies imitate mayflies from the nymphal stage to the dun, sunken terrestrials, sunken insects or small minnows, but they can well imitate fresh water shrimp and even cressbugs. They can be fished year-round effectively, but when the major mayfly hatches are over, most fly fishermen put wets away and go to dry fly. What a mistake. I grant you, dries are more fun but if you can't entice them on top, don't rule out the wet fly. It is the most versatile fly of them all. This experience is a prime example.

The scene was Spring Creek: an area known as Rock where a giant outcropping of limestone towered above limestone waters. It was a warm July evening. The water at its summertime low. I had expected to fish on top, but there wasn't any surface activity, so I reverted to my old standby wet fly, and worked it down-and-across without success. I replaced the grey hackle-yellow bodied fly with a Dark Cahill wet—no droppers, only a tail fly, and sat on the bank until the gut leader was saturated and ready for use. Idly I flipped the fly upstream, mainly to see if the leader would sink. As it passed me in the shallow riff, I saw a flash, and the leader straightened out. The trout, a foot long native, had hooked itself. But, more important, I had made a discovery— two in fact: not only a different approach, but also a fly that produced. I decided to try it again, on purpose. A short distance below, a magnificent limestone spring fed a relatively flat stretch of water. Watercress lined the bank on the spring side and provided good cover as well as optimum temperatures for trout. Kneeling well back from the bank, I cast again and watched the butt end of my leader float by. From my vantage point I watched a big brown drift out and move to the fly. The butt of the leader stopped and I was into a magnificent trout! I jumped into the water which was freezing and deeper than I thought, well up to my chest. I foundered, but managed to hold on and land that fish, a heavy eighteen-inch native brown trout that was truly a prize.

Impervious to the discomfort of wet clothing, I rushed to tell my father of the new technique, the fly, and to show off my trophy. He was impressed with my success and the fish—but failed to grasp the lesson. (Even today we laugh and share the humor of the fact that my father never really knew what patterns adorned the leaders' end. He remembers the names of but a few—the Cahill, Black Gnat and why I'll never know—The Parmachene Belle.)

This story contains a lesson: limestone waters have an abundance of fresh water shrimp and cressbugs that can be well imitated with wets. The Dark Cahill, with its dun fur body and throat hackle must have simulated a cressbug floating naturally in the current. The swimming action of shrimp and the tumbling of a cressbug can be copied with wet fly techniques. A fox fur-bodied wet fly with a tad of marabou across the back and extended as a tail, worked close to the bank with a downstream approach is one system (remember, shrimp are good swimmers). Both the cressbug and the shrimp can also be fished on a downstream drift.

Droppers and Leaders

There are probably as many dropper systems as there are wet flys. My Three-fly system has the simple advantage of odds.

To tie droppers, I use an extended piece of leader off the heavier end of a blood or barrel knot (the two are interchangeable), four inches in length. Using the heavier end allows the dropper to stand out and away from the leader below it and prevents twisting. If I want to add a dropper without cutting back the leader, a dropper can be tied on above a barrel knot with an improved clinch knot, and then snugged against the barrel knot. One other solution: a looped overhand knot with a dropper tied in the loop with a clinch knot, drawn up without a visible loop.

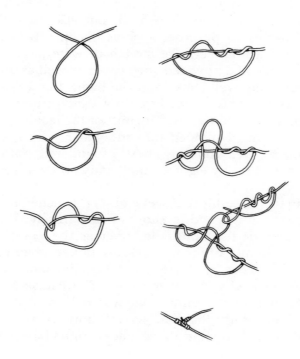

The oldtimers advocated loops on the leader and snelled wet flies with loops for the hookup. The major reason loops were used is that they didn't know better. Loop hookups have several disadvantages: If you get an occasional wind knot because your cast is in the same plane or your line is kicking on itself, you are making a casting mistake. Loops add to the problem. The leader kicks and hangs on the loops. And when fish hit the dropper and begin to roll, you've got one hell of a mess. The leaders twist into a ball around the dropper. Loops also hang up in debris, and they drag. In my scuba gear I've observed loops from underwater, and I saw how the extra bulk of the loops dragged and acted like a hinge, making an unnatural drift.

A sliding dropper isn't worth a damn. Not only because you can't tell where the dropper is on the leader, but the hooking qualities are poor. The extra give on a sliding dropper allows a trout the extra chance to get rid of the fly.

Flyline

The flyline that I find to be most effective for wet flyfishing is a double-tapered floating line. The small diameter front portion of the line will sink, so that you have a line section you can work in subsurface levels, yet you can maintain some visibility with the floating section. Weight forward floaters are too bouyant in the forward section, often dragging the flies on a downstream cast. It is also more difficult to impart motion to the flies. WF lines are fine

WET FLY - EMERGING NYMPHS - 9'

STIFF NYLON					
.017	.015	.013	.011	.009	.008
10"	20"	20"	20"	20"	20"

WET FLY - TWO DROPPERS - 8' 6"

STIFF NYLON					
.017	.015	.013	.011	.009	008
10"	20"	16"+4" dropper 60'	20"	16"+4" dropper 29'	20"

Leader designs for wet flies.

for upstream approaches, though. Sinking lines and sinking tips will belly under water in the shifting currents and they are very difficult to control, particularly in moving water. And you have to pick up the whole cast before you can make another cast.

The Leader

I'm going to give one basic wet fly leader formula, one that George Harvey devised and that I use exclusively.

A twelve-inch section of .017. The sections follow in this order: twenty-two inches of .015; twenty-two inches of .013; twenty-two inches of .011 and .009 and .008—all DuPont stiff monofilament. It isn't necessary to go lighter than 3x or .008.

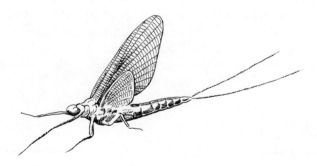

4

STREAMERS:
Matching Minnows

It was a summer day on Letort Creek; the fish were touchy and I was growing weary from the lack of activity. Terrestrials and midges on the surface didn't excite the trout, and nymphs fared little better. Then my fishing companion, Tom Miller, said, "Try a streamer."

The thought was repulsive. Hell, I didn't want to fish "hardware," I wanted to finesse the trout. But after twenty more minutes of finessing, I succumbed to Tom's suggestion. I tied on a multi-grizzly saddle-hackled streamer with a tinsel body and an orange bucktail belly—a baby brown trout imitation. The streamer was fastened to a nine-foot leader tapered to 2X with no weight added.

The results were astonishing. Trout were coming out of areas where there shouldn't have been trout. They seemed starved. Tom shook his head and called me a hardware fisherman with no scruples and little class. But I noticed Tom had a streamer tied to the end of his leader.

Stream problems are often solved by going to another extreme, and streamers are frequently that extreme.

Given my choice, I'd rather fish nymphs, drys, and wet flies than streamers. But catching fish is what it's all about and if it takes a streamer or a bucktail to turn the trick, I'll fish it as hard as the next guy. And I'll try more than one way of fishing it. Preoccupied with imitations of aquatic insects, fly fishermen tend to forget that streamers also imitate live creatures. Streamers have to be fished like *live* minnows. Live minnow fishermen do just that season after season, and fly fishermen can take a few lessons from the veteran minnow fisherman's book. I bait fished well into my twenties, and I still find ways to use the old timers' minnow fishing tactics to improve my streamer presentation. But let's begin at the beginning.

First, know what baitfish inhabit the waters you fish. Limestone streams may have an abundance of sculpins or redfin suckers that form a principal part of the trout's diet. Freestone streams often are populated by dace, shiners, or chubs, with some species being in greater abundance than others. Coastal streams or those that feed large bodies of fresh water may get runs of smelt or sawbellies, and the timing of such runs becomes important.

The naturals determine the basic design, size, shape, color, and action of the imitation. But what is most important is finding the level, or depth, you must fish. In other words, where are the naturals? How do they behave in this water? *That* is the question—not, "How do you fish streamers?" "Why down-and-across." Sometimes.

Baitfish, like trout, seek cover and food in areas of lesser current—expecially cover. Ever watch sculpins on the stream bottom? They hide under anything they can: rocks, streambanks, debris. When they move from one place to another, they move tight to the bottom with a quick, wiggling motion and then scurry for cover. Ever seine for redfins? Where do you find them? In the riffs. You have to dislodge the stones on the stream bottom and push down through a riff to drive the minnows into the net. Schools of minnows inhabit backwater eddies or lie tight to the bank where they can get out of the main current.

Baitfish, like trout, must find areas of lesser current velocity for survival. For example, take one very important baitfish, the sculpin. In my bait days, I'd lip hook a live sculpin, drop it by my feet, and watch. Immediately it would head for the rocky bottom and cover. Lift it off the bottom a few inches and drop the rod tip. The live sculpin would dive like a submarine. If you use split-shot with the bait, they'd wiggle under cover and you were hung up, unless the water was deep or fast.

Even without weight, I'd let them lie on the bottom. They'd wiggle under obstructions and hang me up. The secret was to keep them moving, I saw. As soon as they touched bottom, I gently lifted them, repeating this process the whole way through the drift.

Today I transfer this to fishing my sculpin imitation. If the water is shallow — a shallow riff or a pocket in inches of water — and you have weight tied into your sculpin imitation, use a straight overhead cast upstream. Check the rod tip high, drop your arm or elbow, but keep the rod tip up so you'll have immediate contact with the fly.

It won't take long for the fly to gain the bottom naturally. As soon as you feel it touch bottom, lift the rod tip just a little bit. Lift each time you feel it touch the bottom. Keep the line tight between the rod tip and the fly and follow the course of the drift with the tip.

The speed of the drift is important: most streamer fishermen have a tendency to overemphasize streamer action. A twitch, lift, or pull can move the fly too fast, so that it travels too far off the bottom. *Slow down!* The more time the fly spends down on the bottom — where the naturals are — the more effective it is. Coordinate the feel of the imitation touching the bottom, the gentle lift of the rod tip, and a slow hand-twist retrieve to keep the line tight.

I've watched hundreds of fishermen work sculpin imitations, and most of these anglers fish them like frightened bait — stripping line in like hell and moving the flies erratically across the currents, not *with* the currents and *on* the bottom. On occasion this cross-stream action takes a fish, but they'd pick up a lot more if they would imitate the live sculpin.

For example, for night fishing, I use a weighted fly. I'let it sink to the bottom, move it up a couple of inches, rest it, and then repeat the process. This is a very slow method, but a most effective one. When a live sculpin feeds, it rests on the bottom, wiggles inches ahead, picks up food. Then it rests again. At times it wiggles a few inches up off the bottom to feed on something overhead and wiggles back down.

Positioning the streamer at the right fishing level and giving it the right action: that's the streamer man's game. I know of no better teachers than the veteran minnow-fishermen I grew up with. Guys like Lewie Weaver and Les Rote could make a minnow do the mambo in the stream using live rigs on a fly rod.

Streamers on The Bottom

Some of the minnow fishermen I know liphook minnows and use a natural drift, which is a deadly presentation. The live minnow drifts with the currents, heads directly for the bottom, struggling to find the safety of cover. In the heavy currents, the minnow is bounced and rolled along the bottom, frantically working against the pull of the leader and the currents, trying to keep upright and gain the safety of the rocky bottom. Such a natural, easy prey is hard for a fish to resist. The trout doesn't have to chase it: it simply drifts with the minnow and picks it up.

To imitate this presentation with a streamer, we have to use weights in certain adjustments on the leader work to slow the action of the fly. We want a natural drift—slower than the bottom currents. But our imitation isn't going to make a straight line for the bottom and wiggle for us as a live minnow would. We have to supply the depth and action with the cast, drift, and retrieve.

Use the same casting method as you would in your nymphing techniques, the tuck cast and its variations. Weight the streamer or bucktail, as you would a nymph, in the front third of the hook. A 4XL hook will drop the head of the streamer down toward the bottom—the length of the streamer hook gives that leverage. The streamer drops head down toward the bottom; the tuck cast gives it time to get there.

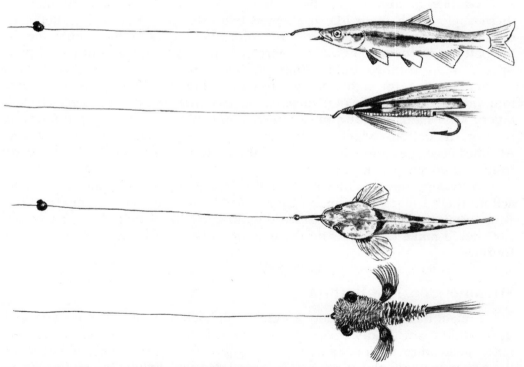

The fly fisherman's imitations should be fished with the same action as live minnows are fished. In this illustration weight is incorporated in the streamer and in the eyes of the sculpin imitation.

Properly regulating the amount of weight you use in a streamer or sculpin imitation is important, as well as placement of the weight in the fly. One way to weight a sculpin imitation is by using split-shot tied into a muddler-style head as eyes. Ed Shenk snugs a split-shot right on the head of his muddle fly. You can tie patterns to fish at different depths by using different sizes of split-shot.

If the streamer is a marabou or a feather streamer, the action of the current on the material supplies the movement, so you can fish a natural drift, just as you would a nymph. Tuck an upstream cast with the rod tip held up, and strip or hand twist the line in as it comes back to you. Use the strip retrieve if the currents are fast—*But you've got to maintain control of the line from the rod tip to the streamer*. If you're shooting a considerable amount of line—thirty feet or more—upstream, watch the line for any sudden stop or hesitation. Trout don't always rip into their prey. A minnow is often simply interrupted and killed, then inhaled on the drift.

The same technique applies to a shorter cast when an upstream approach is impossible, perhaps because of an obstruction across the stream. Tuck the cast across and work for as much of an upstream angle as possible. Keep the rod tip up as the streamer passes downstream of you and lifts off the bottom. Impart any action you wish: lift the tip and strip, or hand twist slowly and bounce the tip. Vary the speed of retrieve. As the fly reaches you, shake line out with the rod tip down and then lift the tip to take up excess slack; this keeps the streamer rolling on the bottom for an extended drift downstream.

When you are working a streamer upstream in pocket water and riffs where you can get close, shorten up on the cast. Use the downer-and-upper tuck cast and *drive* that streamer into the water. As it comes back, use the rod tip to impart further action to the fly, as usual.

The retrieve is very important when fishing streamers in deep water. I want my streamer or bucktail to have as much time on the bottom as possible. But what should it be doing down there? Stream minnows such as redfins and sculpins don't streak around. Sure, a small sucker under attack may dart or dash for safety, and any minnow may dash for safety; but by and large there isn't much chasing going on down there. So once I have the feel of the fly on the bottom, I try to retrieve just enough to keep the line tight to the rod tip, so I can continually sense the fly working on the bottom.

When I work slow, flat water, backwater eddies, or changing currents of lesser speeds, I use a hand-twist retrieve slow enough to keep the fly down there. In slower currents, the slow hand twist plus the action of the current on the fly can be deadly. Even in fairly fast currents, I use a hand twist and lift with a downward strip for a retrieve. The combination of the lift of the

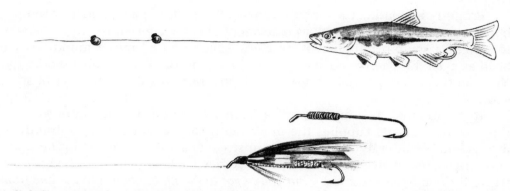

A lightly-weighted streamer fly can simulate the subsurface "strung" minnow technique that the old minnow fishermen used.

rod tip and the downward pull of the line over an extended finger, along with
the line hand making the hand twist, gives constant control with good sensitivity even at a faster pace.

Whenever possible, use the hand twist retrieve. You are more in touch
with the streamer with a hand-twist. Your fingertips are more sensitive to the
motion of the streamer bouncing on the bottom. When the fly is coming back
at a fast pace, you may have to strip it in. Whatever you do, don't trap the line
against the rod. A strip retrieve, with the line passing over the extended index
finger on the rod hand, is more effective than trapping the fly line against the
handle. The extended finger by itself is more sensitive than the finger tight to
the rod handle. The feel of the line across the finger keeps you in touch with
the fly and the action of the rod. The line trapped against the rod handle is
okay when you're simply working to take up slack or when speed is essential.

Some veteran live-minnow fishermen also string their minnows. They attach a piece of leader with a loop tied in the end, insert a needle in the minnow's mouth and push it out its vent. With the eye of the needle open or
broken to catch the loop, they pull the loop through the minnow's mouth and
out its vent, attach a set of treble hooks to the loop and then insert one hook
of the treble just aft of the vent. The piece of leader is approximately eighteen
to twenty-four inches long, usually not more than two feet. A swivel is tied in
the opposite end of the leader, and between the swivel and the minnow the
weight was strung.

A stiff fly rod is used to cast this rig: off the end of the fly line another
three- to four-foot piece of leader is connected to the swivel. Now the minnow can turn in the current without twisting the leader.

When pulled through the water the minnow rolls slowly, just barely turning over.

This crippled minnow is fished with a single split-shot or no more than a pair of split-shot placed above the minnow. The weight didn't pull the minnow to the bottom: The trout came up through the water for the bait. A short line and fairly slow retrieve were used to work the minnow around debris, boulders, tight to stream banks, or under overhanging brush with a gentle rod-tip lift to turn the minnow over. My friend Ed Shenk from Carlisle, Pa. is a master with this technique and a sculpin imitation, an imitation he made famous.

To relate the strung minnow to flyfishing, let's begin by using a floating line. If you want no more than a foot or so of depth use streamers with weight tied into the pattern, or use a split-shot about a foot above the streamer but you will still have to adjust the weight and its placement on the leader depending on the depth and speed of the water.

Using a short line and a relatively short leader (six to seven feet long at the most), your casts should be less than twelve feet. Most casts will be four to six feet, and some will only be two or three feet. The leader tippet should not be less than .011 inch diameter monofilament. You have a chance to catch big fish with this method and you don't want them to break off. Also, the heavy tippet is required because once you hook up with a fish in the tight cover around which you will be fishing the streamer, you will have to work the fish out of there quickly before it hangs you up.

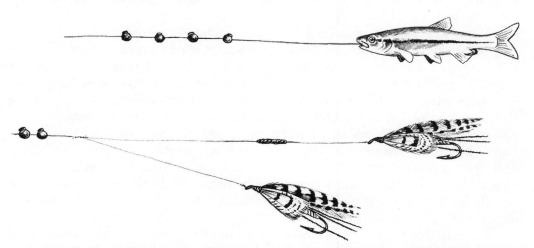

Streamer flies may also be used to bottom fish with a fast retrieve in the same fashion as strung minnows are used.

Your cast can be made straight overhead, and for accuracy, end the cast with thumb and knuckles pointing at the target. In tight brush, a simple underhand flip is sometimes sufficient — or you may want to simply extend the rod and drop the streamer into holding areas. Let the streamer settle for a moment after it enters the water before lifting or imparting any action. If the stream is off-color and a bit high, this short-line method, working close to the brush and boulders, is a dandy. Fish only those areas in tight to the brush piles or roots. Leave the other areas for another day — good fish want to get out of the heavy water when the water level is high and move in tight to pursue their food. Not only are the trout seeking this cover, but minnows as well.

The live-minnow fishermen also use a strung minnow to bottom fish. They use all-monofilament line and a string of six to ten split-shot between the minnow and the swivel. The minnow may be a five- or six-inch chub.

Several techniques are used with this rig: A minnow can be flipped out far across the stream in an arching cast. Once the minnow hits the water, the rod tip is held high until the minnow touches the bottom. Then the rod tip is lowered to pick up the slack. The angler has to strip like hell, at times stopping and changing speeds while lifting the rod tip rythmically as it is stripped in. That minnow will be fairly churning, rising and falling, stopping, and swinging with the downstream currents as it races across the bottom. This presentation is deadly on big fish; the retrieve is tantalizing and deep in the trout's safety zone. The trout don't have time to look it over. It is natural: a crippled minnow, a quick-moving minnow, a darting minnow, and most importantly, a minnow down at the trout's level.

Many years ago, Lewie Weaver and I watched Les Rote use this fast-sinking, fast-retrieve live-minnow method on upper Penns Creek one early-spring morning. Les might well have been using an electric shocker, for each cast seemed to turn over a fish or hook one. One trout, a seventeen-inch brown, was flopped out on the bank, and smaller fish were returned. I can still see the long line of monofilament sail completely across a particular long, flat glide, the minnow thunking between two hemlock trees, inches short of the bank. Les lifted the rod briefly, then lowered it and stripped. The water churned as one hell of a big trout rolled for but missed the minnow. Les chucked one more cast over the spot, and failing to raise the fish again, moved on. He knew that trout wasn't going anywhere; it would be there for another day.

It is possible to implement the same technique with a fly. Instead of using a conventional fly line, you can substitute flat monofilament. Flat monofilament can be handled just like a fly line, but it offers the important advantage

of less air and water resistance, so your fly sinks very quickly and you have excellent sensitivity from hand to rod tip to fly.

When I fish a long line using monofilament, I add a steeply tapered leader to the tip of the flat monofilament. For example, I may come off the flat monofilament with twenty inches of .019-inch-diameter monofilament and then add sixteen-to twenty-inch sections of .017-, .015-, .013-, and .011-inch-diameter leader material. All of the leader monofilament should be stiff material. The tippet section may be loaded with lead: four or five split-shot placed two inches apart beginning twelve to fourteen inches above the streamer. The amount of lead you use depends on the depth and speed of the water.

After the cast, hold the rod tip high, let the streamer get to the bottom, drop the rod tip and strip in the line quickly over the extended finger of your rod hand, and try to keep the streamer close to the bottom. The current and changes in depth will dictate the speed of your retrieve. If the water deepens, slow the retrieve, letting the streamer settle for a mite, but remember that you have a lot of weight at the business end of your leader so don't delay too long or you'll hang up. This fly-fishing technique imitates the live-minnow fisherman's technique, and it puts your imitation at the depth the trout are, moving the fly fast enough so that the trout don't have much time to think things over before striking.

Using the same rig, you can also cover the bottom slowly with a dragging, bouncing retrieve. This is another technique used by the live-minnow fishermen. Shoot your cast across and slightly upstream, check the cast high (at the 10:30 position), and let the streamer and weight drive into the water first. With this technique you should need only two or three split-shot or one wraparound lead strip with a weighted streamer. After the cast, extend your arm and keep the rod tip high until you feel the streamer and weight reach the bottom of the stream. Let the line go slack. Then drop your elbow, keeping the rod tip high, and strip in the line until it tightens and you feel the streamer on the bottom.

Continue to keep the rod tip elevated and move it with the line in the water as the currents swing the streamer around. A gentle lift and touch of the tip may accompany the swing. Strip slowly or hand twist, keeping pace with the current. If you need speed, drop the tip momentarily, strip in a tad of line and wait until the streamer gains the bottom. Elevate the tip again and continue to strip. The streamer rolls, bounces, is lifted with motion, imparted and then dropped again; the streamer is being lifted and then dropped and dragged along the bottom. Each time you feel the bottom, the hand twist or strip with the rod tip elevated, it lifts the imitation off the bottom. The distance that the streamer will lift off the bottom is determined by the placement of the split-shot. The higher up the leader they are placed, the higher up the streamer will drift off the bottom. If you want the streamer tight to the bottom with this bouncing, lifting technique, then place the weight closer to the fly.

When using this technique it is important, as when wet-fly fishing, to maintain a ninety-degree angle between the rod tip and the fly line as the line goes into the water. The ninety-degree angle can be maintained even if the line comes off the rod tip in a slight upstream or downstream direction.

Thus far I've stressed deep-water streamer techniques, each one styled after live-minnow tactics. But, of course, more conventional tactics with a streamer are also effective. When fishing streamers on a small stream, I like to use a floating line—also on any stream when the action is on top, such as when the fish are moving to minnows or chasing them in the shallows. Trout seem inclined to chase minnows late in the season when the water has warmed. A floating double-taper line with a nine or nine-and-a-half foot leader that is tapered to .011- or .009-inch-diameter monofilament (1X or 2X) is effective in low, clear water. This leader design is the same as for basic wet fly leader.

I've fished at night when out of the silent darkness the water exploded. For example, below a federal fish hatchery where a multitude of small rainbows once escaped from one of the ponds and infiltrated the big, flat water below, the fingerlings would lie just under the surface and dimple from morning to night on minutiae floating in the surface film. In time, as summer stretched into fall, their numbers decreased, stored in the body tissues of those cannibal brown trout that picked them off on top. On rivers such as the Delaware I've heard big browns thrashing the surface, chomping on forage fish coming to the top to feed. I've watched big trout nail small fish and then shake the fish with their heads still out of water, slashing from side to side for the kill. Here, surface-stripping techniques come into play. The line is placed over the extended first finger of the rod hand and worked back in a series of short tugs in rapid order or by stripping three to four feet of line in hauls, changing the rod position to compliment the changing currents and position the streamer where the action is. Another approach is to cast downstream and let the streamer hang in the surface, the currents working the fibers of the streamer wing. With either approach, you want to keep the streamer in the trout's feeding zone as long as possible.

Streamers may not always imitate minnows, they might well represent insects at times. For example, several years ago I was fishing a limestone stream in late July. The stream was laced with patches of elodea and the water was

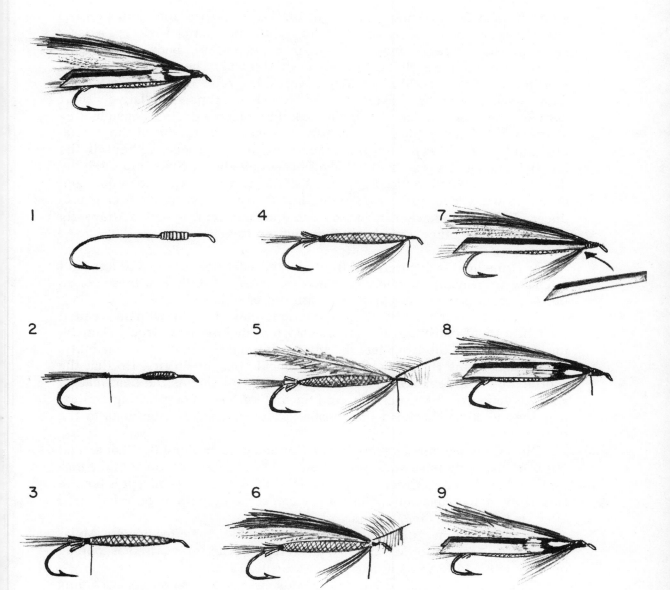

Red-Fin Streamer. 1. Weight streamer hook on front third of hook shank. 2. Cover with thread and tie in orange hackle-fiber tail. 3. Tie in Mylar tubing for body. 4. Add throat hackle (orange hackle fibers). 5. Tie in white marabou for topping. 6. Tie in dark brown marabou over white marabou. 7. Add Mylar strip with black edge painted on it. 8. Tie in jungle cock (or substitute) for eye. 9. Build head and tie off.

a bit off color from a shower the night before. Terrestrial limitations on top failed to raise a fish, and in searching for an attention getter I selected a dark-green bucktail streamer with a pea-green molded-plastic body. It had been shuffled around in my fly box for years without trial. The water was at summertime low; the previous evening's rain didn't raise the level, so weight wasn't needed with the bucktail. I soaked it well and flipped a relatively short cast, angling upstream, and let the fly sink. In moments the line began to drag as the bucktail settled in the weed growth. I eased the fly out of the vegetation and let it settle again, but this time on the lift a trout hooked himself, the line tightened and a red-tailed holdover brown fought for cover and safety by diving into the waving weed growth. For the next hour the technique continued to work, and under similar conditions over the years it's been a producer. I firmly believe that dark-green bucktail represented a dragonfly nymph or some other nymphal activity within the elodea.

Anytime light is diffused and trout feel the safety of darkness or less light intensity from high, off-colored, or muddy water, or darkness, these conditions are conducive to bringing good fish out of hiding.

Streamers fished under these conditions and at night with movement built into them constitute the ingredients for catching good trout. Namely, pushing water so the trout feel the movement and the motion for visibility. The design of the fly, with heavy head hackle tied in tip first (so that the shorter fibers underneath brace the longer fibers) expands the head hackle and the action of the water. The rod-tip motion has a compressing and expanding effect on the head that pushes water and sends vibrations to the trout.

Duck flank feathers or goose breast feathers used as shoulders that extend out from the body push water; marabou and saddle hackles move in the currents and push water. Creativity with this push and motion concept is boundless. How many ways and materials you can come up with to get the desired effect is left to your imagination.

Once the motion is detected, visual aids can add to the effectiveness. Mylar sides on the streamer or Mylar strips taken from Mylar tubing used as topping or belly will add flash as it catches the existing light.

Fluorescent materials used for the body, wings, and so on are becoming popular. But I don't know what effect or advantage, if any, fluorescent colors have with the additional light of day in off-colored water on an overcast day. Would black or dark brown in the same design do just as well? Steelhead fishermen use a wide range of fluorescent materials with success.

Lewie Weaver had a technique with a live-minnow-and-streamer combination. Lewie wasn't afraid to experiment. I remember one cold April morning when the stream was heavily stocked, and the worm dunkers and salmon-egg men were taking it on the chin and bitching about the stocking program. I had been fishing nymphs and had taken a couple of ten-inch hatchery rainbows. The stream, a little limestone gem originating from one large spring hole, was filled with cress bugs and freshwater shrimp, which I was imitating. Lewie was, as always, fishing live minnows and though moving trout, couldn't hold their interest long enough to take one. They would show, roll, or briefly chase the minnow, and all but a couple refused to strike. Then Lewie got a brainstorm. Why not an exciter? A polar-bear-hair streamer with a black chenille body and a rib of tinsel for a dropper above the minnow. He didn't clean the stream out with this combination, but he took more fish than anyone else and doubled his enjoyment. Since that experience I've used a pair of streamers as I would wet flies with success.

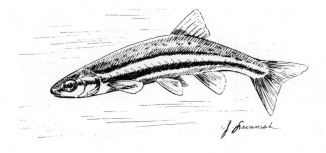

5

DRY FLIES:

Seeing is Believing

The hatch was tapering off. Two other fishermen had already given up and were standing on the bank above me. The glow from a cigarette now and then illuminated their faces, and I could hear them chatting in the darkness. It had been a dilly of a Sulphur hatch, and while now and then a fish broke water, I had had enough. I waded over to join the two anglers.

"We've been watching you," one of them said. "It doesn't look like you did too well."

"That's an understatement," I said. "I'm going home to soak my casting arm."

"We couldn't figure them out either," they said.

"Well, you can bet I'll be here tomorrow night—I'm determined to figure them out.

The following evening I was in the same spot. The trout were offering the same challenge. I worked on my leader until I got a drag-free float for the fly, a size 14 Sulphur-dun imitation, but four unheeded floats over a steadily rising trout prompted another change. "They must be on spinners," I thought. The light was fading, the trout continued to feed, and the spinner produced nothing. "What the heck," I moaned to myself, "don't tell me they're going to whip me two nights in a row!"

Then it occurred to me that I might be missing the boat entirely. I had never checked to see exactly what the fish were feeding on. I held a fine-mesh net in the water and trapped some of the naturals that were floating downstream. They were Sulphurs, all right, but tiny ones. I had been fishing an imitation two sizes too big. In the growing darkness I managed to tie on a size 18, three-hackled Sulphur pattern and I moved up to a flat glide at the end of a pool. I could just barely make out the rings from the rises, but I found several steady feeders. I caught three fish and raised two more before they finally stopped feeding.

My success that evening depended on my taking the time to see what was happening. Dry-fly fishing is a visual thing—observation and the ability to assess and utilize the information you've witnessed is fundamental to effective dry-fly fishing.

The three critical areas of dry-fly fishing—the three *basic* areas—in which you must utilize visual information are approach, leader construction, and casting. Approach includes finding trout and positioning yourself for a cast; leader construction guarantees you a natural, drag-free float; and casting technique allows you to make the cast that will allow the leader to present the fly properly. These three areas of fishing dry flies are the fundamentals—other aspects such as fly selection and hatches can only fit into the picture successfully if the requirements of the three basic areas are first met. The most skilled athletes—and anglers—are simply refining fundamentals to the point that they are not recognized as fundamentals. Let's take a look at the basics of dry-fly fishing and then see how the other aspects fit into the picture.

Approach

The first approach is with a thermometer—make sure the trout are in the stream before you even rig a line. I won't belabor this point, but if you're a dry-fly man you should know that optimum temperatures for dry-fly fishing are in the upper fifties to midsixties. Chapter 1 gives more detailed information on the relationship between water temperatures and trout feeding activity.

Once you've taken the water temperature and have determined that it is conducive to surface-feeding activity, the next move is to "fish" the stream—without a rod. No matter how tantalizing the river is, whether it's the Snake River in Wyoming or Kettle Creek in Pennsylvania, if you don't know the water, don't put your rod together. Walk the stream and observe where fish are feeding. Refer to a topographical map or draw your own map as you walk.

Mark areas where you see fish working. You may see fish feeding on the inner edge of an eddy as the water swings in close to the bank, or find two good fish feeding below a boulder, or several fish feeding at the base of a riff. Mark these areas down; it will be difficult not to run back to the car for your rod, but keep going and cover as much water as you can. Later on, when these fish are not on top, you'll know where their feeding lanes are. And they won't change that much, even when a hatch is not in progress. This is also a way to locate trophy trout. When you do come back with a rod, you will be able to skip a lot of water that's not productive and hit the spots that are. If you can't take them on top with a dry, pop a nymph in behind that boulder where you located them. Covering only the water that you know holds fish is just good common sense.

Now pretend that you've made this preliminary observation and not only have you found an appropriate water temperature and rising trout but you've also found a trophy trout—a trout of a lifetime, perhaps—feeding on the surface. What would you do before making your first cast? Get into the best posi-

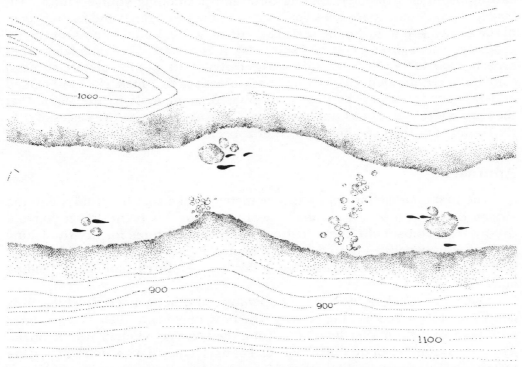

You can mark down where you see trout rising on a topographical map or a map of your own so you know later where trout hold when they are not rising.

tion for making the cast, of course. Two factors to consider in choosing a position are water clarity and the position of the sun.

If the water is cloudy, or if it's broken or riffly water, you can get closer to the fish than if the fish is lying in flat, clear, slow-moving water. I do not hold by the theory that trout can see greater distances peripherally when they are deeper in the water than when they hold in shallow water. Native and hold-over trout will scoot away sooner than freshly stocked trout – stocked trout have been conditioned to a great degree not to fear people.

One day on Young Womans Creek in northern Pennsylvania, George Harvey and I arrived to find the stream at an all-time low due to drought conditions. Nonetheless, I entered the stream and began fishing a dry fly while George watched from the road above. At the base of a pool some seventy feet away from me, George saw a trout rise.

"Did you see that fish break?" he called to me.

"No, where was it?"

"Upstream about sixty feet from you." The trout rose again and I marked its position.

"Just move to your right and cast to it," George recommended. But I looked behind me and felt that my backcast might hang up in tree limbs, so I moved upstream. I stayed low, getting down on my knees. I raised my upper body for a better look as I lifted my arm to cast. I saw the trout's wake as it sped upstream through the pool. I had spooked the fish from a crouch at fifty feet away!

"Why didn't you cast from where you were?" George asked.

"Hell, I was sixty feet away," I replied.

"What difference does that make?" said George. "Can't you cast a dry fly sixty feet?"

There are times when getting as close to a fish as possible may mean fishing to it from a considerable distance. The water clarity often determines how close you can get. But the position of the sun is also important, and it can sometimes help you to offset the disadvantage of low, slow-moving, clear water. When a trout has to look into the sun, its vision, just like yours or mine, is impaired. So if you approach a trout with the sun at your back, it's tough for it to see you.

If a trout is lying in a stream and feeding consistently on the surface to the right of it, there may be several reasons. There may be slight currents carrying surface food to his right, or the majority of food may be coming off the bank to his right, but it may also be that the sun is on the fish's left and if it looks in that direction, it sees a fly as a blob with no detail – or it may not see the fly at all. The fish is forced in such a situation to feed to its right – food on its right is highly visible with distinguishable detail. You can approach this fish from the left—its "blind side"—and cast to him without spooking him.

If making your presentation from the bank, stay back away from the water, even out of sight of the stream. Drop down on your knees or crouch to lower your profile, and crawl to within sight of the water. Use the cover available so you blend into the background. At times when I'm making an on-the-bank approach, I'll make my cast without seeing the water and lay the fly line over as much as thirty feet of bank and depend on my sense of feel to detect the rise. Ease into position, as though you were trying to stalk a gray squirrel on a bright November day. Keep your eyes on the fish, move slowly, watch and wait. There, he rose again. How close can you get? Can you avoid drag from where you are, or is there a better position for making that initial cast?

Wading into position might be your best approach if you can do so. If you can, bear in mind that trout face into the current. In most situations this means that they are facing upstream, but if they're holding in a backwater eddy, they may be facing downstream. Try to approach a feeding trout from behind the fish—its chances of seeing you are fewer than if you approached from another angle.

When you enter a pool or a long piece of flat water, ease in and try not to push any water. Once in the stream, let the rings around your boots or waders die and observe what is happening from this in-stream vantage point. See which bank you want to work and where the fish are feeding before you make a move. When you do move, slide your feet but inches at a time and let the rings die after each move. This is especially important if you've chosen flat water to fish. You can't push waves of water ahead of you and expect to catch fish. In fast, broken, or riffly water you can move into position more readily than in flat water because the speed of the current prevents waves from being pushed ahead of you, and the trout doesn't have the range vision he has in flat water.

In some situations, if the water isn't too deep, you may want to lower your body into the stream, crouching or going down on one or both knees. When approaching a trout from below, inching along and maintaining a low profile often allows you to get surprisingly close to a fish—especially in riffly or broken water. In such water I've sometimes approached within a rod's length of a rising trout. In flat water, I can usually approach within easy casting range. The low-profile approach isn't only for fishing from the bank.

Getting as close to our trout as possible without spooking him is important; how close, as stated, depends on the clarity of the water, the sun, and the surroundings. "Close" may be twenty feet or forty feet. Getting as close as you can for that initial cast can benefit you in several ways. First of all, it

In flat water an inch-by-inch approach is the best way to wade into position. *Photo by Paul Blankenhorn.*

You can't push water when wading and expect to catch trout in flat water, day or night. *Photo by Paul Blankenhorn.*

helps you cast with accuracy. You can pinpoint the cast. If the wind is a factor, a shorter cast will give you better control. Secondly, being close gives you better visibility. The trout broke the surface, or did he? Is it actually feeding on top? When you're close you can watch individual flies coming over the fish. If you see that fly disappear, then you know the trout is surface feeding. But if that fly doesn't disappear, nor do the preceding ones, then switch to nymphs or wets.

Finally, getting as close as possible in a position to make an accurate cast helps you to overcome drag. At this point, drag is the single most important thing that dictates a take or a refusal by the trout.

A specific trout maintains a distinctive lie on the bottom. His chin rests on a specific stone, and when he moves for food or to chase away a competitor, he returns to the exact spot or a spot inches from it. All of the overhead food that comes to it is carried its way by distinct currents, currents that the fish watches for twenty-four hours a day, twelve months a year. You can bet the trout knows what mayflies look like when they drift over — every minute detail — because its life depends on it. If suddenly your fly drifts over it, and small, imperceptible currents — imperceptible to you but distinct to the trout — pull through the line, leader, and fly, the fly drags. It doesn't resemble the natural at all in its drift. The trout may stop feeding, now alerted that something is wrong, and race or drift to the safety of cover.

Once you've found a surface-feeding trout and have positioned yourself for an accurate cast, the next important thing is to use a leader that doesn't drag the fly once your cast is made.

Leaders for Dry Flies

The area you fish dictates the length of the leader. If you're in freestone mountain country or in any tight brush situation, an effective leader may be no longer than six feet and seldom longer than seven. It's almost impossible to control ten feet of leader in tight quarters. In open waters nine to ten feet of leader will suffice, depending on the size and air resistance of your imitation. Forget twelve-foot and longer leaders; they're too tough to control accurately, especially if there is any wind.

Construct the leader with both stiff and soft monofilament, the butt end coming off the fly line and the upper half of the leader with stiff monofilament. Why stiff? If you're fishing small, tight streams where there are over-hanging tree limbs you've got to push that fly back under. It's impossible to do it with all soft monofilament because the leader will collapse on you, and I don't give a damn what casting technique you employ. If you use all stiff monofilament, you can't get an extended drag-free float once you do get it back under the trees.

I fished a mountain stream one afternoon with a good fisherman. He was a fine caster and his leaders consisted of all soft nylon material. The leader was a tad long for the brush, but he said he could compensate for the length and softness of the leader with his casting. But his leader kept collapsing on him. One trout was feeding under some rhododendrons, about fifteen feet back under, with only a couple of feet of clearance between the limbs and the water. Try as he would, the leader collapsed each time before the fly reached the trout. His casting mechanics were correct, his leader wasn't. Stiff nylon for the butt and the first two sections helps punch your leader back under obstructions when you need to.

I've used a variety of different dry-fly leader formulas, and I've bought leaders manufactured in different formulas. But generally there were two problems with these leaders. First, the butt sections were so heavy and long that a leader needed to be twelve feet or so in length to properly turn over. Second, most were designed to straighten the leader out. The leader formula that I recommend is lighter in the butt than other formulas and it is designed to land on the water in snakey curves. A leader that completely straightens out immediately starts to drag the fly; one that lands in curves gives slack to let the dry fly drift without drag.

A straight leader results in a dragging fly and a warning to a rising fish. A leader that lands with S-curves allows a drag-free float.

On mountain streams where casting may be impeded by overhanging limbs and other obstructions, I'll use 3X for the tippet, particularly when there is ample water in the stream. When the streams drop to a summertime low, or I find more casting room in brush or mountain country, I'll shorten the 3X material to twelve inches and add sixteen to twenty inches of 4X material. The tippet diameter and length must also be adjusted with respect to the air resistance and density of the fly. For example, with a size 12, three-hackle Humpy I might use a 3X tippet because it is a bulky fly tied with a good deal of deer hair. But with a size 12 three-hackled Adams I'll possibly go to 4X for the tippet. In any case make sure the fly and leader compliment each other, and the leader is lying in soft curves on the water before you fish.

The dry-fly leaders I use are based on a formula developed by George Harvey. Mine may vary from George's in the length of sections by an inch or so, but the diameters of the monofilament and the principle behind the leader's construction are the same.

It wasn't until George sat down with me and explained the concept that I began to see how important leader construction was to catching trout. I'll stick to the formula that follows George's concepts, but I won't stop experimenting, looking for something better – and if I know George, neither will he.

The tippet material should not be lighter than 6X (.005-inch diameter), and preferably heavier – as heavy as you can get away with. It should be strong enough to pressure a good trout, but light enough to get an adequate float. In my opinion, anything lighter than 6X has two strikes against it: first, you tire a large trout to the point of no recovery when playing it; second, you're using a lighter tippet to compensate for your own inability – it takes considerably more angling know-how to take a trout on 5X than on 7X or 8X.

The tippet length can be from twenty to forty inches, depending on the size and the air resistance of the fly. If the tippet piles up on the water, it's too long for the air resistance of the fly. If it straightens out, it isn't long enough. What you want is for that soft tippet material to lie in a series of S-curves on the water. Check it before you start to fish. Make a cast, then look and see what the entire leader is doing out there. Adjust it until it works. Just don't tie a tippet on and fish, as most fishermen do. Make sure it's right.

The formulas for dry-fly leaders that I use are shown in accompanying illustrations.

The third critical area in dry-fly fishing is casting. Once you've made a good approach and are equipped with the proper leader for the stream situation and the fly you're using, you must be able to get the fly to the fish with a cast that will complement your efforts so far.

People often seem to get the wrong idea that the cast should be employed

10' - 10' 6" – FLAT WATER

STIFF				SOFT			
		0X	2X	3X	4X	5X	6X
.015	.013	.011	.009	.008	.007	.006 or	.005
10"	20"	20"	12"	14"	18"	25"-30"	

10' 6" LEADER

STIFF				SOFT		
			0X	2X	3X	4X
.017	.015	.013	.011	.009	.008	.007
10"	20"	20"	20"	12"	18"	22"-28"

11' LEADER

STIFF				SOFT			
			0X	2X	3X	4X	5X
.017	.015	.013	.011	.009	.008	.007	.006
10"	20"	20"	20"	12"	12"	18"	22"-30"

Leaders for dry flies. Bottom two formulas were developed by Pennsylvania angler George Harvey.

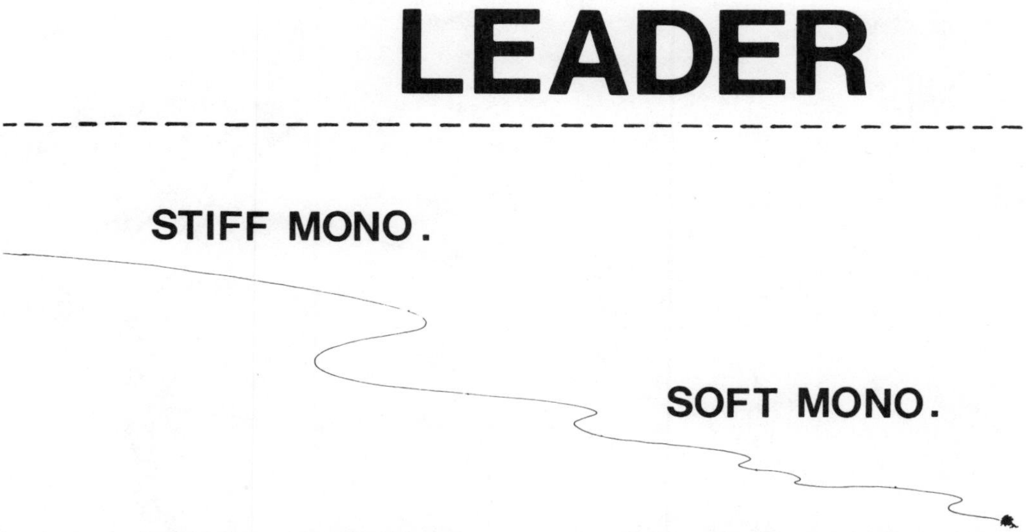

LEADER

- -

STIFF MONO.

SOFT MONO.

A properly constructed dry-fly leader with stiff monofilament in the butt sections and soft monofilament for the other sections will fall with S-curves in the soft material to allow a drag-free float.

To check the cast, stop the rod sharply overhead on the forward cast, then drop the elbow and the rod tip—this allows the leader to lie in S-curves on the water.

In the push–cast the thumb pushes forward and up into the forward stroke – stop the rod abruptly, then drop the elbow and the rod tip. This stacks the leader as it collapses on the water in soft curves.

to overcome drag. Generally speaking, most anglers feel that if you have enough extra fly line on the water you will get an extended drag-free float. But this is not so; you can have a considerable amount of slack line on the water – in fact the whole line – and still end up with a dragging fly if the leader is straight.

The casts you use when dry-fly fishing are a means to get the leader to perform properly. For example, a mend in the air lifts the line upstream and it will fall to the water at an angle from rod tip to fly. The fact that it is lifted upstream is beneficial to the float only in part. Sure it can give you more float time, but only if you had a good check of the rod tip before the lift, and dropped the elbow after the lift, and the leader isn't straightened out. Only then have you given the soft monofilament of the leader time to react to the check and lay loosely on the water. It's the leader that performs off the mend if you check it in the air properly.

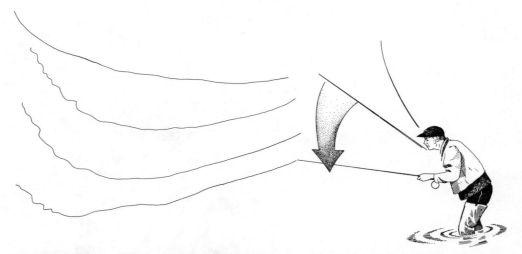

In the drop cast, as the loop begins to unfold on the forward cast the elbow and the rod tip are dropped as shown.

In most of the casting techniques, the line straightens out. The push cast, the drop cast, a wide loop, all of these casts straighten the line out, but not the leader. Granted, with a good check on a cast, and with the elbow dropped, the line will have a series of curves on the water and some slack will help to obtain a good float, but it's the combination of the casting technique and leader construction that does the trick.

Check Cast

Check the rod sharply overhead on the forward power stroke. If you can't remember the time, 10:30 is when you see your rod hand directly in front of you. This cast changes the level of the line in the air. Remember to drop your elbow and the rod tip, and the leader will fall to the water in a series of S-curves. This cast may be used in a variety of upstream, downstream, and across-stream situations, but it is best used when casting directly upstream to a rising fish.

The Push Cast

In this cast you push completely through the forward stroke when you

To make the open-loop cast, use a longer power stroke – the thumb pushes the rod tip in an upward plane. As the loop opens, drop your elbow and rod tip. The line drops, the leader collapses with a lot of curves on the water.

In the underhand lift, the cast is begun with an upward lift to the backcast as shown.
On the forward stroke, the wrist kicks as shown, and the leader and fly travel upward at
the end of the loop—then drop the elbow and the rod tip.

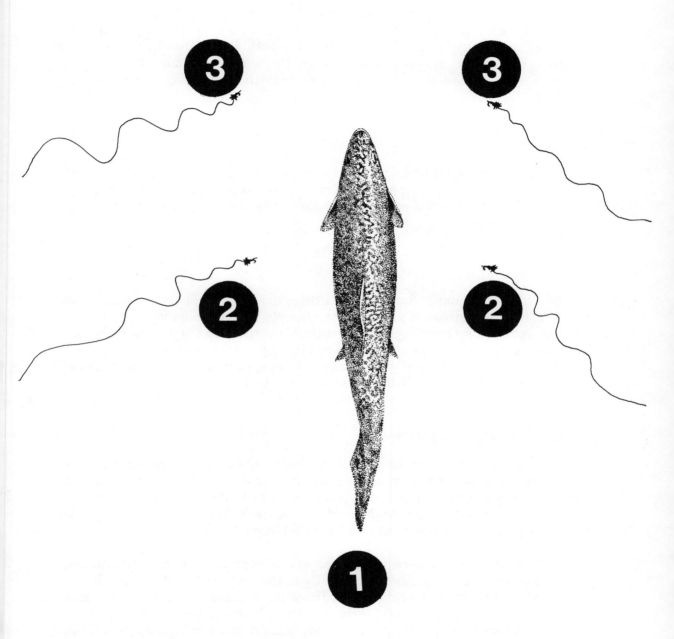

Casting order, presenting a dry fly to a rising fish in flat water. In each cast the trout sees the fly first, not the leader.

deliver the fly, as shown in the illustrations. As the line straightens out, the loop climbs at the completion of the cast, and the leader falls or partially collapses in the water. This cast, when used with an upstream approach to a trout, gives more drag-free float to a dry-fly in a specific spot than does the check cast. It may also be used in across-stream and downstream presentations.

The Drop Cast

This is an excellent cast for upstream work when you're covering pocket water. This cast is the best I know for giving extra float time to a fly in fast water. Like the push cast, the drop cast collapses the leader so it lands in curves to give slack.

The Open Loop Cast

The longer your forward power stroke, the wider the loop you cast. If you start the power stroke at your ear, for example, and finish it out in front of you with your rod tip traveling in an upward plane the loop climbs. As it begins to open, you can drop your elbow and rod tip and the line and leader drop to the water. This cast is great if your fly needs more float time in a backwater pocket and there are fast currents between you and the pocket.

The Underhand Lift Cast

This cast comes off the side of the caster. On both the backcast and the forward cast the line stays lower than the rod tip. As the forward loop unfolds, a sharp upward flip of the casting wrist kicks the leader and fly upward and it settles to the water with considerable slack. This cast is used to get up under overhanging brush and limbs for additional float time.

Now that we have examined matters of approach, leader construction, and casting, you are ready to get the fly to the fish—but where to put it? My approach is to make the first cast in flat-water situations so that the fly lands behind the fish. If it turns for it the first thing it sees is the fly, not the line or leader. If the fish doesn't turn for it, my second cast is off to one side or another—not over it. Again, if the trout turns for the fly, it sees the fly first. The third cast is above the fish, but off to one side.

Whenever possible I'll try to approach the fish from behind him, casting upstream. I'll pop that fly just behind the fish and hope he spins around and takes it. It can feel the vibrations of the fly on the water in flat-water stretches; it knows the fly is there.

If you are fishing a hatch that has brought many fish to the surface to feed, don't spend too much time working on one fish. If your leader is properly constructed and your casting is accurate, then each cast after your first diminishes your chances. If you're certain you have chosen the correct fly pattern and all the other requirements of leader construction, approach, and casting have been met, but you fail to take the fish, move on to another trout.

It was hell for me to learn and accept this. I'd stay with one finicky trout and change tippets and flies and invariably put the fish down in the end. And even if the first cast was a bad one and may have alerted the trout, I'd stay there and cast until I got a cast in there that I was satisfied with. It was simply casting practice.

To wade past and put down feeding trout that refuse your presentation and to move on to one that will take requires discipline. But remember that

In the midseason and late-season periods terrestrials often attract trout to the streambanks. Throughout the season, crustaceans are available in aquatic-weed growth along banks. A careful approach will help you avoid spooking bank-hugging trout. *Photo by the author.*

most hatches are of short duration, and you've got to do your fishing while it's there.

Hatches and Fly Selection

My approach to hatches is a simplified one. Sulphurs can include several species of mayflies. I'm not concerned about the specific identification of an insect, but it's basic size and color are important. If someone says he took a fish on a size 16 Sulphur we are communicating. I know that mayflies have Latin names and that Ephemerella dorothea, invaria, or rotunda are Sulphurs and they differ in detail, and to be able to communicate with the angling fraternity, I feel it is necessary for me to know the basic mayfly families and hatches, but I don't have time for an in-depth entomological study of the hatches. That could take a lifetime, and I've got too much to learn about catching trout to take the time.

I am constantly aware that the size and unique characteristics of some of the flies—an olive body, a touch of orange, the down wings of a caddis—can make the difference between catching fish and going fishless. I am also aware that an oversize tail or wings or other details that you've been careless about when constructing a fly can make the difference.

Generally speaking, where mayflies are concerned I follow this simple approach: I tie my early-season patterns in shades of dun, black, and dark brown in hook sizes 12 through 20. These flies cover most of the early-season hatches for which we use patterns such as the Quill Gordons, Hendricksons, Blue Quills, and so on. Sulphurs (which are sulphur in color) in sizes 10

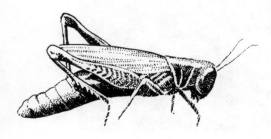

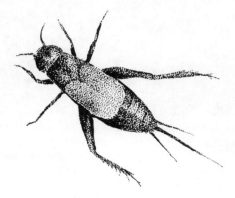

through 20 will match most of the hatches that come in May and June. Both the dark flies and the Sulphur flies may also match many of the hatches that occur in July and August, such as the *Isonychia* and the Yellow Drake. There are occasions, however, when trout in different parts of the country will be keying in on specific hatches and local anglers may be able to tell you what patterns work best. There are also specific hatches of caddis and stoneflies that require your observation when tying flies to represent them.

spider

Imitations of terrestrial insects can often turn a day of unsuccessful fishing around. Even when trout are finicky and taking tiny midges or mayflies, they will often turn quickly to grab a deer-hair beetle or ant that you cast over them. Beetles fly and crash on the water; carpenter ants fall off limbs and leaves onto the water with a splash; grasshoppers and crickets jump and tumble to the water. Many times a forceful presentation of the fly to the fish can stimulate the fish into action. But don't get me wrong, there is nothing wrong with a delicate presentation of a terrestrial imitation. A tiny fur ant with a couple of wraps of hackle dimpling and settling on the surface is sometimes all that will turn the trick. Be open-minded. But even following a "crash-to-the-surface" presentation, the fly should float without drag.

Terrestrial insects push water after they land in the stream in their attempts to escape. Trout are sensitive to the disturbance. Pulling a grasshopper imitation, for example, off an overhanging grassy bank and giving it a twitch or a couple of forceful jerks can draw the fish's attention. I've often gathered hoppers from streamside and popped them into the stream behind a visible trout. The trout often spins and rushes for the struggling natural. The grasshopper may have been thrown too far behind the fish for visibility, but the vibrations it made transmitted the message.

variant

In many trout streams the fish become conditioned to terrestrial activity. Late in the summer, you will find a majority of the trout looking up for their food. Yet there will be days when the fish aren't showing. But don't waste time traveling the banks looking for rises. During the late summer when the trout have started to feed on terrestrials, it is often productive to fish blind, casting to the major currents in which the insects drift and currents close to cover. There may be few if any insects coming to the trout, but the trout are there looking for food.

skater

For example, on summer mornings, before the sun has warmed things up enough to stir terrestrial insects, I've had excellent fishing with grasshopper and ant imitations. On heavily fished waters the trout at this time of day have been rested. The fish will still move to food, and you have a chance to be the first one on the water.

Once trout have been introduced to the terrestrials and these insects become a mainstay in the fish's diet, the trout will accept just about any terrestrial—ant, beetle, grasshopper. The trout aren't usually as selective as they are
during the mayfly hatches. But, of course, if there is a profusion of one kind
of terrestrial, grasshoppers or oak worms for example, those are the insects
you should imitate. Remember, however, that the requirements of the three
basic areas of dry-fly fishing—approach, leader construction, and casting—are
equally as important and perhaps more important with terrestrials as with
imitations of aquatic-insects. These basics may be more important with terrestrials because of the typically low, clear water conditions of late season
when terrestrials are most successful.

Trout move well to terrestrials into the fall, and once the autumn weather
begins, the trout feed less selectively than earlier in the season because they
are storing up fat for the winter.

One style of dry flies that call for special techniques in fishing are the
oversize hackle creations known as spiders, skaters, or variants. These far-out
relatives of the dry fly are fished so that they skim, skate, or tumble across
the water's surface, and at times they have utterly amazed me with their effectiveness. In many instances fish that won't look twice at a drag-free presentation of a conventional mayfly imitation rush to grab these flies.

This style of fly can be fished both in an upstream direction or a downstream direction, and the key is usually imparting enticing motion. They
seem most effective during periods of low, clear water. Often these skimming
creations can be used as locators. A fish, for example, may show under the fly
but refuse to take. If this happens, you can change to a terrestrial imitation
and position yourself for a good float over the fish; often the fish will take
after their interest has been aroused.

Nor do these flies have to be constantly moved. There are times when I
simply drift these powder puffs in tight to cover or through a riff and move
fish. It never fails to surprise me when the fly disappears in a rise. Also these
flies are sometimes good for matching hatches in appropriate sizes and
shades. The skittering motion perhaps imitates a flopping dun on the surface.
Here, it is movement that comes into play, and not just the skating motion. If
those stiff saddle fibers are in abundance, and if they are arrayed in equal circumference around the hook (whether two hackles facing opposite directions
are pushed together as in a skater or a long saddle hackle is wound and braced
forward with a hackle stem as in the variant construction) it's the lateral motion from side to side that aids as well as the skating or skimming.

Al Hagg, a longtime fishing friend, enjoys fishing for brook trout in the
upper reaches of the mountain freestone streams in Pennsylvania. However,

In tying the three-hackle dry fly, the hackle with the most fibers removed from the stem is wound last, bracing the first two hackles forward. *Photo by Paul Blankenhorn.*

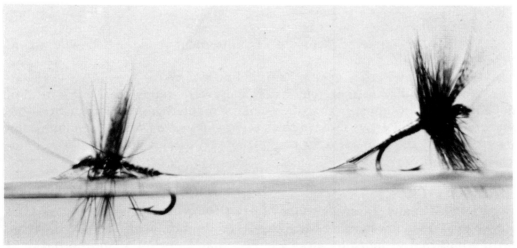

Fly on left is tied with two hackles whose fibers were not spread equally around the hook shank when tying. Fly on right is properly tied three-hackle dry with hackles braced forward for maximum flotation. A three-hackle dry fly with the hackle fibers spread equally around hook shank will ride on the water in such a way that air and water can move it naturally. *Photo by Paul Blankenhorn.*

when we go together, Al doesn't fish. He says he just enjoys watching, and I enjoy his companionship. On one occasion our choice was a big, brawling stream that had questionable water quality—too acidic I was told. But we were curious. Al followed me with foodstuffs packed on his back and a frying pan in his hand. As I covered the water ahead of me, it began to look like the pan was excess baggage. The leader was working properly, and the deer-hair dry fly floated drag free in beautiful holding water. "Maybe the water is too acid," I thought.

A half-mile later we came upon two Pennsylvania State University students camped at streamside. When they saw Al with the frying pan they broke into laughter. "Talk about optimistic," they said. In two days they had only two trout between them. Thirty yards upstream I looked back and the boys were damn near rolling on the ground laughing.

I tied on a variant, reconstructed the leader so that I could control the fly with a combination of rod elevation and a stripping retrieve. On the second cast, I skated the fly around the lip of a house-sized boulder and a ten-inch brookie pounced on it. Every pool and pocket yielded a fish or evidence of one as I guided the fly down and across the interchanging currents and close to the cover of the boulders that created them. Within an hour I had a limit of eight fine brook trout that averaged from nine to twelve inches in length.

We walked back downstream and greeted our bemused student acquaintances.

"How many?" they queried.

"My limit," I countered. The look of amusement changed to bewilderment when they saw the trout.

"How did you?," they asked. I offered no advice.

"Would you like to share our fish?" They were delighted. After a meal of golden fried trout, home fries, coffee, complemented with good conversation, we left. I turned after we crossed the stream and yelled, "Sell those damn spinning rods and get yourself a fly rod!" They waved and nodded.

Tying Dry Flies

I've tried many different styles of dry flies over that last forty years. As long ago as 1946 I was using Mucilin-soaked dubbing tied on a size 22 hook, with wings tied in more for my own eyes than the trout's, and no hackle. I also tried sparsely tied one- or two-hackle drys, thorax patterns, parachute patterns, and many other types. I've caught trout on all of them, but the pattern that produces most effectively for me is a dry fly tied with three hackles.

My formula for the three-hackle fly starts with a standard tying approach:

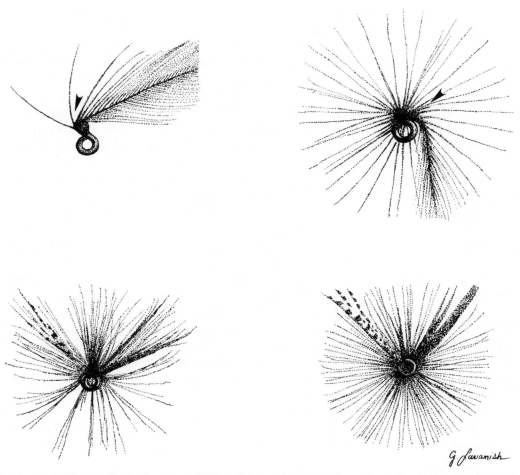

The Three-Hackle-Dry Fly. **Top left: break in first hackle; top right: break in second hackle; bottom left: fly tied without tying hackles off at break spreads fibers unevenly; bottom right: fly with each hackle tied off at break spreads fibers evenly around hook shank.**

hook in the vise; thread on the hook; wings set back one-third the hook-shank length behind the eye, divided and well braced; tail with enough stiff fibers for support, straight or divided, as you prefer. Then you add the body, and now the clincher.

Select three first-quality hackles with short, stiff, glossy, narrow fibers, with flexible stems and little or no webbing. I use Metz necks exclusively because I feel they are the best available in the widest selection. Strip what little webbing there may be from the base of the hackles, slightly more from one hackle than from the other two. Put the three hackles together, with the one having the most webbing removed nearest to the hook bend. Tie these hackles in behind the wing and underneath the hook, with the curve of the feathers (the dull side of the hackles) facing toward the hook eye.

Now spin and weave the magic. The first or front hackle is wrapped completely behind the wing and tied off underneath. The second hackle is wrapped behind the wing, except for the last two or three turns, which are wound in front of the wing and are tied off where the fibers "break" from the stem. (If you take a hackle, tie it on a hook and wind it, you will see that the fibers suddenly spring or "break" from the stem of the hackle at one specific spot. If you tie your hackle off at exactly that point, your fly will end up with an equal number of fibers spread around the circumference of the hook shank.)

The third hackle, the one with the longer stem, braces the other two. With your thumb and first two fingers, pull all the fibers toward the eye of the hook and wind the bare stem of the last hackle behind the other hackles. This creates a base and supports the fibers by thrusting them forward. Now start winding the hackle, weaving it back and forth among the other hackle fibers as you move toward the eye. This motion interlaces the stem of the last hackle between the other two. When you reach a point in front of the wings, take two or more turns, and then pull the fibers back toward the wings with your thumb and fingers. Take one or two final turns with the hackle in front of the fibers you are holding, and tie it off.

There you have it: a fly constructed so the hackles, which have been braced forward, will provide maximum flotation. Pick up the fly, cast it back on the water, and the braced hackles snap forward and back into place for another good float.

There are certain duties a good dry fly must perform. It has to float or it isn't a dry fly. It must float well with a minimum of false casts. It must be durable enough to withstand the rigors of casting, continued floats and strikes. It must be visible to the angler in heavy water, during dimly lit early-morning and late-evening rises and on those long casts that you seldom need but are sometimes forced to make.

The three-hackle dry has another unique feature. The hackles, with an even number of fibers around the circumference, support the fly at almost any angle and enable the fly to rock from side to side with the interaction of both wind and water currents. Movement can be an important criterion, and I know more often than not that it's been the wiggle of a mayfly that enticed a trout to take it.

6

BRUSH FISHING:

The Dry Fly and Small Streams

I was fishing under a canopy of hemlocks, rhododendron, and mountain laurel thinking about a friend, Ralph Dougherty, who described this kind of fishing well: "It's like trying to cast in an eighteen-inch pipe."

It was high summer, and in between pools the water, cool and clear, was hardly deep enough to hold a fingerling. But I like small mountain streams this time of year, because I know there will be fish. The stream is tight with rhododendron and hemlock forming a tunnel, and even so bright a day the thicket blocked out the light. The pools were shaded. On this particular afternoon, the trout were extra tough, and on occasion trout would move out long before I could get into position, their wakes pushing through the pool. How keenly aware they are and what a disadvantage the angler is at. I managed a couple of seven-inch trout. In here, a nine-inch brookie is a trophy.

On one pool, a large hemlock leaned out over the water, its root system reaching like so many fingers into the pool at its base, and then gradually the gravel bottom shallowed at the tail. I managed to shoot a cast to where the hemlock trunk met the water. The fly danced along its rough bark edges and headed for the tail. Quietly it disappeared in a dimple. I raised the rod tip expecting a wiggling, parr-

sized brookie to come flying across the surface. Instead: solid weight—the throbbing of a fish far too large to exist in such a small stream. My first reaction was that a trophy nine-inch trout had wrapped my leader around a root, but as the trout yielded under pressure, eighteen inches of brown trout came into view. That fish must have migrated several miles in periods of high water, either in the spring or winter or after heavy June rains. Upon beaching the fish and rapping it smartly on the head, I could almost hear the smaller native brookies cheering in joyous celebration, "The monster is dead!"

These stream conditions are not restricted to the mountain regions of the East; the same challenges can be found in mid-western and Western states. Often this tight fishing is the best game in town, especially in mid-season.

The dry fly game in the brush is totally different from fishing open waters. Approach, casting, and tackle all change. But as always we must start with the fish.

Trout have a social arrangement in the stream that can best be described as a pecking order. They arrange themselves in the water according to size, the bigger fish in command of the best currents that provide a food supply and are adjacent to cover for safety. For the most part, fishermen don't recognize this phenomenon because they fish water where fish are not visible. But in meadow and mountain pools this arrangement becomes obvious—and it dictates the strategy necessary to take trout consistently.

As water levels drop in Eastern mountain freestone streams, particularly in the end of June and through July and August, the trout congregate in the pools with low, clear water, and temperatures in the fifty-five-degree to sixty-five-degree range. The best fish may drop to the tail of the pool where the dominant currents pull the majority of the food to it.

The pecking order may change according to factors that influence the water temperature and other conditions. If the water temperature has risen a degree or two during the day, and especially if there has been an extended warm spell with the air temperatures in the eighties, the best trout will move into the riffs for oxygen. The pecking order will now establish itself with the smallest trout at the tail of the pool or below the riffs.

Heavy currents also may push water into secluded cover areas and change the trouts' order, moving larger fish out of the main currents to establish feeding lanes elsewhere. Showers late in the summer will push more terrestrial food to the fish—a goodly portion of their diet in small freestone streams. High water later in the year will bring good trout out into the open late in the year. The commanding currents carry that food supply, so the best trout is looking for food at the edges of major currents. Also, high water that is

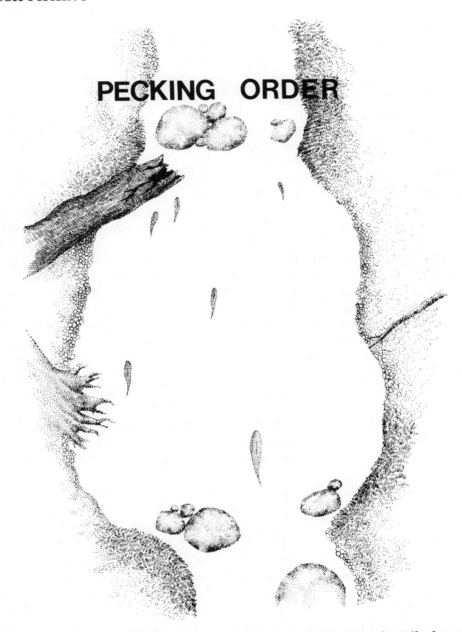

PECKING ORDER

Pecking order in a mountain stream: If you take a good fish from the tail, chances are the others in the pool are small and you should move on. Under some conditions, the pecking order may reverse itself. If you take a small trout or a fry at the tail of a pool, shoot your next cast to the head of the pool.

slightly off-color makes it easier for good fish to pick off smaller fish. When the water is off-color, you can get closer to them, and they'll still come up through to feed.

Approach and Casting

The approach to these small streams is all-important: the slightest mistake will send the fish at the tail scurrying through the pool like Paul Revere. I've watched anglers lower their profile in a crouch or on bended knee, slip cautiously up to a pool and come away fishless, pool after pool. They claim the stream has been cleaned out by early-season bait fishermen. When these streams are low and clear there is no way you are going to get that close to the fish. Numerous times I've heard the advice, "Crawl on your hands and knees and poke your rod tip through the brush, and . . ." And baloney! You might get close enough in broken water to poke your rod tip over the bank and flip a fly to the surface. In early season or after a heavy rain, when the water is up, you might also be able to get that close. But in flat, low, clear water, forget it! With the first movement of that rod tip over the water, the trout are gone.

The low-profile approach is correct—down on one knee so that your casting stroke is lower and you are less visible—but you must stay back at least twenty feet from the pool you want to fish. Distance in the brush and pinpoint casting control is the secret.

Impossible? Not at all.

When the pool comes into view, study it. Before you fish, ask yourself the following questions: Can I make an upstream approach, or is it physically impossible? Is there so much brush and so many obstructions that it's impossible to cast?

I once read an article on brush fishing in which the author stated, "always fish upstream." More baloney! Your best approach at times is at the head of the pool. If it is impossible to make an upstream casting approach, check out the major currents leaving the pool. If the currents are fast-moving, but there is good holding water at the lip of the pool, at the edge of a boulder, between two boulders, a log or other debris, ask yourself, "How can I best approach and cast to avoid drag?" You might as well heave a stone into a pool if you drag your fly over a wild stream-wise trout. Once in awhile, if you have most of your leader off the water, you can raise a fish if the drag is not extended—but not often.

I once fished a willow-shrouded meadow stream that held native browns that were extremely sensitive. I came upon a long, deep, flat pool with plenty

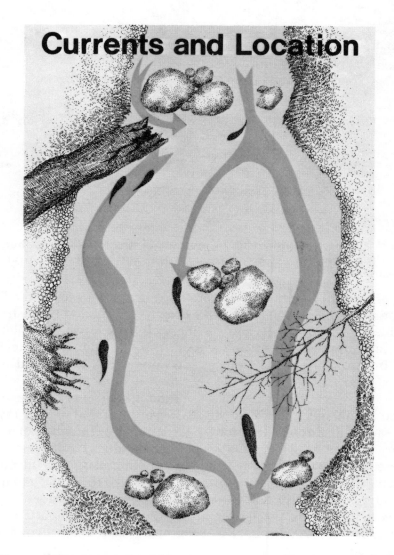

Currents and Location

On a small mountain pool, study the pool with respect to best currents and best cover for trout before fishing. With this information you can determine what is the best position from which to cast to get a proper float. Four or five well-placed casts a brush stream will cover even the largest pools adequately. Cover only that area above the last cast with each new cast.

An upstream approach is preferable in most small-stream situations, but there are times when it is advantageous to cast from the side and lay your line over the bank. *Photo by Sharon Bernard.*

of casting area at the tail, but there were few obstructions to lay the line on or over on the lip of the pool to aid me in a drag-free float. So I reconstructed the leader, added a longer tippet, and staying well back, opened the loop of my cast wide and dropped the fly and a good deal of leader fifteen feet up into the pool. Immediately a fine trout swirled under it, disappeared, and then came back. Had the fish taken the fly when it hit the water I might have caught the fish, but it didn't. By that time the lip currents had devoured the slack in both line and leader and the fly began to drag. I cussed my luck as the trout raced up through that long pool sending out a wake of water and ending any chance of fishing that pool successfully. Trout were scurrying everywhere, and the wake of one trout after another disrupted the pool's tranquil surface. Moral: Don't fool yourself. When you're in the mountains or brush country, drag is still one of your most important considerations. Planning the cast to employ the leader in avoiding drag is important on small streams because you seldom have a second cast. Let's make a good approach to a typical pool:

You're in position, well back from the pool you want to fish. Your approach was low and you dropped on one knee in the water to avoid spooking fish, and to allow more rod movement.

Now look around you. What are your options? Where must you place your backcast? Can you use a backcast? If you can, then strip enough line off the reel and out through the rod tip to cover the water in front of you. Lift the rod tip and look in the direction of your backcast. *Concentrate on where the forward cast must go.* That's an important distinction.

If you try to establish the direction and amount of line needed on the actual backcast (as some anglers advocate), your attention and vision is focused on the backcast. When your head turns as you shoot a forward cast, unless you're lucky, you won't be able to control the loop for real pinpoint accuracy. And you sure as hell can't control a distance shot under the brush.

Once you establish the direction of your backcast, be conscious of it, but concentrate on what is in *front* of you. *What* cast *where* is needed to avoid drag? What area must you concentrate on for your first cast, what are the currents and cover? Must you cast under overhanging limbs, or beyond them? If you can't get to where you want to go with the cast, is there a better vantage point, not just for rod movement, but for reaching the area you want to cover? Maybe you shouldn't even attempt a cast where you are.

Control the fly. Grasp the leader inches above the fly before you put the line in motion, otherwise your fly will get hung up on every weed or stick in the vicinity. False casting must be kept to a minimum, otherwise you're in the trees three-quarters of the time. Establish the position of your backcast. Concentrate on where you're casting in front of you. Put the line in motion with the rod tip and shoot.

Three-hackle flies with hackles braced forward for the best flotation are essential. On each cast, whether it be a roll cast, a push cast, a circle cast — whatever — the fly must float with little or no false-casting. In many cases false-casting is impossible, only the motion of the lift and the power stroke dry the fly. The more supporting fibers there are, the more flotation, and the less fuss. A combination of three hackles and deer hair or other high-floating animal hair is best.

The other important aspect is that of movement. Three hackles with the circumference of fibers spread evenly around the hook enhances movement as the currents, even though imperceptible to the fisherman, move the fly.

If you cover the tail end of a hole without a rise, keep in position and shoot higher — but don't stand up. Chances are there is a good trout located somewhere in a gut or pocket in the middle of that pool or hidden from your view at the tail with the rest of the school facing upstream above it. *Cover as much water as you can from one position.* Cover the best currents at the tail of the pool, and don't overlook shallows at the edge of the tail. Good trout will often be in inches of water near or under cover or where there is a minimum water velocity to contend with. But once you spook them, forget it. Try to make that first cast count. If you get it in there with no drag you should take a trout; they're competitive and won't often let something that looks like food pass by.

If you don't raise a trout at the tail of a pool, but take a small trout toward the head of the pool, concentrate on the riff at the very head. Likely the best trout will be there.

If you botch the first cast, for example, by hanging the leader over a limb or bush, once you shake and move those limbs trying to get your fly off, it's all over in that area, so move on. But if the cast is made and the fly does not hit a productive area of the pool, don't lift it—fish it out, let it lie. Food is scarce and trout will move a considerable distance to investigate. Many times when I've all but given up on a cast, much to my surprise the fly disappeared in a swirl.

As the water levels drop later in the season, trout move into the pools. Earlier you may have picked up trout in pockets and riffs between the pools as well as in the pools themselves. The trout were spread out over a much larger area. The trout now move to the safety of the holes and congregate. The feeding surface area of the pools is now much greater than elsewhere and more food is available in them. Skip the riffs and shallows, hit the pools and the deepest pockets and move. Don't stay in one pool. Use the strategy discussed earlier and travel; you'll catch twice as many fish and maybe ten times as many as you would if you spent a long time in each pool.

If the first cast raises a fish and you miss it, you may shoot another cast in the same area, but nine chances out of ten, you're wasting your time. It's gone. I've often observed that the trout dart for cover after simply missing the fly. Something was wrong with that bug, something wasn't natural.

Cover the water with the fly. If you have covered the tail of the pool with a good drift, shoot higher, but cover only that area above the last cast. If there was a trout there you would have taken it. You know where the productive areas are: hit them, drift your fly over them, and move. Remember, every cast after that first one, your chances go down. Three or four casts should cover a pool—and that would be a long pool. Two casts in a small pool should do it.

Remember, the trout at the tail are usually well camouflaged and have maximum visibility. Once frightened, it will race up through the pool alarming the other trout.

And if you take that trout at the tail and he's a good fish, move on. If it's a sizable pool, you may try shooting a cast higher or to the top of the pool. But the disturbance caused by the first fish you caught will probably end the fishing. You've taken the best fish anyway, so don't overharvest the pool—leave

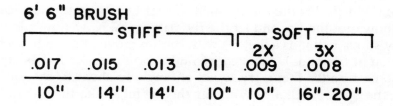

5'6" TIGHT BRUSH

STIFF				SOFT	
				2X	3X
.017	.015	.013	.011	.009	.008
10"	12"	12"	10"	10"	16"+

6' 6" BRUSH

STIFF				SOFT	
				2X	3X
.017	.015	.013	.011	.009	.008
10"	14"	14"	10"	10"	16"-20"

7' 6" BRUSH

STIFF				SOFT		
				2X	3X	4X
.017	.015	.013	.011	.009	.008	.007
10"	14"	14"	10"	10"	12"	16"-20"

Dry fly leaders for brush fishing.

some for breeding stock. If I kill some trout on a small stream to eat, I don't kill fish from that area again the same year. I go to another section of that stream or to another stream, and give the remaining trout a chance to grow and spawn. If by chance you spook a fish at the tail of a pool, quickly punch a cast to the head. There is a chance that the fish at the upper end hasn't received the word yet.

I prefer an upstream approach whenever possible. The trout are facing into the current and for the most part that means upstream. Therefore, fishing upstream you can usually get closer on the approach. However, I don't limit the water I fish, and sometimes the most productive area of a pool is the center, but it's impossible to approach from below. If space permits and I can attack the pool from the bank, I'll move well back from the water's edge and cast twenty feet of line or more across the ground and over the bank to the water's edge, no rod-tip poking through streamside grasses, only the fly and leader dropping in the pool. If I simply don't have the casting space or am blocked from the water's edge, I'll move to the top of the pool, staying well back, checking my cast at the 10:30 position, dropping my elbow, and drifting the fly with the currents feeding the pool.

Another technique I might use is to lift the rod tip high as the loop of line unfolds to bring the fly back toward me, depositing it in the pool with enough slack in the leader to allow a drag-free float. As the fly continues to drift, drop the rod tip and, using the water resistance, kick out more line for a continued drift. Mend the line in the direction of the main current for a drag-free drift. At the end of the drift, lift the rod tip high, skitter the fly on the surface, then drop your elbow, not the tip, and let the fly drift again. Now slowly lower the rod. If the fly sinks, fish it as a wet fly with rod-tip movement on the retrieve.

If a portion of the pool is blocked by limbs, branches, or leaves, and it is impossible to cast under them, try to get an angle to shoot to the top of the pool and let the currents that flow under those limbs take the fly under – at times it's the only way. Let the currents work for you.

To achieve even more distance under overhanging brush, as you drift the rod forward on your cast and make the power stroke, use a single line haul, which is no more than a downward tug of the line with the free hand. This adds speed (and distance) to the unfolding loop.

Remember that your approach must most of all be careful. If, for example, a log lying on the bank extends well into a good pool you want to fish and you bump it or step on it, shock waves from that vibration will put fish down.

Casting

In our modern society, we either change with the times or get lost in the shuffle; so it is with fly-casting in the brush, the nitty-gritty of brush fishing. As the conditions change, so must your casting. Below I describe a cast that will help you fish effectively when you encounter different small-stream casting situations.

If you don't have enough room behind you to make a full backcast, then try the circle cast. All casts should begin after you have picked up enough line so that you've established tension through the line and the fly moves. This principle is equally important to the circle cast. To make the circle cast, pick up the line with a circular motion of the rod. Anytime after the fly is in motion, you can drift the rod forward and apply a power stroke. *When* you apply the stroke depends on where you're casting. Once the line and fly are in motion, the power stroke that you apply straightens out the line and heads it toward the target. The line circles and straightens out with the drift and stroke. It's as simple as that.

With some practice you'll find that you can make any cast you would make with a standard cast with the circle cast—you can shoot line, throw wide or narrow loops, or mend line in the air.

Let's see how a circle cast can be used to avoid drag at the tail of a pool. If you can lay your fly line over a log, stone, or the streambank to keep it off the water, you can get a drag-free float for a distance under most circumstances. Many times your best drag preventative is a tree limb or log above the water. Sure, you have a chance of hanging up, but if the cast is a good one your chances of raising a trout are well above fifty percent. Once you hook a trout the tension and movement of the fish will free your line, if not you can lift the line off the limb or log as you play the fish.

The bank, however, is frequently your best bet for drag prevention, but

The circle cast picks up the line with a circular motion. Once the line and fly start moving, the forward power stroke can be completed at any angle or position. The line follows the circular motion of the rod on the pick up. Front view of the circle cast motion at right shows this motion on a vertical plane, but it can be used on any plane.

The author executing a circle cast in a tight, small-stream situation. Note the path of the line and the load on the rod tip as the author squeezes off the power stroke. *Photos by George Lavanish.* ►

The author making a cross-chest underhand cast to avoid backcast obstructions on a small stream. The aim is to cover the lip of the pool with a drag-free float. On this cast, power is relaxed as the loop unfolds and the rod tip is dropped. *Photos by George Lavanish.* ▼

this requires a mend in the air off the circle cast and an extended drift of the rod tip upstream and toward the opposite bank. This throws a belly in the line when the first few feet of line falls on the bank. Then the fly, leader, and line fall in an upstream arc with the fly drifting downstream ahead of the leader and line. This same cast can be employed without using the bank, simply casting upstream using the same technique but easing off the power stroke as you drift the rod forward and pointing the rod tip in the exact direction of the arc. This is not for distance, but to give you enough time without drag to cover the immediate few feet to the tail of the pool.

You were able to solve a difficult small-stream casting problem with the circle cast—and the line never went behind you. Because the number-one problem you'll encounter in brush fishing is lack of backcast space, the circle cast and variations of it provide the solution. You can combine the cast with the push cast, the drop cast, or the standard roll cast in many situations.

Whether you are using a straight backcast, a circle cast, or another cast, if you want to achieve greater accuracy and a tight loop, here's how to do it. Once you start the line moving in a circle cast or have started a backcast, you drop and drift. That is, after lifting the line, drop the rod by lowering your elbow so that the rod is in the plane you want for the cast you're making. Then drift and make a power stroke toward your target. It helps when you make the stroke to use your thumb as a sort of gun sight—and you should end your cast with thumb and knuckles pointing at your target. Remember, where the rod tip goes, so goes the line and leader and fly. In any cast when brush fishing, your power stroke is only a two-inch punch. You squeeze the rod handle (thumb goes forward and last two fingers come back) and punch a short, quick stroke.

If you are in a situation where you want to cast around a corner, here's how to do it. Using the curve cast, drift your fist around an imaginary corner and as it turns the corner make your power stroke. Your thumb and knuckles should be pointing at what you want to hit. The line goes up and around whatever it is you're trying to get around. To further enhance the cast when you complete that power stroke, push your thumb up. This opens the loop, your leader now falls in loose coils, and your fly is drifting naturally without drag. This also gives you more float time. To go around something and back under employs the same mechanics except that you drop your elbow so the thumb and knuckles point at exactly what you want to get under.

An invaluable cast and one that will serve you well is the switch cast. Grasp a length of line from the rod tip and hold it a foot or so above the fly. Pull the line back. Make sure your fly is free as it dangles below your thumb and forefinger. The rod tip is now loaded, acting as a spring or switch. Release

The difference between a circle roll cast and a standard roll cast is that the standard roll cast requires that the rod be loaded behind you on the power stroke. You begin the circle roll just as you would a standard roll cast, but you pick up the line with the circular motion of the roll so that only a portion of the line is on the water. Now, with the line mostly off the water, you can drift forward and make the power stroke in front of you. Making a power stroke in front of you gives better control to punch out a lower cast with a tighter loop. The line portion in the air loads the rod in a circle cast while the line tension on the water loads the standard roll cast.

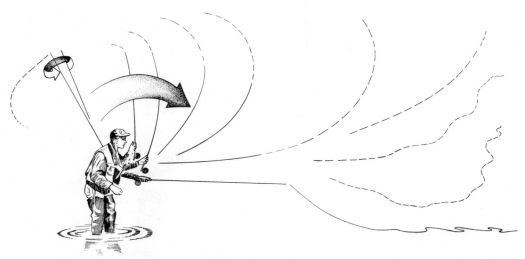

The circle push-cast is invaluable when covering the lip of a pool in brush fishing because it allows you to pile up enough slack to defeat the very fast currents between you and the lip of the pool. Shock the forward cast, then drop the elbow and rod tip.

the fly and the tip flips the fly forward. You should push the thumb of your casting hand into the rod to help load it for the cast. This is an ideal cast where there is no casting space whatsoever. If you want to get back under the brush with this cast, sight over the rod tip and lower the tip just under the limb you want to go under. Make sure the line is at the same level as the tip. Don't have the line hand lower than the tip or the fly will go up in the air higher than the tip and will hang up in the branches you want to go under. The thumb directs the cast and you can feel the rod load through it as pressure is applied. That pressure transmits through the thumb when the rod is fully loaded. Release the leader and fly by simply letting go, don't flinch and spring it with a sudden jerk—a smooth release gives you better control. If you want to hit a specific spot, use the rod tip as a guide and on the release point it at what you want to hit.

Tackle

Leader construction in brush country is another critical factor in drag control. The density of brush dictates the length of the leader. There is no way you're going to handle nine feet of leader in a thicket. Depending upon how open a stream is, your leader may range from five or six feet to seven feet. Keep this in mind: you're going to be required to go back under brush as well as avoid drag. An accompanying illustration shows my leader formulas.

The drop-and-drift cast begins with a normal backcast or circle cast, but before coming forward you drop your elbow until the rod tip is in the correct plane for the cast you want to make, then you drift (make a power stroke) forward.

A small-stream situation that calls for a tight loop off a drop-and-drift cast: drop the rod tip after loop upfolds.

Short sections of stiff DuPont monofilament in the butt will straighten out the leader so you can get way back under the brush without the leader collapsing. A long, soft-monofilament tippet will land in snakelike curves to give you a drag-free float. The tippet length must be adjusted to the air-resistance of your fly, and you'll have to find the right length for different patterns through trial and error. Any of the sections of this leader may be adjusted in length for different situations (longer sections for open water, shorter sections for tighter water).

My choice of a rod is a seven and one-half foot, stiff, graphite rod that takes a six-weight line. A rod for brush fishing should be at least seven feet. A double-taper line works well in most cases, but if I'm in tight quarters and need a little more punch to get back under brush, I'll use a weight forward.

An example of a stream situation in which you would combine a curve cast with an open loop to achieve a drag-free presentation around the corner of a streambank.

NIGHT NYMPH - WITH DROPPER - 7'6"

————————— STIFF NYLON —————————

.019	.017	.015	.013	.011
12"	20"	20"	16"+4" dropper	22"

NIGHT FLY LEADER - 6'8" WET

————————— STIFF NYLON —————————

.019	.017	.015	.013
20"	20"	20"	20"

NIGHT FLY LEADER - WITH DROPPER - 7'4" WET

————————— STIFF NYLON —————————

.019	.017	.015	.013
20"	20"	16"+4" dropper	20"

NIGHT DRY FLY LEADER - 7'4"

—— STIFF —— —— SOFT ——

.017	.015	.013	.011	.010
12"	20"	20"	12"	20"-24"

Leaders for night fishing.

Don't worry about that super-soft, delicate presentation that a four- or five-weight line may give you; you've got to get that fly in there and it will drive you crazy to have a line so light that it collapses on you.

A short rod – six feet or even six and a half – means you've got that much extra line on the water. Line that's difficult to control. With a short rod you can't lift enough line off the water and over currents to control a drag free float.

Your line should be a floating line, and it must float or you're hung up on everything. As the line tip sinks it pulls the leader and fly under debris, rocks, and so on. Dress it before you start, then stop after an hour or less, dry it and dress it again. I know it takes time and you become involved with the fishing, but it will save you time and get you more fish in the long run.

Helpful Hints for Small Streams

If you cast over brush to help you with your drag-free float, or if you cast over a pile of debris to hit a productive spot, as the line floats back to you, wiggle the tip back and forth while you lift to begin a new cast. The line in motion lifts the fly over the debris. A direct lift almost guarantees you a hangup.

If you hang up on the forward cast, don't lift the rod tip and pull. Point the rod tip at the limb you're hung on, gradually gather the line in with your free hand using a hand-twist retrieve. When you feel the line tighten, take the line between your thumb and forefinger and spring it. The spring loosens the leader wrapped around the branch and often it drops off. Repeat the process three or four times. It takes time to loosen it. It works. Ralph Dougherty gave me that hint, one he used when fishing among the mangroves in Florida for snook.

If you hang up on a backcast, it is easy to reach up and grasp the leader. With a direct, gentle pull, it will at times come free. If it is high or somewhere you can't reach it, run the rod tip up to the fly and lift or shake. If the line has sunk and you're wrapped up in the debris under the water, do the same thing: run the rod right down in the water to the fly, but don't apply so much pressure that you'll snap the rod tip. In or out of the water, if you can't get it, pull directly on the line with the rod pointed straight at the fly and break the fly off.

When using three-hackle drys, those well-braced hackles act as a snag guard. When I punch my line into hard-to-get places, over or under limbs and branches, as I take up the slack I'll keep the fly coming, pulling the rod tip slightly up, and continue to gather in the line, gently. Many times the fly bounces through the limbs and branches as if it were without a hook point. Be patient, it pays off.

When George Harvey and I fish the small streams, he travels light. He laughs at me with my vest bulging with all the unnecessary paraphernalia. George carries a wicker creel that contains a box of flies and a towel sewn into a bag that he can wet to hold trout if he wants a couple of brookies for the table. George carries enough leader material to adjust a leader. No nets that catch on everything. No heavy vest. Just a fly rod and a basket.

7

NIGHT FISHING:

The Big Ones Come Out at Night

The late-summer White Fly hatch was in progress on the Yellow Breeches, a lime-stone trout stream in Pennsylvania. The hatch was in full swing when Tom Miller and I arrived on the stream at 8 P.M. Flies swarmed in the air like a miniature snowstorm, and I began fishing a dry fly. Tom moved down below me to fish wets in broken water.

This was my first encounter with this popular hatch, and the imitation I was using left something to be desired. It was only with persistence that I was able to raise two fish—without landing either. My lack of success couldn't be blamed on a lack of feeding fish; there were trout rising everywhere.

I slipped down to Tom who was positioned in the riff at the head of a long, deep stretch. Tom had just released a trout. I took the hint, put on a pair of white wets and cast down and across the riff. I let the flies swing, using no rod action, but keep-ing the rod tip up and using a slow, hand-twist retrieve. I missed the first fish, but hooked and landed the second. It was now dark, 10:30 P.M. Occasionally I could hear a fish break water, but nothing that sounded like a good fish.

I waded to shore and changed to a heavy leader and a pair of size 1/0 wets, slipped back to the top of the riff, and worked my way down through the top half of the deep hole. Halfway through that pool my line straightened out and I was into a good trout. I worked for an angle to turn his head, exerting maximum pressure, when suddenly the hook pulled out and like a breaking bowstring the line snapped past my ear and back into the trees behind me. With considerable effort I managed to untangle the line, leader, and flies from the tree limbs above. I didn't bring another fish up to the big wet flies. Tom had changed to big wets also, though not as big as the flies I was using, and hadn't raised a fish.

It was time for another change. It was also midnight. Still using a weight-forward floating line, I stripped the big wets from the leader, lengthened the leader to nine feet, and secured a size 1, 4XL, black Woolly Worm with a marabou tail. I added two split-shot fourteen inches above the nymph and worked upstream trying to get a natural drift and feel the bottom in the process. But the water hugging the far bank was deep and the floating line continued to lift the nymphs off the bottom. More weight wasn't the answer, nor was a sinking-tip, nor a sinking line, nor a lead-core shooting head. All of these lines belly because of their weight and diameter. The answer: flat monofilament.

Now I tied a pair of size 1 Woolly Worms to the leader, thirty inches apart, and wrapped a strip of lead fourteen inches up the leader from the bottom nymph. Now, when I made a tuck cast upstream against the far bank, I had control of the line and flies. The flies ticked, ticked, ticked along the bottom. Because of the small-diameter monofilament I was using, there was little drag and water resistance.

As the flies straightened out at the end of the cast, a trout ripped into the tail nymph. After landing this fish, I repeated the cast, and again at the end of the swing, the nymphs still bouncing and rolling along the bottom, a trout took. And then twice more the method worked. I had found the right combination, finally, for taking trout that night.

Fishing at night, as with fishing during the day, requires that you remain flexible and open-minded in your approach. The evening I just described on the Yellow Breeches illustrates several night-fishing approaches—dry-fly fishing during a hatch, conventional wet-fly and nymph fishing, and nymphing with a monofilament line. Night fishing is not simply throwing big flies into a stream in the dark, figuring that a huge fish is going to snap them up as soon as they hit the water. There is a great deal of technique involved; stream knowledge is required; and there are special tackle considerations that come into play when you're on the stream at night.

But you might ask, "Why fish at night to begin with?" My answer is that it's the best way to catch large brown trout, especially on streams that endure heavy angling pressure. On such streams the wise old browns—the really big ones—shy away from exposing themselves in daylight hours in favor of feeding at night. Certainly fishing at night doesn't include many of the "fringe benefits" that daytime fishing does—the visual pleasure you may take in your surroundings and so on—but if you want to catch big fish, after dark is the best time to do it. You may also find a certain excitement in being on the stream at night that will compensate for the more conventional pleasures of fishing during the daytime.

Preparation, Locating Fish, and Tackle

Planning and preparation are prerequisites for a successful night on the stream. It is pure folly, and dangerous, to fish a stream that you've never been over previously in the daytime. If you don't know your water and surroundings, pitch darkness is a poor time for exploration.

Wade the pools when you can see; learn and get a feel for the bottom; learn to avoid sudden dropoffs. If the pool is too deep to wade, learn the shoreline and become familiar with the surroundings.

This photograph plots the positions that trout take up in a pool. It corresponds to accompanying illustrations. *Photo by Sharon Bernard.*

Here are examples of the things you must consider before fishing any stream at night:

How far above the water are those hemlock boughs?

Get a feel for the casting—how much line will you need to cover an area?

You've already checked out the boughs, now how tight must your loop be to shoot back under them?

The currents—have you checked the possible feeding lanes that trout will position themselves in?

Did you notice the cover close to those currents—that submerged log, or the root system projecting from the gnarled willows providing cover for trout as well as feeding stations?

Look for those shallow riffs at the head of the pool where the broken water and pockets are—big fish move up into them to feed at night.

Trout will leave the holes and move either to the head of the pool in the riffs or to the shallows at the end of the pool in the safety of darkness. If it is midseason or late season, they may move to cold tributaries or spring holes. Knowing this, plan where you'll fish. Many times you are hampered by heavy foliage or deep water with not much bank to move on, or a steep, rocky, hard-

It is a good idea to get a feel for the necessary casting stroke you'll need during the day-time. Here the author tries out a tight-loop cast to reach under overhanging boughs in the daytime. He can return at night and know how tight his loop must be and how long the cast must be. *Photos by Sharon Bernard.*

At night, big trout drop down to the tails of the pools or to riffs at the head. This trout is holding in the tail of a pool. *Photo by Sharon Bernard.*

to-navigate shore. At times, pools are all but impossible to fish, but don't give up on them—you can bet if they are difficult for fishermen, they harbor good fish. In this case, look for a location that will permit rod movement and work a short roll cast, keeping in mind which bank harbors the best currents, and then work them slowly with short, down-and-across casts that swing in tight to the bank. If you are fishing a tough spot to get around in, it's a good idea to go in before dark and wait.

This past year on one of my favorite streams in central Pennsylvania, I picked up a twenty-inch brown in inches of water tight against the bank. As the flies swung across the current, I used a slow pick-up of the line and rod tip with the flies coming to rest on the bottom at the end of the swing. The fish inhaled the tail fly, and for a moment I thought my flies were hung on the bottom. But soon I felt the weight and surge of a good fish.

Water temperature is extremely important in trout fishing, day or night. Night fishermen who neglect this aspect are in deep trouble. So many trout streams in this country are marginal, and as the sun raises the stream temperature in the summer, trout migrate. Either you hit the cold spots or work the extremely deep pools at night when the water temperature drops as the night air cools the water. But even if a stream is not marginal, night fishermen should still pay attention to spring holes and cold tributaries.

On many occasions upon arriving at a stream at 9 P.M., I've found temperatures of seventy degrees or more. Then as the colder, heavier night air descends into the valleys the water temperature drops and by midnight can change as much as five degrees. This change will stir sluggish trout into activity. Seldom have I found big fish feeding at night in water exceeding seventy-five degrees, and if they feed at all at this temperature it will be in the riffly water where they have sufficiently more oxygen.

Very large trout feed almost exclusively at night, usually in the darkest phase of the moon. During the lighter stages of the moon, in the early-morning hours, they feed usually between 3 and 5 A.M. When these fish feed, most likely they will go for something substantial—a ten-inch sucker, a nine-inch trout, or a crayfish the size of a small lobster. This is why large streamers are often effective. Such meals will keep a trout contented for perhaps two or three days.

Weather conditions also play an important part in night fishing and the activity of the trout. Heavy fog that lies on the water's surface turns fish off. I've never done well under these conditions. Perhaps it results in poor visibility for trout, restricting their view of the silhouette of the fly, but I don't know. I've taken enough beatings under these conditions to know not to fish them. If, however, the fog is high above the water due to cold water temperatures as in a spring-fed limestone stream, for example, as the cold air intermixes with the warmer air of a hot summer night, it seems to have little effect on the trout's feeding patterns.

A summer storm, depending on air and water temperatures, may produce a surface fog. Summer storms may or may not be conducive to good night fishing. On occasions, when heavy storms disturb the clarity of the water with silt from runoff, a fish's visibility may be hampered. Off-colored water in the daytime diffuses light and can readily move good fish, but at night I prefer clear, low water. After a storm, however, if the water's clarity has not been greatly affected, I've had prime fishing. Summer lightning storms at night turn me off. Other than the safety factor, I don't enjoy getting drenched from the heavy rains of such storms. There are too many good nights to fish. The barometer is often a good indicator, as it begins to climb or starts to drop as weather fronts move in and out. I've had superb fishing with changing fronts.

Rain can be a major turn-on to trout. Many years ago, during a summer drought, the streams I was fishing were unseasonably low. But one night, at 2 A.M., a soft, warm rain began to fall, and in the next hour I landed three brown trout of about eighteen, nineteen, and twenty-two inches. Rain often raises the oxygen level of the water significantly—stirring trout into activity.

The theory that storms wash food into the stream and that off-color water adds to the angler's chances for success holds true in daylight, but at night further restricts the vision of fish. Imparting movement to your flies so that they move water becomes very important under such conditions. You've got to practically hit the trout on the nose with the fly. The trout can feel movement of baitfish and nymphs, but they have a tendency to move less themselves. Bouncing nymphs and wets on the bottom in a specific spot close to cover might get you a fish in cloudy water on a bright moonlit night. But I'll wait for dark nights and clear water if I can.

Bright moonlight nights may stir the hearts of lovers, but not night-feeding trout. Seldom have I done well on moonlit waters. The light intensity turns trout off. If I'm forced to fish under these conditions, I'll seek heavily shaded areas, as in a forest patch or a deep chasm where light doesn't reach the water. If it's the only time available for me to fish, I'll wait until 3 A.M., when there is less light, and fish until dawn. On brightly lit nights, another alternative is to fish flies in deep water where there is less light intensity. This calls for fishing nymphs on the bottom in most cases.

As far as wind is concerned, a light, warm breeze doesn't seem to affect the fishing at all. But I've never done well at night when there has been a cold wind blowing.

Seasonally, you can take trout at any time of the year at night. You may have to work at various levels, though. The high, cold waters of the spring, or the chilled waters of the fall, or the frigid waters of the winter may require that your flies dredge the bottom of the stream. However, if the waters are low in the spring and fall, trout may come up through them to take your flies — be prepared to fish at middle depth and on the bottom at these times of year.

Trout in moving water — fast water, broken water, water with any appreciable velocity — are either feeding on the bottom or near the surface. They may come up through the water, off the bottom, to take something at a higher level, but you won't find them hanging suspended in midcurrent. In slow-moving water and in lakes you will find trout at different levels, but in water with more current, they're either holding near the bottom or the top.

Finding the right depth of drift is as important at night as it is in the daytime. Once a hatch is in progress, the fish will intercept nymphs coming off the bottom or drifting or swimming above them, but the trout won't suspend themselves and fight the current. Once they pick off a nymph above them, they return to the bottom. If the trout are feeding on or near the surface they will hold near the top just under the surface and position themselves to feed. The difference between success and failure is more often than not finding the right level at which to fish your flies.

Because night fishing is to a great extent the pursuit of very large trout, it is often desirable to locate the big ones before fishing. Below is a list of approaches to finding big fish.

1. While fishing, if observant, you can spot one. Once in a while you can see one out in the daytime. If it's early in the morning you may spook one that has remained out at the tail of a pool. If the water is clear enough, you may spot one from a high vantage point, a high bank or overhanging tree. Look for the head or tail sticking out from under a rock or log, or a tail sticking out from an undercut bank.
2. Big, deep holes usually hold one. Keep working the heads and tails of those pools. If there is one there, sooner or later you'll move him or see him. It takes time.
3. When the big-fly hatches are on, such as the Green Drake, this is one of the few times big fish come to the top. Mark the spot that is his feeding lane. Not only do you locate them, but you know basically where they feed.
4. Learn to recognize good holding water. A log jam or a fallen tree where the water is deep enough for good protection or a big boulder with a deep gut along its side with shallow riffs adjacent to that cover are examples of holding water for big fish.
5. In streams where there is an abundance of small fish, brookies or parr-size browns on native waters, and you hit a pool where you can't raise a fish or the small fish can only be found at the tail and the pool is sizable, it's a clue that a big fish dominates it.
6. If you've taken a good fish in one spot, you know that spot has the factors necessary to support such a fish. Over the years, on streams that I've learned well, I waste little time covering water because I've learned the specific locations that hold good fish. For example, in one spot I've taken sixty fish over fourteen inches long.
7. Sometimes another angler will share his information. I'll listen closely, for example, to early-season live-minnow fishermen when they talk about a spot where they raised a large fish.

The tackle you use to fly-fish at night can be the same outfit you use for fishing during the day, except that the rod should be eight to nine feet long with enough backbone to cast heavy, size 1/0 and 2/0 wet flies. The line to use is a floating line or flat monofilament when conditions dictate. Leaders should be short and strong, and different tapers are recommended for dry flies and wet flies later in this chapter. Your reel can be your single-action trout model.

Some accessories become more important at night, specifically a flashlight. In fact, two flashlights are best: one small one for tying on flies and leader material and a larger one for finding your way to and from the stream. For a small light you can use the kind with a flexible neck that you can attach to your vest; I prefer a larger light mounted on the front of my Fye chestbox and a Flexlight in a holder on the side of the box.

You should avoid shining light on the water you plan to fish for any period of time. If you need to look at the water, you can shine your light on it *for an instant*, but no longer. A quick look should tell you what you need to know — current speed, distance to the other bank, obstructions, and so on. When using light to tie on flies, turn your back to the water to guard against illuminating it and putting the fish down; you can also shield the light with clothing or go to the streambank away from the area you're fishing. When walking to the stream it's a good idea to put your fingers over the larger flashlight to keep the light from shining too far ahead of you and onto the water.

Before going to the trout stream at night, prepare your tackle and accessories at home so you won't have to fumble with leaders and flies and insect repellent at streamside. You should rig up your rod at home, so when you reach the stream you're ready to go.

Fishing Dry Flies at Night

The slurping sound of a heavy trout surface feeding drifts out from the edge of the hemlock boughs in the darkness. The sound and an occasional reflection reveal his position.

Only a few times each year do hatches bring big trout out of hiding to surface feed in the cover of darkness. The Green Drake, Sulphur and Cahill, Brown Drake, Hexagenia, and White Fly are among these hatches.

Each hatch has distinctive characteristics and differences, yet they are alike in basic stages, moving from stream bottom to top, water temperature in the sixties or high fifties, and the lack of light trigger nymphal movement and hatching activity. When nymphs begin moving prior to surface activity, so do trout. The fish are waiting, watching, pouncing on the wiggling nymphs as they show themselves on the bottom, emerging from beneath the stones and silt.

When fishing to rising trout at night, approach the fish as close as possible. At night you can practically get on top of them if you are discreet enough. If you come up from behind you can get within feet or even inches of a trout both in riffs and slow-flowing water. If you approach from the side in shallow water and there is still some light, keep your profile low. When approaching in flat water, inch along carefully and don't push water — the shock waves will warn the fish of your approach. Approach slowly in riffs, too, because in very low light it will help you spot rises that otherwise you might wade past.

If you are familiar with the water you are going to fish and you know where the trout feed, wait until darkness falls and the trout establish a steady feeding pattern. If there is one particular fish you're after, get into position before darkness and wait. Don't wade around; sit still. On streams where angling competition is stiff, I go to the riffs, away from the congregations of anglers at the pools and holes, and fish slowly upstream. You can get so close to fish that you can make out their rises even in broken water at night. You can find some super fish in this type of water, especially if the water has boulders and guts that give trout cover during the day. Also, big fish often move out of the pools and holes to feed in the riffs at night.

If the rising trout is across the stream from you and you can't reach him easily with a cast, move to him. Shorten the distance for better line control and casting accuracy. Strike at anything that looks like a rise to your fly.

Trout do see at night and they can become selective, conditioned to feeding on certain hatches. If, for example, the fish have zeroed in on Sulphurs, an occasional Green Drake may float over the rising trout unnoticed—or at least unattacked. Approach rising trout at night with the same match-the-hatch tactics you would employ during daylight, and don't be afraid to try nymphs and wets if your dry flies don't work.

Drag-free float is imperative for most daytime dryfly situations. But at night it's not as critical, since the fish react more to vibration and motion and the silhouette on the water. Sometimes I even drag my dryfly at night over a feeding fish. You can shorten up the leader and use a heavier tippet, even say 2X. After all, you don't want to lose a bragging fish. And drag is not as important when fishing broken water at night. The leader design on page 161 incorporates a strong tippet on a leader that will help give you a drag-free float.

I made a surprising discovery one night fishing the Green Drake hatch on Penns Creek. I discovered that at night trout are attracted more to flies that are flopping or in some way moving on the surface than they are to the free-floating flies. I had had little success that evening when I stopped to rest for a while and observe the rising trout and the flies that were hatching. What I learned must surely have been learned long ago by live-bait fishermen who impaled live drakes on hooks and fished them on the surface on a short line.

Four fish were feeding directly in front of me in the backwater at the top of a long, flat pool. The current hugged the bank below the backwater and sent a constant stream of flies eddying in front of me. Down on my knees for a closer look and to lower my profile, I watched. Those flies that were floating spent, or dead, were not taken by the trout. Neither were the duns with upright wings that floated by unmoving. But spent flies that were still squirming on the surface and duns that wriggled and flopped about were taken readily. The moving flies must not only have sent out vibrations for the trout to home in on, they must also have made themselves easier for the night-feeding fish to see because of the tiny commotions they made.

I backed away from the water and cut the materials off a size 8 short-shanked hook. Then I slipped down below the eddy and collected several of the live duns. I put all the naturals but one in a plastic box; the one I kept out I impaled on the bare hook shank and returned to the backwater.

The fish were still feeding, so I positioned myself for a cast. With a short line and leader, I dropped the hapless fly above the trout nearest to me. He took a drake inches from mine, but wouldn't take mine. I tried another cast, and still nothing. Then I noticed that my natural was not alive – not moving – so I changed to another of the naturals in my box, this one alive and fluttering. I slid the hook beneath the wings and flipped the flopping fly above the trout and waited. Without hesitation the trout sucked it in. I repeated the process and caught all four of the feeding trout.

With this inspiring example, I tied on an imitation and moved farther down the pool until I found another trout feeding near the bank. I crawled within a rod's length of the fish and dropped my fly upstream of him. I extended my arm, followed the fly with the rod tip, at the same time gigging the rod tip and dappling the fly. The trout came quickly to the fly. Movement was imparted to the fly as the fly was drifting naturally, not dragging.

When fishing dry flies at night, then, because you can usually approach very close to rising trout, you can use a short line and impart natural motion to your imitation to excite the trout into striking.

I have made other night-fishing observations that pertain more specifically to the Green Drake hatch. However, it is possible that these observations hold true for the other nocturnal hatches of large flies, such as the Brown Drakes and the Hexagenias. One aspect of the Green Drake hatch that the majority of anglers overlook is the early-morning spinner fall. Excellent dry-fly fishing can be had to Green Drake spinners from 5 A.M. until dawn. Secondly, earlier in the evening when hatching activity has been heavy and many anglers have been fishing, they may put the fish down as the hatch tapers off and the trout stop feeding. However, hatching is sometimes heavier on different stretches of the stream, and if you wait until the exodus of fishermen is over, and the road dust has settled, you may find feeding activity to flies that have floated a long distance downstream and brought the trout out of the feeding lull. This can be super fishing, because the crowds are gone and rising fish are feeding leisurely and regularly. Once again, these observations pertain specifically to the Green Drakes, but you might discover similar feeding and hatching patterns on waters that have other large mayfly night hatches.

Fishing Nymphs, Wet Flies, and Streamers at Night

To most fishermen, night fishing with flies means casting wet flies or streamers, usually size 4 through 10, downstream and across, or perhaps fishing a night hatch until 11 P.M. But when I fish at night, I usually use wet flies and streamers as large as 1/0 and 2/0, or I bounce a nymph or sculpin imitation on a short line on the stream bottom. Because I limit my dry-fly fishing at night to the few hatches that occur after dark, most of my night fishing is done under the surface. Also, nine out of ten big fish are caught under the surface. And fishing under the surface means finding the right level.

If trout are moving at night and are coming up through the water for wet flies, by far the most successful technique is a down-and-across cast. The down-and-across cast covers more water than other approaches and the motion of the wet flies alerts the actively feeding trout. This is especially true, as we shall see, when you make more than one pass through a specific section of stream.

If the trout are not moving up through the water for the wet flies, you will want to fish big nymphs on the bottom with a short line and leader. Bouncing the nymphs deep covers the bottom level when that's where the trout are feeding. Using nymphs and a natural drift, it's best that you know the specific locations—the deep pockets, runs and guts—where trout hold and feed.

An in-between technique, in terms of the level you're fishing and attention-getting action you're imparting, is fishing a sculpin imitation. By imparting a slow, pumping action to the bulky fly, you create more action and cover more water than when deep-drifting nymphs, but not as much as with the wet-fly system.

For the best results with a nymph, the fly should be bouncing naturally along the bottom. With a sculpin imitation, you cover an area off the bottom as well as on the bottom. The big wet flies and streamers cover the water from top to bottom, depending upon water depth, current speed, and speed of retrieve. Let's look at techniques for fishing these different imitations.

Bottom activity at night may include a wide range of trout foods. Stonefly and mayfly nymphs, hellgrammites, and many other food forms become active at night. The imitations I tie for nymphing at night don't specifically imitate any one or another of these forms because I don't feel exact imitation is required. As long as the nymph imitation is big, lifelike and fished properly, it will take trout. Most of my night nymphs have dubbing, chenille, or marabou bodies; heavy palmered hackle the length of the body; grouse, partridge, or dark mallard fibers for wings; and a head of heavily webbed hackle. Another fly I use on numerous occasions is a Woolly Worm.

In my experience, darker patterns of both nymphs and wets take the most trout. Perhaps this is because the fish can more easily see the silhouette of a dark fly against the sky than they can see the silhouette of a lighter fly.

When trout are taking nymphs on the bottom at night, they are looking for food drifting to them naturally or with a little action – but on the bottom. Getting the nymph there is the key.

Use a short upstream cast (ten to fifteen feet) so that your fly will drift through a productive area. I recommend the downer and upper tuck cast (described in Chapter 2). After you make the cast, extend your arm as the nymph reaches the bottom. Lead the line and nymph completely through the drift with the rod tip. This is an effective way to keep the line tight and feel the action of the nymph on the bottom.

As the nymph reaches the end of the drift, lift it slowly. Then bounce your rod tip and impart a little action as you continue to lift. Sometimes trout will follow the nymph to the top before taking it.

As you are fishing out a cast with nymphs, try not to rush. Give the flies as much time on the bottom as you can. You may tend to lift the rod tip and move the line faster than the water. Try to avoid doing this, because it pulls the nymph off the bottom and moves it at an unnatural speed.

When nymphing shallow water and pocket water, use a short (six- or six-and-a-half-foot) leader. It is easier to control than a longer leader, and sometimes there is enough light to see the end of the fly line. If you can see the end of the line, it will give you an idea of how fast your nymph is traveling and where it is. Here's the formula of my night-nymphing leader: twenty inches of .017-inch diameter monofilament, twenty inches of .015, twenty inches of .013, and twenty inches of .011. I try not to use a tippet lighter than eight-pound-test line, and ten-pound-test is preferable. If I'm after a trophy trout, I use .013-inch diameter for the tippet. There have been times when I've wanted a heavier leader than the one described above, and I'll use twenty-inch sections of .019, .017, and two sections of .015. I use all Dupont nylon for these leaders, which is stiff monofilament. I prefer stiff material because I think it sinks quicker and drifts better. When confronted with deep or fast water that I can't get my floating line and short leader to sink fast enough in, I exchange the floating line for flat monofilament and attach the short leader to it. The nymphing-with-monofilament technique is described in Chapter 2.

Sometimes I will add a dropper and fish two nymphs on a cast. The drop-

Short-line nymphing at night.

per should be about four inches long—long enough for the fish to suck the fly in and short enough not to wrap around the leader. The dropper can be the extension of the heavier monofilament preceding the tippet. Simply leave a four-inch length coming off the blood knot when you tie on the tippet.

If you are fishing nymphs on the bottom without success, you may want to switch to a sculpin imitation and work the fly on the bottom, coming off the bottom to see if the fish are feeding at that level.

Sculpins move at night—they are night feeders. Your imitation should work the bottom. To get the weight needed to sink the fly, tie in split-shot for the eyes of the pattern. Use different sizes of split-shot for different weights that may be required to fish the pattern at different depths. Your imitation should be similar to the sculpin's outline and the fly should also have movement built into it. Use marabou for the tail and body, goose breast feathers for the wing, and deerhair spun and trimmed to shape for the head. The action of the wings and the bulky deer-hair head pushing water sends shock waves to the fish.

You can use the same upstream, short-line technique just described for fishing nymphs at night. But once you let the sculpin imitation settle to the bottom and extend your arm, lift the fly off the bottom occasionally during its downstream drift. Use a slow but continuous rod motion throughout the drift.

The free-swimming baitfishes such as chubs and dace are not a major food source for night-feeding trout. This is because, unlike sculpins, they are not active at night, tending to seek cover instead. On some occasions, however, I have seen and heard large trout slashing the stream's surface at night in pursuit of minnows. In this instance, a streamer fished on the surface with a down-and-across swing keeps the fly in the trout's feeding zone. It may also sometimes be productive to fish a streamer in the same manner as a sculpin imitation. But when I refer to streamers, I don't mean slender, feather-wing patterns; I mean flies with a heavy marabou-fiber wing and bulky hackle heads.

Big wet flies can be used at any depth from top to bottom. There is greater variety to the technique of fishing wets at night than fishing nymphs or sculpin imitations. Many times at the head of a pool I will fish the riffs

Straight downstream riff technique with big wet flies at night.

with a straight downstream cast, letting the flies swing and move in the current. Then I'll retrieve them very slowly with a little touch of the rod tip. Once I've retrieved the flies, I'll let them drift back downstream and repeat the process. If you're fishing wets down and across a pool, swing the rod tip with the line. That keeps the belly out of the line and keeps the line tight between you and the fly—a necessity if you want to hook fish and a necessity if you want to feel your flies drifting at the right level.

Night-feeding trout are slow and deliberate; seldom do you get the headlong rush or explosive strike that you sometimes do in daylight. Once in awhile as you lift your flies in a riff, a trout will take in a flurry, but that is the exception rather than the rule. In most cases, trout will simply inhale the fly and stop it.

If you want to add movement to your flies, lift the rod tip. Maintain a continuous but slow hand-twist retrieve and swing with your flies until they straighten out below you. Don't pick them up immediately—a good fish may

When you're fishing big wet flies down and across a pool at night, swing the rod tip with the line to avoid a bellying line as shown at left. If the line bellies as shown at right, you can't stay in touch with your flies—and you'll probably be unable to hook a fish if one takes. *Photos by Sharon Bernard.*

have followed your fly for some distance. Gradually lift the tip until the flies are ready to be airborne for the next cast. Keep that rod tip at a ninety-degree angle to the line coming from the tip. Remember: trout don't grab, they inhale —and the extra slack from the rod-and-line angle will enable you to hook more fish.

Big trout will move up through water to take big wet flies and you should both vary the speed of your retrieve and the depth of your flies. The slower you retrieve, the deeper the flies will be fishing.

You can also control the depth at which you fish your flies by varying hook sizes and amount of weight in the flies. For example, in three feet of water or more, I ordinarily use a pair of 2/0 wet flies tied on Mustad 36890 hooks. This is a turned-up, looped-eye salmon hook of stout wire with a black enamel finish. Two flies on these hooks should give enough weight to sufficiently cover the deeper areas of a stream, depending, of course, on current speed and the speed of your retrieve. But in the shallows or in areas of slow current, these flies will hang up. If so, remove the top fly or both and replace with a lighter wire hook, one size smaller. If the hang-up problem continues, remove the dropper altogether and replace the tail fly with a lighter wire hook, one or even two sizes smaller.

When I need to lighten the tail fly or both the tail and dropper, I use a size 1 French V-M hook number MD, which has a turned-down eye, round bend, and standard-length shank. The wire is lighter, and I can in most cases cover the shallow water without hanging up. But both of these hooks have one important thing in common: the gaps are wide enough that when the hook shank is built up with dubbing or chenille, there is still hooking and holding power. It took me a while to learn this hook-gap lesson. My early attempts at wet-fly fishing the big flies were with flies tied on standard, size 2–6 streamer hooks with a limerick bend. The number of fish landed in relation to the number lost forced me to look for a hook with a larger gap. Also, the size of the trout I wanted forced me to go to the bigger hook.

When forced to lighten the hook, not only do I sacrifice hook size, but I also change body materials. My preference for body material in wet flies is for dubbing; it absorbs water, moves, and gives bulk. It's meaty. Heavy chenille is my second choice, but when I need a shallow-water fly I either go lighter on the dubbing, use a smaller-diameter chenille, or go to a more bouyant material, such as deer hair. But at no time will I sacrifice the movement tied in the fly. The hook size may be smaller but the wings, palmered body, and heavy head hackle remain. Incorporating movement in a fly (and fishing it to give motion) is more important at night than at any other time.

The only time I use smaller wet flies at night is when the larger patterns

Big wet flies for fishing at night: these patterns should be tied to move water and move in the water rather than as specific imitators. *Photos by Lefty Kreh.*

don't produce or are only bumped by the trout. Usually there are three reasons why the big flies fail: first, the fish may be going off the feed; second, the fish are only inquisitive; or third, the fish are small. In such situations, it is sometimes effective to go to size 6 or 8 wet flies.

There is more than one approach to a pool or a specific spot, and working a pool from both sides, for example, can increase your chances for success because you're covering more water. When you have a location that you know holds fish, and a down-and-across presentation isn't working, try for another angle to present your flies. Move farther upstream, wade out a little farther, and cast so that your flies will have more time in the spot, giving the fish a longer look at them. A fish will sometimes follow flies on a swing and hit them, but at other times you have to put the fly right on top of the fish and keep it there to entice the trout into taking.

On an across-and-downstream drift, let your flies drift tight into the bank, or work tight to the bank on a straight downstream cast. The bank offers good cover, less current speed, and a good food source (terrestrials, sculpins, and other foods also looking for cover). Trout are often located near the banks or they may follow a fly into the bank. Once your flies drift in tight to the bank, let them settle on the bottom, then gently lift them an inch or so, and let them settle again. Repeat the lift-and-settle process. Another tight-to-the-bank technique is to let the flies straighten out downstream and retrieve them with a slow lift of the rod tip and a slow hand-twist retrieve. Try three slow hand twists to one lift of the rod tip.

When fishing water where you have all the cover on one side of the stream — perhaps a line of alders or a cedar sweep — or when cold spring holes or tributaries enter on one side of the stream, mentally divide the stream in half and work in close to the fish-holding side of the stream. If you try to fish such cover from too far away, your flies will swing out of the productive zone. So work in close and keep your flies where the fish are.

Once you become accustomed to fishing at night, you may find that the sounds of the stream will help you recognize what you can't see in areas you know well. On a very dark night, for example, a quiet riffle or a gurgle behind a boulder might tell you that here is the spot that holds fish. If you know the

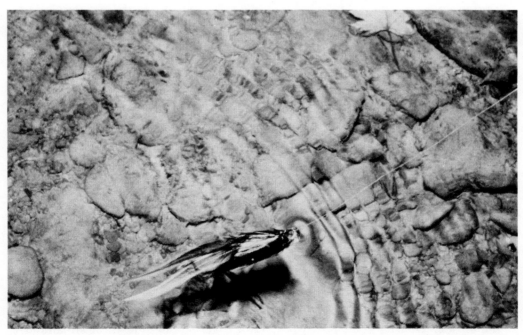

Here's why: the shock waves made by moving elements of the fly attract the fish at night. *Photo by Sharon Bernard.*

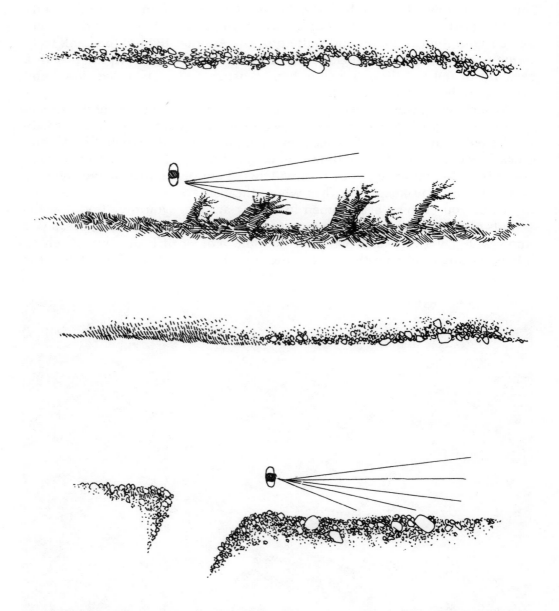

If you have an entering cold-water tributary or cover on one side of the stream, mentally divide the stream in half in order to concentrate your efforts on the fish-holding side.

water, odd shape stones under foot can guide you to a hot spot, or tell you this is it.

When fishing the big wet flies, as soon as you make a cast, give the rod tip a short lift and move the flies. You should do this on every cast as soon as the flies hit the water. There are several reasons for this. The lift puts you immediately in touch with your flies. If you have overshot your target and the flies have landed on the bank, a lift will often free them and plop them into the water. Sometimes a good trout will hold very tight to the bank or under other cover, and an immediate movement of the flies may alert the trout and stimulate it into striking. Finally, an immediate lift of the flies can tell you right where your cast landed—whether it was too long or too short.

When I fish at night with nymphs, sculpin imitations, or big wet flies, I try not to cover more than three areas a night. But I cover each area thoroughly. I'll go through the tail end of a pool, for example, two or three times, resting in between each pass. On many occasions, I've caught a fish on the last time through. Sometimes the first or second times through alert a good fish, and on the next pass he finally takes.

Here is a checklist of approaches to fishing for trout at night, including the different techniques covered in this chapter.

1. If there is a major hatch on top and the trout are moving for surface food, fish on top with dry flies. However, take into consideration the size of the trout that are feeding on top. If the fish are mostly ten or twelve inches long, you might consider fishing big wet flies under the surface—sometimes bigger trout are eyeing the smaller surface-feeding fish for a meal.
2. If there isn't any hatching activity, try wet flies.
   A. Cast down and across, varying the speed of retrieve and the rod tip action.
   B. Next, slow down your retrieve and try heavy 1/0 and 2/0 flies.
   C. If you find action at the tail of the pool, and the big flies hang up on the bottom, try lighter and/or smaller flies.
3. If the down-and-across approach doesn't work, cast upstream and fish the big wets bouncing on the bottom. Hold the rod tip high, and lift the rod tip periodically throughout the drift.
4. If the trout don't want the wet flies and refuse to come off the bottom, try nymphs. Use a short, upstream tuck cast and lead the nymphs through the drift with the rod tip. If you can't keep the nymph rolling and bouncing on the bottom, try the flat-monofilament technique with nymphs.

Next, try a sculpin imitation, lifting it off the bottom periodically through-out the drift.

5. To be successful you may have to fish through a specific area several times. Concentrate on a specific spot that you know holds good fish, if you can. Vary your techniques until you come up with a winner. It isn't always possible. If I had a dollar for every time I struck out at night, I'd be a rich man.

PART TWO

1

WATER TEMPERATURES

Trout react to a variety of stimuli, but their basic metabolism is keyed to temperature, which in turn affects oxygen levels. As water temperatures increase to between 55° and 65°, trout body tissues demand food; they're hungry. The oxygen content is prime, then, at between 9 and 11 parts per million (unless the water is polluted). If water temperature continues to rise, oxygen dissipates and metabolisms slow again. At 70° feeding winds down. In the mid-70s the oxygen content drops to 7 ppm and trout migrate to colder water with more oxygen. Increase the temperature to 80° and, unless ample oxygen is added somehow, trout literally suffocate.

An increased metabolic rate, which brings on the feeding that we look for, can, however, lead to starvation: Winter is giving way to spring; the water has been cold during the frozen months, in the high 30s, low 40s. Then there's a thaw, a sudden rise in air and water temperatures; it becomes unseasonably warm for two weeks and the water reaches the high 50s and low 60s. The sudden increase in both temperature and the trout's metabolism without an also-reactivated food chain can result in starvation. It can be the cause of an early fish kill. Ever catch a trout with all head and a stringbean body? This may be the reason.

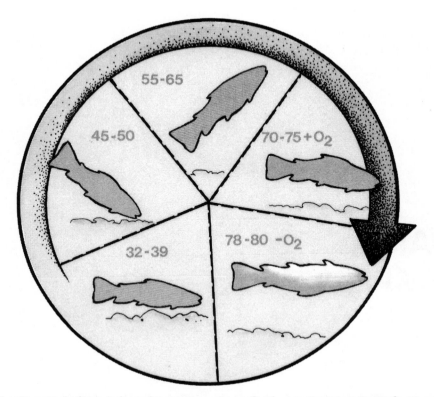

Trout's basic metabolism is keyed to temperature. Optimum temperatures for trout, 55° to 65°F, increase their need for food, but once conditioned to colder temperatures trout can readily feed at 45°F.

An important factor is conditioning, or acclimation. If there's enough oxygen and trout are trapped, they can survive at temperatures of 70°-plus—but they're not healthy. I once fished a private stream where the water was 78° and the fish had nowhere to go. A few rainbows were feeding on the surface, but the browns were on the bottom in stress.

I caught one rainbow, which succumbed without a struggle; it was landed in seconds. I tried to revive the fish, but to no avail—the lactic acid buildup was too rapid. I stopped fishing.

On the Yellow Breeches at the Allenberry Resort near Carlisle, Pennsylvania, in midsummer hot spells the water can be 72° to 74° from one bank to the other. The rainbows are more active than the browns during the day. Most browns are under the vegetation, in the shade, or in the riffles where there's more oxygen. Cooler air in the morning and evening will push water temperature down, which moves more fish, but the fact remains that these trout can be caught at 74°. They have been conditioned to these temperatures.

Cold water is the other extreme. Immediately below the Navajo Dam, on the San Juan River in New Mexico, the water is a constant 37°. Only rainbows are found there, and they feed readily. Those fish are conditioned to cold. A few miles downstream, in 50°-plus water, brown trout begin to appear, and fishing is excellent for both species until air temperatures drop (morning and evening). Then they're tough to take. I tried night fishing when temperatures slid from the 50s to the 40s and took a beating for a solid week from dark till 4 A.M. Yet immediately below the dam, at 37°, I caught rainbows after dark. Why? Temperatures at the dam didn't fluctuate.

In many trout streams across the nation, trout can be fished for and caught year-round. In December I was taking brown trout in Arkansas on the White River in 50° temperatures and I was also catching browns in Pennsylvania on a limestone stream with water temperatures at 45°. Rapidly fluctuating temperatures can turn trout off, but once temperatures hold for a period of time and the trout condition to them, the fish can feed actively. Optimum temperatures from the mid-50s to the mid-60s stir the metabolic process, but the conditioning process is equally important.

High lakes in the Rocky Mountains are fed by snowmelt. Water temperatures seldom rise above 45° in midsummer, yet the cutthroat and brook trout that inhabit the lakes feed readily on top and just under the surface – and they're active. One afternoon, where an icy tributary entered a lake, the local trout population went crazy over a brace of wet flies fished near the surface. It's acclimation – conditioning.

In early season, when my Pennsylvania waters are high and cold, I'll move to smaller mountain streams where there's less water to cover and there are brookies. In the bigger stream in the valley below, finding fish in all that runoff can be a problem and the native browns may have lockjaw. Brook trout have a lower optimum temperature range for feeding – 45° to 65° – than the browns; they may feed actively at 45° where browns might not move.

Water chemistry – its alkalinity and acidity – is another consideration in finding fish.

In normal conditions in a healthy environment, the pH level may be 7. Drop it to 4, and the stream becomes too acidic for survival unless a conditioning process has been going on. Studies by Swarts, Dunson, and Wright, with the assistance of William Kennedy of the Pennsylvania Fish Commission, found that native brown trout and certain strains of brook trout could withstand lower pH levels; through acclimation, the trout become conditioned to acid water. Selective spawning of resistant genetic strains, from the embryo to swim-up fry (in low-pH environs—4.4 to 4.7), enhanced resistance to acid conditions.

Another study, by Pennsylvania fisheries biologist Joe O'Grodnick, found that certain strains of brook trout can withstand a pH factor as low as 4.4.

Each year I fish a mountain stream that drains from a bog. Several miles downstream I catch native brookies and browns, the browns being predominant. Closer to the bog, the stream has only brookies. Immediately below and within the bog there are no fish. Understanding the pH-conditioning factor tells me not only where to fish, but for what species.

The term pH is used to express hydrogen-ion equivalents per liter and represents the degree of acidity or alkalinity. The scale runs from 0 to 14, with 7 being neutral. Numbers less than 7 denote acidity and numbers greater than 7, alkalinity.

Acid can be produced by the decomposition of plant material, as may be the case with the waters draining from a swamp. In coal-mining areas, iron sulfide mixed with water and air leaches out of the coal as sulfuric acid; when this drains into the waters of freestone streams, the pH is dropped to a level where living organisms cannot exist. The burning of fossil fuels causes sulfur dioxide to be oxidized into sulfur trioxide, which forms sulfuric acid and enters streams in the form of rain or snow. This can spell disaster to freestone waters with little or no alkalinity. In limestone country, water and limestone produce calcium carbonate, which has a high pH and acts as a buffer against acid runoff.

If you wish to determine the pH of a stream, an instrument that can record it for you is made by the HANNA Instrument Co., Aquatics Eco-Systems, P.O. Box 1446, Apopka, FL 32704-1446.

These days, there is a third factor that may affect early-season trout fishing. From the time they lose their egg sacs till they're stocked, hatchery trout are conditioned daily to overhead feeding. Once released, they're still looking for food in the upper level. I've taken stocked trout of all three strains—brook, brown, rainbow—in early season in water temperatures between 40° and 50° with wet flies just under the surface. They were looking up for food.

2

NYMPHING

POCKET WATER

Pockets, those washed-out basins or cavities behind boulders, logs, and debris in midstream or along the banks, hold trout for many reasons. Pockets offer velocity changes and shelter where fish needn't fight the currents. As water cascades over and around objects, it becomes aerated, another boon to trout. The same flows also dislodge aquatic insects and trap terrestrials, tumbling them into the pockets, where trout wait. In the slower current, trout have more time to pick off nymphs. To migrating fish, pockets are rest areas, and the gravel downstream could be a spawning site. The broken water even offers fishermen an advantage: Fish can't see us as well as they can through flat water.

• A most valid approach to upstream nymphing is to employ the tuck cast. But a tuck cast is not always the prescription in upstream nymphing; in pockets only inches deep, you want to straighten the leader. The tuck cast can hang you on the bottom, and line control becomes difficult. In the shallows, a straight line from rod tip to nymph will put you in control.

191

• In pockets of moderate depth—a foot or two—modify the tuck cast. Instead of stopping the rod tip sharply overhead, as you would for a deep tuck, drift the rod farther forward. This will reduce the angle at which the nymph is delivered. A deep tuck cast lets the weighted nymph enter the water at a sharper angle, creating slack at the end of the leader and giving the fly more time to sink. The modified tuck doesn't permit the nymph to settle as deeply.

• One important aspect of the mechanics of the tuck cast is that you must feel the pull of the weighted nymph on the backcast. As soon as you make the backcast, drift the rod forward so that the line and weighted nymph will load the rod tip. That "tug" made by the weighted nymph as it straightens on the backcast is the signal for the forward casting stroke. If you employ the forward cast before you feel the bounce of the nymph on the tip, the nymph will drop and more than likely will hit you on the back of the head. It's an attention getter!

• For a natural drift, you have to avoid as many cross-currents as possible (thus the upstream approach). Eliminating drag is every bit as important in nymphing as it is in dry-fly fishing. Ask yourself how you can best get an extended, bottom-rolling, natural drift, because that's the secret of deep nymphing.

• Casting accuracy is important. If you get those first and second casts on target, your chances of a hookup are good. On each succeeding cast to the same spot, your chances drop. Ninety percent of the time the trout saw the nymph on the first cast; if it dropped and drifted drag-free, and if you selected the right fly, you should be into fish.

• Don't become mesmerized by one pocket and pound it. The more water you cover, the better your chances. Get those first couple of casts in there, then move.

• Weight adjustment is important—most of us stick on a split-shot or two and then seldom change weight through the day.

Pockets vary and so require different weights. Adjust not only the weight on the leader but the weighted nymph as well; the depth and speed of the water may call for both. The type of weight—shot, sleeve, wrap-around, wire— isn't that critical. I prefer split-shot, without ears; ears add to hangups on the bottom. Sleeves are too long—I want my weight more specifically located on the leader—and with a good tuck cast, they can fly off. Wrap-around is fine in shallow water, but in deeper pockets I want heavier, more concentrated weight to get me to the bottom faster with control.

What you're after is good, natural contact with the bottom. If the nymph hangs, take some weight off; if the nymph comes back too fast, add weight. The closer the weight is to the nymph (maybe only 6 to 8 inches away) the deeper it

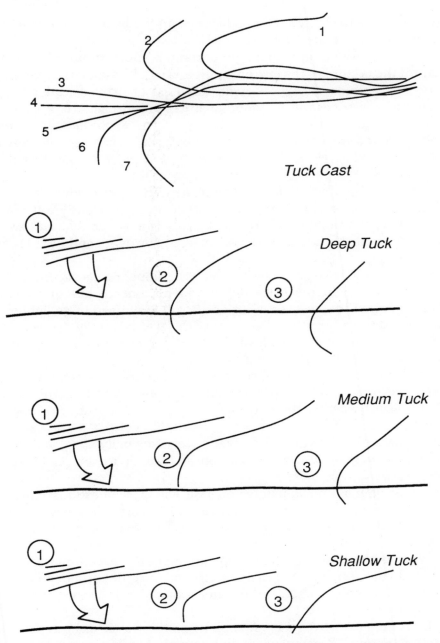

Tuck Cast

Deep Tuck

Medium Tuck

Shallow Tuck

The depth of the water is the guide for a tuck cast: in shallow water you want a tuck with a lesser angle; for water 1 or 2 feet deep a steeper angle; and for deep water a sharp, steep angle.

will ride. Moving the weight 16 to 20 inches up the leader will lift the nymph off the bottom. Experiment a little.

Leaders themselves are equally important. A short, stout, thick leader can lift a fly off the bottom as the currents pull through it. Adjust the overall length and also the sections of the leader. In this kind of fishing, leader length depends upon • your casting freedom—overhanging brush, etc. • water depth and speed • water clarity and how close you can get to the fish • your own ability to cast and control the leader • the elements • visibility (can you see the end of a long leader?) • the distance between you and your quarry • the need for control.

Learn to be flexible; don't start with a preconceived idea. Is the water clear? Are the fish spooky? Are you working deep pockets? You may need to lengthen your leader. If you're fishing off-color water that isn't too deep, shorten up. You must control the leader at a specific depth and be in touch with the nymph.

Often the base leader is okay and only the tippet needs adjusting. Lengthening it can give you the extra depth you may need, but tippet diameter requires attention too. In a gin-clear creek you may need to go lighter. In the toughest conditions I never go below .005" (6X). A trout may detect a dragging nymph, but a trout won't see a leader of that diameter. Besides, I want to land the fish and release it, not worry it to death.

One more thought: In these conditions, I usually prefer stiff mono for the base sections of the leader, tapering from .017" down to .011". Stiff mono sinks faster; it doesn't wave in the currents as much; and it straightens better, for more control.

Don't use sinking-tip lines in pocket water; they belly, drag, and hinge, and it's impossible to maintain immediate control from tip to nymph. Use a floater, in most cases a double-taper.

Examine your approach before you cast. Ask these questions: How can you position yourself for a natural, controlled drift? A direct upstream approach is often best. But with obstructions, an upstream approach may be impossible. A downstream drift might do.

• What is the best cast? This depends upon the depth and speed of the water. Will you straighten the cast, modify the tuck, or use a deep tuck?

• How close can you get? If the water is off-color or broken, you can move in; on clear water you can't.

• How much weight, in the nymph or on the leader or both, is needed to reach the bottom? Remember, if the nymph hangs up regularly, remove weight. If the nymph comes back too fast, even if you think you're on the bottom, add weight.

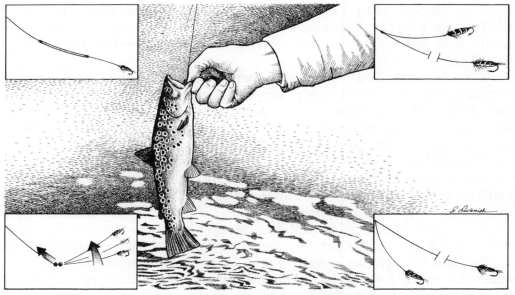

Adjust the weight: The closer the weight to the nymph, the deeper it rides; 16 to 20 inches up the leader, the nymphs lift. A strip of leadcore spliced into the leader might give you the needed drift. Try two weighted nymphs—a lightweight to ride up and a heavyweight to roll the bottom, or two heavyweights for a balanced bottom roll.

It's all just common sense, isn't it?

Fish a stretch of pocket water with me on a day in May; maybe I can share with you an idea or two.

Insect activity, or the lack of it, can give direction and insight as to what to fish, when, and what casting strategy you might use.

On a limestone stream one May, the sulphur *(Ephemerella dorothea)* mayfly had been hatching all week, and the trout were becoming conditioned to the nymphal activity. It was cold this morning; the water temperatures were in the 50s and the air temperature in the low 60s. There were no sulphurs visibly hatching, but this spring creek has a year-round supply of cress bugs, so I rigged a pair of weighted cress bugs, added more weight, and covered the bottom, working upstream.

In the deep pockets a deep tuck cast was needed. I stopped the rod tip high—the casting stroke was no more than a sharp squeeze of the rod handle, with an almost imperceptible recoil of the tip, the tip lifting up into the cast. I used my wrist and forearm, keeping the upper arm close to the body. The nymphs entered the pocket at a steep angle and settled to the bottom. I concentrated on the end of the leader where it entered the water and raised the rod tip to pick up the slack line. The leader bounced, signaling a strike, and I set the hook into a 13-inch native brown trout, then released the fish and continued on.

I slid in below and close to a midstream boulder. It was a deep run. I shoved my elbow in tight to my body and, using only the wrist, punched a "down and upper" cast that drove the nymphs forcibly into the water. The rod tip remained up on the cast and I had control of the line and nymphs on impact. I saw and felt the take but lost the fish.

The riffs began to shallow as I continued upstream, and with shallow water there was more clarity. I could see the gravelly bottom, even from a distance, and I knew the fish could see me. In the deep pockets I could get closer to the fish, but now I had to lengthen my casts.

Once again I changed my casting strategy. I used the same casting stroke, but I drifted the rod farther forward, to ten o'clock, before employing the stroke. Now the nymphs entered the water at a lesser angle, not as steep; I didn't need as much depth. I adjusted the weight. I decided to use one split-shot in some pockets, none in others; the weighted nymphs could give me the depth I needed.

In the short pockets at the head of the riffs, with a lot of broken water, I could get closer to the trout, as in broken water the fish had less visibility. I shortened the cast and used a "down and upper cast," and struck on a one-two-three count. In a short pocket, trout can pick up and eject nymphs so quickly that if you wait for the leader to stop or for a visual signal, it's too late.

The cast was short, my arm along my side, the wrist doing the work. As the nymph entered the water, I began to count "one-two-strike," and to my surprise, I felt the roll of a trout that was just as surprised as I was! I never saw any indication of a strike—this was blind striking, and it's a technique you want to remember.

I feel that a pair of nymphs—a tandem—is more effective than a single nymph because you are doubling your chances. You can fish two different levels simultaneously by using nymphs of different weights, such as a light-weight nymph 2 feet above a heavy nymph rolling the bottom. Trout may visually react to one nymph, miss it, and take the other. Often fish are moving up off the bottom chasing nymphs to the top, and a nymph drifting up off the bottom is just the ticket. If fish are not chasing or intercepting a nymph, rolling the bottom is the answer. A pair of flattened nymphs rolling the bottom will balance each other; they rock, bounce, turn, lift and drop, and almost crawl.

I've suggested keeping the nymph 2 feet apart, not only for technique (fishing two different levels), but also to help avoid the tangle you get when a trout rolls and churns as it is being landed. There have been more times than I wish to remember when the tangle has been so severe that I've had to reconstruct the leader and retie the nymphs. Another solution for this problem is to use a small swivel attached to the leader where you want your dropper, then attach the leader for the dropper on the other end of the swivel. You also can tie in a swivel below the dropper and above the bottom nymph. When the action is fast, and tangles have been taking away your "catchin' and grinnin' time," these tactics can help.

By midmorning on that May day, the sun's warmth replaced the early-morning chill. The waters began to warm and now and again an occasional sulphur would take flight. I keyed on the insect activity and changed to a pair of sulphur nymphs. Also prompting this change was the lack of action with the cress bug imitations, hinting that the trout were keying on something else.

By midafternoon there was considerable hatching activity, and some of the struggling duns never made it. Here and there trout intercepted the insects with splashy rises. The rising fish enticed me to fish a dry fly—I enjoy taking fish on top—but the greater activity was on the bottom, so I returned to fishing the nymph. I took some of the best fish of the day during this period—the nymphal activity on the bottom had stirred and enticed a few of the larger fish from hiding.

As daylight began to fade, sulphur spinners swarmed over some of the riffs, and many trout were showing on the surface. Now I rerigged—the top nymph with no weight, and the bottom nymph a lightweight one. I was catching fish, but only occasionally on the bottom nymph. I replaced the tail nymph with a no-weight one—only the brass wire ribbing gave it weight—and I straightened out the cast—no tuck cast here. I wanted the nymphs just under the surface and still used the same quick, short, squeezing stroke, but now I drifted the rod even farther forward before applying the stroke, which was all wrist: I kept my wrist straight, pushing the thumb forward and down, the flies coming directly overhead. This changed the level so there was no tailing loop and the nymphs wouldn't tangle. Bringing the cast straight overhead in this manner, with the thumb, wrist, and reel lined up, gives the caster accuracy, control of the angle at which the nymph enters the water, and a straight line from rod tip to nymph for line control, and it also prevents you from casting a hook or a cowtail.

The line and leader straightened on the cast; I elevated the rod tip and stripped the line as it floated back to me, keeping the line straight between rod tip and nymphs. The line stopped and I was into a fish.

As darkness fell, only a few duns continued to hatch, the spinners left the water, and just an occasional trout broke the surface. Once again I went back to the bottom, and night techniques took over.

I've used the above scenario to illustrate how you must change your tactics as conditions change. Learn to recognize insect activity or the lack of it, and adjust your techniques and casting approach accordingly. It's observation and flexibility that are paramount.

Tippet adjustment is vital to success both on the surface with a dry fly and on the bottom with a nymph. Paul Blankenhorn, a friend who helps me with photography on occasion, and I were nymphing a section of pocket water on a big Pennsylvania limestoner in early season. Paul was a beginning fly fisher and I was trying to help him. From 8 to 10 that morning the trout were active. I landed several fish, most of them stocked trout but a few nice natives. Paul caught a couple and was gaining confidence in his ability to catch fish on a nymph.

After lunch we continued to nymph pocket water. Paul caught three fish and I couldn't move a one; the pupil was giving the instructor a lesson. Frustrated, I waded ashore, sat on the bank and watched Paul. We were using the same upstream nymphing technique. Moments later Paul waded over to me and sat down.

"What are you doing differently, Paul?" I asked.

"I don't know," he replied. "The only thing I've done since this morning was change the tippet. How long is your tippet?" It wasn't long enough. I had changed nymphs several times, broke off on a couple of hangups, and shortened my tippet several inches.

The pockets were relatively deep, the water fast, and though the leader was 9 feet long, the currents on the line and the heavier leader sections, along with the shortened tippet, lifted the nymph off the bottom. I replaced the tippet with a 20-inch section of 4X (.007") soft mono. The change put me on the bottom again, and now, with the proper weight adjustment for each pocket, I was back in business catching fish. It is literally a game of inches. Leader makeup is determined by the conditions you face and your needs.

SIGHT FISHING

I was fortunate to be raised in trout country—central Pennsylvania. Our limestone streams, fed by cold springs, held trout year-round and were a perfect classroom for a trout-bit kid. Thompson Run, a tributary to Spring Creek, came from a large spring just outside town. In the warm months, after school, we'd throw our fly rods across the handlebars of our bicycles and speed to the fly hole, the first fishable pool below the spring.

To get there first was an advantage; in that crystal water, the trout were spooky and the first drift of a fly through the pool usually worked. The first *good* drift—frequent failures instilled in us all the need to begin with a stealthy hands-and-knees approach. (When the last straggler arrived, we no doubt resembled a band of Indians about to ambush the cavalry: Porky, Don, Max, the Wahl brothers, and me, fly rods poised as spears, waiting for the trout to meet the hatch.)

Clear water gave the edge to the trout, and as spring gave way to summer and the water level dropped, it became doubly tough—those trout could see you a mile away. They were equally visible to us, and thus sight fishing became a way of life.

I suppose I was fifteen or so that morning when a major breakthrough came in my angling tuition. A good trout, maybe 14 inches, lay at the head of a riff. Its dark, almost black form made the fish easy to spot, and the broken water let me get close. But instead of casting, I watched. The fish was feeding—drifting, picking something off the bottom, always returning to its original position, sometimes lifting or dropping as it moved.

The trout refused what I had to offer; it stopped feeding and took off. I was determined to find out what that trout was after. I pulled a handful of vegetation from the stream bottom—it was alive with insects later identified as freshwater shrimp and cress bugs. Some of the shrimp were touched with orange. The color caught my eye and my imagination. At home I fashioned what I thought was a look-alike, oversize because a #16 was the smallest hook I had.

Next morning I returned. The trout was in the same position. The first cast was off to the side, but the trout moved quickly to the nymph. I saw its mouth open, and moments later it lay at my feet.

Watch the fish. If a trout isn't cruising, it will be feeding to the right or left, and you've got to know before you cast. The trout will be lying in a velocity change, and the current bringing most of its food will be to one side or the other. Its food may be falling off the bank, so the trout will work to that side. Or if there is underwater growth—watercress and elodea, with cress bugs, shrimp, nymphs—next to major currents, the fish will position itself to intercept dislodged food or dig into the vegetation for food.

A fish may change its location: It's feeding to the left, you're about to cast, and it moves to feed to the right because the currents changed. Or the sun moved, blinding the fish on one side so it has to feed on the other. Wait and watch, and then cast.

One day I was leading a Penn State angling class on a field trip. The lesson was nymphing; twenty-five students were lined up on the bank above and behind me. They could readily see the trout I had pointed out. It was a few inches from the bank and feeding to its left, toward the bank. I lectured, "This fish is feeding to the left, the currents are bringing the bulk of the food to the left, and the greatest portion of nymph life is in the vegetation next to the bank, also to its left. Now watch this—if I cast to the right of the trout, it won't budge for the fly."

Sure enough, the trout never moved.

"Now," I said, "if I can get a cast between the trout and the bank, the trout should move for the nymph." As luck would have it, the nymph fell inches above the trout and between it and the bank. The fish eased over, picked up the nymph, and I landed a plump brown. The cheers turned to laughter and guffaws when examination of the trout found it had only one eye—it could only see to the left!

When you've determined which side the trout is moving to, time your cast so the trout isn't turning, lifting, or chasing, so it can pay undivided attention to your nymph as it comes by. Don't cast too far upstream; that gives the fish extra time to examine the imitation, particularly in slower water. If the nymph is heavily weighted it can sink out of the trout's sight before it arrives. Speeding currents and velocity changes lift and drop the nymph; on such a tough moving target, the trout has to make a snap decision.

Not only must you be aware of which side the fish is working, but you need to know its level too. Is the fish on the bottom? Or lifting? Is it doing both? Weight or no weight, in the nymph or on the leader or both—these things are crucial to depth and natural drift. The amount of weight and the length of the tippet depend on the trout and the depth and speed of the water. You've got to be flexible.

• For a bottom-feeding fish in deeper water, you may have to lengthen your tippet, go to a finer tippet, change to a heavier-weighted nymph, or add weight to the tippet. Remember this rule: The deeper the ride, the closer you slide (the weight to the nymph).

• If you want the fly to lift, go to a lighter nymph and slide the weight farther up. If the fish is lifting, tie on a lighter nymph that sinks slowly in the short distance it must travel, or use no weight at all for a natural drift just under the surface or in the surface film.

• If a trout visibly refuses the nymph, go to a smaller fly, change the pattern, or both. A finer tippet can make the difference too, though in my experience you don't need less than 6X (.005″) for the most sophisticated feeder in the clearest water.

Think about this too: A natural, no-drag drift can be just as important for a nymph as for a dry fly. A refusal may be the result of an unnatural drift, not the choice of fly. Improper tippet length and poor leader construction may have caused that poor drift.

- Too much weight in the nymph or on the leader will prevent natural drift—the nymph can hang on the bottom, where the trout will lose it or never see it (and if the nymph becomes covered with weeds or algae, no trout will touch it).

- Check the cast—stop the rod tip sharply overhead—then drop the elbow, then the rod tip. I'm throwing some slack in the leader because I'm after a natural drift. I'm using all stiff mono except for the last 2 feet of soft tippet. The line straightens out, most of the leader straightens but not the tippet, and I've got control of line and leader from rod tip to nymph. The cast and the leader complement each other. Too long a leader, 11 feet or more, is often too tough to handle when sight fishing; you don't have leader control or accuracy.

- There are times when an upstream approach is not practical or possible. With downstream nymphing, the distance the fly must drift, the depth and speed of the current, and the sink rate of the fly for a natural drift at the fish's feeding level are all considerations.

- The up side of downstream nymphing is that the nymph, not the leader, gets to the fish first, so you don't "line" the fish.

- Check the cast high with the downstream approach, meaning stop the rod tip high, pull it back, and then drop the elbow and then the rod tip—this puts extra slack in the line and leader for an extended downstream drift.

Check the cast, drop the elbow and rod tip. The line and most of the leader may straighten, but not the tippet.

Trout that have been fished over can be lightning quick when they sample a nymph; they may eject a fly as quickly as we blink an eye. The cue for striking: any movement of the trout to the nymph.

• Sometimes the fish nosedives, or it moves to one side, lifts, or turns around; more often than not, the trout has picked up the nymph on the turn. When you see the fish turn — lift. Often the flash of the trout's side as it turns signals a take.

• The opening of a trout's mouth — you can see the white inside — strike? The increased wiggle of the trout's tail as it moves to the nymph can signify a take. Often when I see the tail go into motion I lift; a trout can be so quick that there is only a second between the tail and the take.

Here's a final tip: Trout don't grab, they inhale, and you've got to give them a chance to pull the nymph in. You can be too fast. With experience, you will find the middle ground.

THE RUNNING LINE AND BIG-RIVER SYSTEMS

A nymphing technique that I've used for years is quite effective in big water with heavy currents. I stumbled onto it at the end of the 1940s when monofilament hit Centre County, Pennsylvania. Butch Kerstetter, Les Rote, and Lewis Weaver all threw big minnows with mono, using a fly rod and an automatic reel for quick line pickup; it was deadly for big browns on Penns Creek. I learned the system and I adapted it to nymphing . . . with great success. I could take fish I could never reach before, in those deep, fast runs.

In 1984 I was asked to host the first all-fly-fishing series on national television, with Larry Matthews and Ashbrooke Communications, for ESPN. There were eight shows, and one was with Steve Rajeff, the world casting champion.

With a caddis hatch bringing a few trout to the surface of a heavy-flowing river, Steve was doing an admirable job working the top and catching fish, but after a time the surface activity stopped. A fly line, with its heavy diameter and resulting water resistance, lifted the nymphs off the bottom in the heavy current. It was impossible to get an extended bottom roll.

We needed action for the cameras. I broke out the mono gear (20-lb. Cortland flat), added two #14 pale yellow caddis pupae and enough weight to roll the bottom, and we were into fish. A 20-inch brown trout closed the show.

One effective rig works like this: Parachute cord or shoestring filled with split shot or brass BBs and sealed at the ends (sometimes referred to as a caterpillar or slinky), is fastened to a snap swivel that runs free on the leader

2 feet above the nymphs or nymph and is restricted by a barrel swivel at the 2-foot mark. The advantage is that the weight slides, rolls, and crawls over the bottom, resulting in far less hangups and a more natural drift. A law in some states, such as New York, when fishing for steelhead is that the lead not be closer than 2 feet from the fly; this system meets that requirement.

One- and two-weight level flylines can be used in the same context. This small-diameter line has less water resistance plus the ability to cast well with weight on the business end. This system can be very effective when nymphing deep, fast waters where you need to cover the bottom over a greater distance.

Tom Johnson pointed out to me on the Pere Marquette that when salmon spawn they churn up piles of gravel, dislodging a myriad of black stonefly nymphs and mayfly nymphs. In those situations, salmon can be taken more readily with nymphs than egg-sac imitations. The steelhead that follow the salmon can be taken with both, but nymphing can really be the ticket.

When nymphing in big waters, deep and fast, I find that a weighted point fly and a weighted dropper with split-shot between the two (plus, if needed, a couple of shot above the dropper) is most effective. The number of shot and the weight in the nymphs again depend on the water. You can fine-tune the drift by adding or removing shot and nymphs of different weights.

Weighting systems vary for deep water. The slinky or caterpillar off a swivel (upper left). Here more weight is added between the nymphs (upper right). Split-shot is added to the leader above the nymphs (lower left). Weight is attached above and between the nymphs (lower right).

SOLVING WEIGHTY PROBLEMS

To be successful in nymphing, there are a few major considerations: The presentation (that is, the cast that will get the job done); the imitation; and getting the nymph down to the fish at whatever level necessary.

A great percentage of the time that means rolling your nymph on the bottom. I want to be prepared for whatever situation I face, so I carry split-shot of every size, loose in a pocket of my vest, along with a knife to open them. When a change is needed I simply grab a handful of shot and select the size and number for the water I'm about to fish. Weight regulation is so important. (Everywhere—at times my fishing vest feels like a sack of potatoes draped over me, particularly after a day of wading heavy water).

Vance McCullough, who now heads the angling program at Penn State University, and I were after early-season steelhead in New York, fishing a tributary that feeds Lake Seneca. The air was cold, the water was cold, and I was cold that early spring morning.

Vance gave me the first shot at a deep hole that we knew harbored fish. But after twenty minutes of bottom-bouncing a nymph, I had nothing to show and let Vance give it a try. Within minutes my partner was into a fish and, after landing a bright, fresh-run 8-pound steelhead, promptly took a second one that could have been a twin, then lost a third. "What the heck you doing, Vance?" I inquired.

"Same thing as you, but I added more weight."

He did, considerably more. I was dealing in split-shot, but he was working with buckshot—#4, three of them. It was a heavy-water chute, and deep, and even though my nymph was rolling on the bottom, those fish were in no hurry in that cold water.

I feel the answer to successful bottom nymphing is to give your flies as much time down there, right on the bottom, as naturally as you can.

When working shallow water, inches of water, maybe the only weight you need is what's tied into the nymph. But when tying weighted nymphs, don't put the same amount of weight into each one. Work with different amounts, and color-code the heads of the flies so you know at a glance if it's a light-, middle-, or heavyweight. When working deeper pockets and glides, a *pair* of heavyweight nymphs may be the answer, or the addition of weight on the leader *with* the heavy nymphs.

Be flexible, learn to adjust and to read the water, experiment till you get that good bottom roll—and in time, with experience and experimentation, a glance at the water will tell you what you need; if not, work at it till you get a good bottom drift.

But you can't always judge the weight to use by looking at the water.

Insects or trout showing – or the lack of both – may give you direction, but not always.

Tim Chavez, a friend and a top guide on the San Juan River in New Mexico, and I were working some heavy, broken water. Seeing little if any action on top, with only a few insects appearing, I decided to roll the bottom. Tim tied a long tippet (2 feet or more) onto his leader and added only a mite of weight, and while I was scouring the bottom with a caddis pupa, Tim was catching trout no more than a few inches under the surface, with the same caddis pupa.

The secret this time was one small shot and a small pupa. The active trout were up and I was far below them. Once I made the change, I too caught fish.

Weight selection can be a matter of common sense. If you hang up repeatedly, take weight off. If your nymphs come back to you too fast – without spending time on the bottom – add some. If your nymph rolls and then hangs up, either adjust the amount of weight or pull the weight farther up the leader. If you want to slow the drift a trifle, pull the weight closer to the nymph, maybe 8 inches, or add a little weight.

Tippet length and diameter are also considerations. The longer the tippet with a smaller diameter, the faster the weight drops. A short, thick tippet may lift the nymph off the bottom as the currents pull on the leader. A 20-inch tippet of 2X (.009″) may be the ticket in heavy pockets that hold heavyweight trout.

Sometimes weighted nymphs or split-shot aren't the best way to go. Mini sections of lead-core trolling line can be spliced into the leader. This arrangement can be deadly in both upstream and down-and-across-stream tactics. I attach the lead-core with a speed nail knot within the leader and adjust the length and density of lead-core for the depth and speed of the water. The fly can be 8 inches, 16 inches or more below the lead-core, depending on the clarity of the water or the desired depth. But a too-long section of lead-core in the leader will drag and hang up, so you don't get a good natural drift, nor are you in touch with the nymph.

FLY SELECTION

Clear spring creeks, with a population of native or hold-over hatchery trout that have been conditioned to man, can be both challenging and frustrating. If a trout is approached properly, it may not run and can be worked over, but it can also be superselective. Our essential need is a natural, drag-free drift – on top or bottom. A perfectly natural drift is every bit as important for a bottom-hugging nymph as it is for a topwater dry fly.

When faced with these conditions, I'll work with the leader – maybe shorten it for pinpoint casting control and accuracy. I'll lengthen the tippet for a deeper drift and go to a smaller diameter (typically .005"-6X) to help eliminate drag. Then I'll try a smaller size of the same nymph.

Fly size can be critical. In my angling classes at Penn State University, one session was an on-stream entomology lecture. I'd lift a stone from the water's edge and find it covered with a myriad of nymphs and crustaceans, and proceed to identify and discuss them. The predominant insect on those limestone waters was the cress bug, and very few were large; most could be imitated on #16 to #20 hooks. Trout become conditioned to what they see most of, and the same bug in a larger size can be a turn-off, particularly if the fish are being pounded by a multitude of anglers using larger flies. Trout in clear water don't cotton to unnatural drifts and oversized flies. They stop feeding with the first cast and by the second one they're long gone.

Water conditions dictate size. If the water is high or off-color or both, then I switch to a larger size. A #12 cress bug becomes more effective in this situation, and the trout can see it better.

When you lift a stone from the stream bottom and examine it for insects, what you find tells you the nymphal life the stream produces, but it won't necessarily tell you what to fish at the time. Unless the mayfly or stonefly nymphs, or the larvae of the caddis, are mature (the wing case of the mayfly or the two wing cases of the stonefly are well developed and the caddis larvae are sizable), it's unlikely there's enough stream-bottom nymphal activity to stir the fish. Tiny, undeveloped nymphs or a caddis worm that's hardly visible on the bottom of a stone don't turn the fish on.

One word to delete in our fly-fishing vocabulary is "always." So many times the adult nymph or larvae are small but they are active. While fishing the San Juan River in New Mexico, Tim Chavez clued me to a small, dark-brown #20 caddis pupa that had the rainbow population doing cartwheels. An upstream cast, a dead drift, and just enough weight to sink the fly was the technique—yet size and color of the fly remained critical.

Fishermen often succeed with specific flies and thus label the rivers accordingly. We hear, "If you want to take trout on the San Juan, you better stock a supply of San Juan Worms or Woolly Buggers." Possibly good advice, but don't stake your entire trip on it—be prepared to be flexible.

NYMPHING THE BRUSH

I had a speaking engagement in one of the southern states several years ago, and I was asked to go fishing with a few members the following day. After the show that evening, as we sat around the table and talked fishing, a member said to me, "When you fish a mountain stream for brookies, how many fish do you catch in a day?" "That's a tough question," I replied. "Sometimes several, sometimes a few, and at other times, none. There are so many variables." "Don't evade the question," he said. "How many?" To avoid answering the question, I asked him how many trout he took in a day's fishing. "Eighty-five," he said. "That's a lot of trout," I remarked. "You certainly are a fine fisherman! I can't do that." "Come on," he said. "You're putting me on!" With that the conversation moved on.

It was cool on that October morning when we arrived at the stream. My new acquaintance was anxious to fish the first pool and show me the action, but none was forthcoming. Nor did the second pool produce. I could tell that he was disturbed and a bit bewildered; these pools had produced for him all summer, so why not now?

On his recommendation, I too had fastened a dry fly on the end of the leader. "It's your turn," he offered. "This next pool always has trout in it." I felt sure I wouldn't raise a fish, but I went through the motions. The others looked on, first enthusiastically, then with growing impatience.

Stooping down, I took a water temperature. It was in the low 50s. Without a word, I adjusted the leader and tied on a pair of stonefly nymphs, both weighted, and patiently waited my turn.

My frustrated friend refused to give up on the dry fly and offered a list of reasons the fish hadn't been biting. Someone had probably fished the stream earlier in the morning; most of the trout had been caught out; they just were not feeding.

The onlookers wanted to see me fish and encouraged me to work a piece of water. I tucked a cast at the head of a deep run, and as the line drifted back to me, it twitched, and I hooked, landed, and released a 10-inch brook trout. Others followed. The colder temperatures had those fish on the bottom. There were plenty of fish, good ones too, and they were receptive to a nymph.

Probably the most difficult and challenging aspect of fly fishing for trout is nymphing a tight, brushy stream. The casting stroke is restricted for the most part, and weighted nymphs, unless you understand the casting strategy, tend to fly into the air and wrap around overhanging limbs. It is a real challenge—the ultimate—distance with weighted nymphs and little or no casting room.

Here is the casting strategy: First you have to feel the tug or pull of the nymphs on the rod tip, on the backcast. Second, drift the rod tip beyond the level of the limb you need to go under, then do nothing more than squeeze the rod handle—that's it, anything more than a squeeze and you're in the trees. Easy? Hell, no, it's as tough as any casting you will do, but what a great feeling of accomplishment you get when you succeed! Be ready for the frustrations that go with it, however. So many people today want instant success with limited effort. With the writings, videos, clinics, state-of-the-art rods, lines, and other equipment, much of the labor and creativity has already been done for the beginner. With a few years' experience, expert status might be claimed, but it has not been attained.

Fly fishing is full of exasperations and setbacks, especially in the early stages. Let me share with you one such experience I had as a teenager attempting to fish a small mountain stream in Pennsylvania.

The water was low and clear, the trout skittish. The only way I could get a fly to a fish was to clear enough line off the rod tip, crawl to the water's edge, and let the currents carry the fly downstream, kicking out extra slack line for the distance needed to raise a fish. But I wanted to cast for the trout.

Previous attempts at casting in tight quarters ended in disaster, and this day was no exception. Even though I crawled through the rhododendron to keep a low profile and crouched in the water, the trout still spooked, and if I did get close enough to cast, I would hang the fly on the overhanging branches. When I tried to shake the fly free, the overhead movement of the limbs sent the trout scurrying.

Pool after pool netted the same results, and my anxiety was being replaced by anger. A large hemlock at streamside afforded me cover and a vantage point from which I could see into the water directly ahead. A patch of sunlight filtering through the dense foliage revealed a splendid foot-long brook trout, its white-tipped fins illuminated by the sunlight—a prize to be captured.

The trout was in a tough place, in a lip current at the tail of the pool and directly under a limb. I hung the backcast in my excitement, crawled back to untangle the fly and leader, and returned to my position at the tree. The fish was still there. The forecast was predictable: too much arm and wrist movement, the thumb pushing skyward, and the line, leader, and fly soaring over the limb. The trout vanished.

In a frenzy I crashed through the brush to a clearing and began beating my rod into the ground, shattering the rod tip. Then I sat down on a log and let the tears flow. Once I regained my composure, I vowed I would learn to fish the brush and catch those trout.

3

WET FLIES

Opening Day of fishing in Pennsylvania, April 15, 1940. I was eleven. It was dark and cold that morning, and a light snow was falling when my father and I arrived on the famous Spring Creek in central Pennsylvania.

Fishermen had already begun to line the banks, their voices and occasional beams of light from flashlights revealing their presence. It was an eerie scene, with almost a carnival atmosphere. I quickly lost track of my father in the darkness and, groping for a place to stand, walked into a fisherman and mumbled an apology. Suddenly a voice rang out, "It's five o'clock, time to start." I baited up with a lively red worm, my hands nearly frozen, and dropped the worm into the dark, swirling waters at my feet. Then a tug—I lifted the rod tip gently and again felt the tug-tug of a feeding fish. I set the hook, and an 11-inch brown trout came flying out of the water and bounced on the high bank behind me.

With the crowds of fishermen around me also landing fish, it was a chaotic scene—thrashing fish, shouts of excitement, cursing—and then it stopped. By then daylight had replaced darkness. I could see there were far more fishermen than I had imagined, and only an occasional fish was being caught . . . except by the fisherman standing across the stream from me. I watched *him* take three fish in a row. "What are you using?" someone called out.

"Wet flies," was his reply, and then he moved on.

"Wet flies on opening day? Flies are for later in the season," I reasoned. "You fish worms on the first day."

Later that morning I told my father about the wet-fly fisherman. Dad tied on three flies, one a #10 Black Gnat (a Spiegel Company special). I met him at noon at the car and he excitedly told me of a large trout he had almost landed on the Black Gnat.

That experience, along with the helpful on-stream advice of knowledge-able fishermen such as George Harvey and Clyde Scheffler, made me realize that fly fishing was a year-round activity and wet flies were effective from the first of the season to the last. By the time I was a sophomore in high school, I was taking trout—on flies—on the first day of the season and beaming at the attention I received from other anglers.

Wet flies are effective for many reasons. They imitate a wide variety of insects—mayflies, caddis, stoneflies, terrestrials—as well as small minnows. Native or hold-over trout condition to hatches and the food supply in the stream and thus consider wet flies to be natural food.

Wet-fly fishing is an excellent way to start a beginner or a fly fisher who wants to learn all aspects of the sport. In my view, the best initial approach is across and downstream. With this method you have better line and casting control, and by working a short cast and gradually lengthening the cast to cover a wider arc, you cover more water. The more water you cover, the better your chances of catching fish.

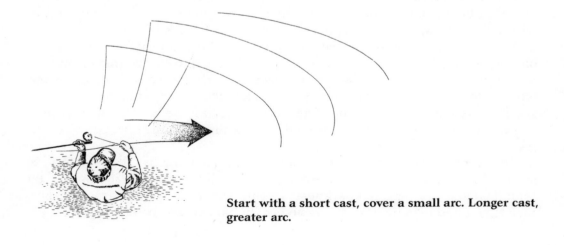

Start with a short cast, cover a small arc. Longer cast, greater arc.

Keep the belly out of the line; follow the fly with the rod tip throughout the drift.

Techniques are as numerous as you are creative. You can imitate a myriad of insect activity. Try a natural downstream drift with a slow hand and twist pickup, bounce the rod tip to impart movement to the flies throughout the drift, or let the flies sink, then lift, then sink again, or change direction and fish upstream. They'll all be effective at different times in different situations.

In review, here are the reasons I feel a beginner should start with wet flies, or a veteran should remember to use them.

• Hatchery trout are conditioned to being fed from above; they look up for their food. Wet flies in early season, even if the water is cold, can take trout near the top, just under the surface.

• On a downstream and across method you can cover more water; beginning with a short cast and gradually lengthening the cast, you can cover a large arc, thus your chances of catching fish are better.

Use a weighted nymph for a tail fly and two wet flies above; thus you are fishing three different levels.

A 90-degree angle from rod tip to fly allows enough slack line for a trout to suck in the fly, giving better hooking quality. *Photo by George Lavanish.*

- In covering more water you learn more about holding water. You learn to cover more productive water.
- Wets imitate a wide variety of mayfly nymphal activity. Insects make up a large portion of the diet of 8- to 14-inch trout—as much as 80 percent; thus wets imitate a large proportion of the trout diet.
- With three flies you have a better chance of picking up a fish, not only because you are offering a choice of flies, but also because you are improving your odds.
- A colorful dropper can well imitate the flash of a small minnow, increasing the range of foods offered.
- The leader is not as critical as in dry-fly fishing. You don't constantly have to struggle for a drag-free float.
- With a weighted tail fly and two droppers, you can cover three levels—a great way to prospect for feeding trout.
- As the light fades in the evening, you can rely on your senses of touch and feel, thereby increasing your fishing time.
- You learn line control, how to keep the belly out of the line.
- You learn to control the line angle, keeping a 90-degree angle from the rod tip to the fly for hooking qualities.
- Wet-fly fishing gives you wide areas in which to experiment with techniques and methods. You can imitate a myriad of insects with drifts, action, and so on. You are limited only by your imagination.

4

STREAMERS

When I was a lad, I fished central Pennsylvania's Spring Creek almost every summer day. One morning I planned to fish a favorite pool that had a long, deep riffle through its length, but another angler was there when I arrived. Chagrined, I found myself a seat from where I could watch and waited impatiently for the stranger to leave. He was fishing a large streamer, and I thought, *What does he expect to catch with that?* Then the angler cast his fly to the head of the riff, and a brown trout, larger than any I'd ever seen, rolled over the fly and disappeared. I couldn't believe what I had just witnessed, nor could I believe that the pool harbored a trout well over 20 inches. I never saw that trout again, but I was never without a streamer after that! You shouldn't be, either.

When fishing streamers, let water temperature be your guide. The activity of the fish depends on its metabolism, and water temperature, combined with oxygen, is the stimulus. When fishing cold waters in early spring for native trout, or fishing western or northern waters fed by snow run-off that keeps them in the 30s or low 40s, give your streamer maximum time on the bottom. As water warms, the trout's body tissues demand food and in the optimum range (55 to 65 degrees) the fish is having a Big Mac attack. Now the trout will chase prey, and a faster stripping retrieve can be the answer. (Of course stocked trout, conditioned to having their food arrive from overhead, break the rules; they look *up* for their food, and a streamer fished near the surface may be successful on a cold morning in early spring.)

Rod angle is critical to presentation. I've written earlier about the 90-degree angle from rod to fly, to create slack that will let the trout inhale the fly. The angle of the rod also helps control fly depth. If you're working down and across the stream and hold the rod tip up, the fly rides higher. If the trout are chasing minnows or baitfish, this may be just the ticket. If you want your fly deeper but can't or don't want to add weight, drop the rod tip to the right or left, maintaining the angle. The fly will sink lower in the water column, yet you'll still have enough slack for the fish to suck in your fly.

When fish are deep, roll the bottom by casting the streamer up and across the current, then drop the rod tip and create the angle to one side of the drift to produce slack. Now lead the fly through the drift with the rod tip, lifting and dropping the tip to give the fly action. For more depth you can drop the rod tip underwater.

I watched Finnish anglers use this technique during the 1989 world championships in Finland. They would make a fairly long cast quartering upstream, then lower the rod tip to the water, at an angle to the left or right, and lead the streamer through the drift with the tip. They gave the fly action with the rod tip, *but did not retrieve.* This technique is effective when the fish are in a lane or drift line, and you can cover a lot of water from a distance.

Tuck the cast upstream so your streamer sinks readily. Elevate the rod tip and strip line in as the fly drifts back to you, lifting and pumping the rod tip throughout the drift. This action imitates a wounded baitfish trying to stay upright as it drifts along. An easy kill for a trout, and a technique you don't want to be without.

At times no action at all is the answer. Make another upstream tuck cast, but work the streamer or sculpin as you would a nymph on a dead drift. A trout will jump on a dead minnow in a minute.

Another idea is to let the fly come to rest on the bottom, then give it a twitch, then let it lie again. During a demonstration on the Yellow Breeches, Ed Shenk stopped his retrieve to talk to the class. While he was talking, his sculpin imitation dropped to the bottom; when he lifted the rod to continue his demo, he had a fish on.

In the clear waters of a western Pennsylvania stream on which I was doing a demo, the fish would halfheartedly chase my streamer and then turn away. When I let the fly settle to the bottom, the fish would turn, drop down, and suck it in. If the fish returned and didn't take the fly, I would give it a twitch and let it rest again. Sculpins live on the stream bottom, scurrying from rock to rock. When they rest on the bottom away from cover, they're an easy meal.

If you want your fly to ride deeper, drop the tip of the fly rod to the water, to the right or left, but keep that 90-degree angle. *Photos by George Lavanish.*

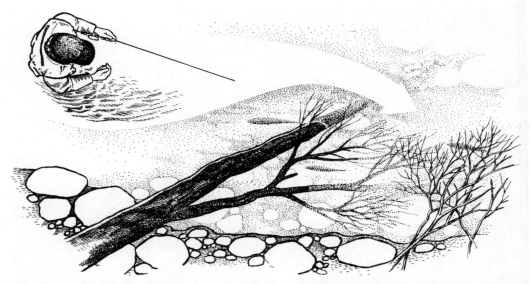

Work in and around brush piles, cedar sweeps, and logjams, at times with no more than a couple of feet off the tip.

Many anglers cast a fair amount of line when fishing streamers and cover a lot of water. Covering water is a good idea, but don't disregard the water right in front of you. When I'm fishing I work in and around brush piles, cedar sweeps, and logjams, sometimes with no more than a couple feet of line out of the tip. I've done well on streams in Michigan dropping my fly down into a hole *within* a logjam (I use a short, stout leader, so I can railroad a fish out of there). It adds excitement. I feel the throb of a heavy fish deep within the logjam and I wonder if I can land it. Will I even see it? Or will it break me off? It's worth the chance.

In Italy a member of the U.S. team, Bob Experti from Jackson Hole, Wyoming, introduced me to a technique using a white streamer with a nymph trailing 14 to 18 inches behind. The action of the streamer excited the fish, and if the fish didn't take it, more often than not it pounced on the nymph. Thanks, Bob. My late friend Lewis Weaver, a great live-minnow man, used a pair of Grey Ghost streamers with the same result. If a trout would show or roll for the dropper fly and miss it, it very often would take the tail fly.

I think we all look back at periods in our youth and reflect on the gang we ran around with and the hangouts we frequented. One such gathering place for us was the fly and tackle shop in Calder Alley in State College, Pennsylvania, owned and run by the Hartswick brothers, Max and Tom. They didn't have much of an overhead, and the shop was a shed—an old horse stable with the floor concreted, a kerosene heater for heat, and benches to sit on.

It was a favorite place after school for the teenage fly-fishing buffs, college students, and the elderly as well. A lot of stories were told—a fair amount of prefabrication, off-color stories, some funny punch lines, and a considerable amount of harassment. More than once tempers flared, but a lot of ideas, tactics, and fly patterns were discussed and passed around.

One afternoon Max handed me a dark green bucktail streamer with a pea green body made from a toothbrush handle softened with acetate, then shaped on the hook shank.

"Will this work, Max?" I asked. "How should I know," he retorted. "Try it. If it's any good, let me know."

That bucktail fished slowly on the bottom, inched along, and was a killer at the famed Fisherman's Paradise project on Spring Creek, as well as the other spring creeks in the area. Evidently it represented a nymph, possibly a dragonfly nymph. Whatever it represented, it was effective and a well-guarded secret. Back in those days on the hard-fished streams, there was little sharing and a lot of secrecy. It was a competitive atmosphere; you had to be in tight with a veteran angler to get a scrap of info. They were the top guns and they were determined to stay that way. I don't think I ever did tell Max how well that fly worked.

5

DRY FLIES

The trout was on top, tight to the far bank, and its feeding area was well chosen for self-preservation: a pocket behind a submerged stone, with a tree limb a foot above the water and heavy with foliage and grapevines serving as a protective umbrella. Halfway between me and the fish were two heavy tailing currents, and from bank to bank was a distance of 60 feet, most of it too deep to wade.

To try for this fish, naturally I'd have to position myself carefully. I'd have to get around as many of the currents as possible, to avoid drag. I'd also have to get as close as possible, for casting accuracy and for line control; I could cut the distance by 15 feet by wading, but the heavy currents were giving me fits. To get on the other side of the stream—the best approach of all—meant a half-mile walk. It didn't seem worth the effort, and besides, this was a casting challenge.

I was using a 9-foot rod, which helped me reduce a lot of drag by lifting line over some of the currents. It would help me mend line too, crucial for a natural drift. To give the fly time in the critical area (close enough to the trout for it to be willing to take the fly) meant constructing a leader that would get me under the limb *and* give me ultimate float time.

I did mend the line, in the air and on the water, but as the fly drifted in, it dragged and that ended the show—the trout disappeared. Frustrating. What could I have done to produce the longer float I needed?

There are three basics that are fundamental to a drag-free float: POSITION, for best casting vantage and to eliminate as many interfering currents as possible; LEADER, specifically one that will turn over, with a tippet to match the density of your fly, and that will give you the necessary soft curves up to the fly; and a CAST that complements the leader. It may need a mend in the air, but with changes in the levels of the elbow and rod tip to create slack in the leader. Thus goes fact versus fiction.

For years I've read volumes about mending and float time. The reach cast, the snake cast, hooking off the mend, slack-line mends—much of it is misinformation that can reinforce mistakes and take away from the angler's joy (catching fish). Add in the frustration of putting fish down or simply being unable to raise them.

Do line-mending tactics add to the length of the float? They are a means to that end, but they are only one element of successful technique. We're told how a reach cast—lifting your fly line upstream—can extend your float, or how shaking the rod tip to make waves of line on the water (the "snake cast") can give us the ultimate float because of the extra line on the water: But we can have the entire fly line in waves on the water and still get immediate drag if the leader straightens out on the cast. I've also read how you can plop a beetle on the water off a mend and have a trout immediately grab your offering; I've watched trout damn near kill themselves trying to stop when the leader straightened out—even though the trout moved to the disturbance; it saw a dragging beetle. Without the proper casting mechanics and the proper leader, mends simply add time to a drift, *extending* the drag. In many cases we can't see this, but the fish does.

How many anglers really work with both leader and cast to achieve those soft curves of tippet up to the fly? And how many take the time to observe and analyze what mending in the air or on the water does to the leader and tippet?

The reach cast, the snake or curve cast, the parachute, steeple, or puddle cast off the mend—all these tend to straighten even a properly constructed leader out, if what I call "level changes" are not employed. Some feel a long, light tippet is the answer, but it isn't unless your cast complements it; a long, fine tippet can straighten out very well and drag quickly. Shocking the rod on the forward cast, dropping the elbow and then the rod tip, is imperative.

I've had trout follow what I thought was an ideal float only to refuse it at the last moment; it wasn't perfect. I didn't have those soft coils of leader—not line—up to the fly. Either I didn't make the leader properly or I didn't shock the

A plop of a beetle on the water can attract a trout, but if that leader straightens and drag sets in, the beetle often will be refused.

cast — making an abrupt stop on the forward cast, shaking slack in the leader — and change the level of the elbow and the rod to give the leader a chance to work — those soft curves to the fly.

The reach cast is an excellent mend *if* you first shock the forward cast. The forward stroke is a mite of a stroke, hardly more than a squeeze of the rod handle, with thumb pushing forward and down and the rod stopping sharply at eleven o'clock. Then drift the rod upstream on the reach, drop your elbow, then the rod tip. If your leader is right, you've got a natural drift.

With the snake cast, shock the forward cast as with the reach cast, then shake the rod tip, drop your elbow and then the rod tip. Now you've got not only waves of line on the water, to compensate for currents, but soft waves of leader too, up to the fly. The shock kicks slack out to the leader, the level changes collapse the leader, and the soft leader material pulls back and stacks up.

The parachute cast off the reach is a combination shot. Here you push your thumb and the rod tip up into the cast, shock the forward stroke when it's at a steep angle, then reach; now make the level changes by dropping your elbow

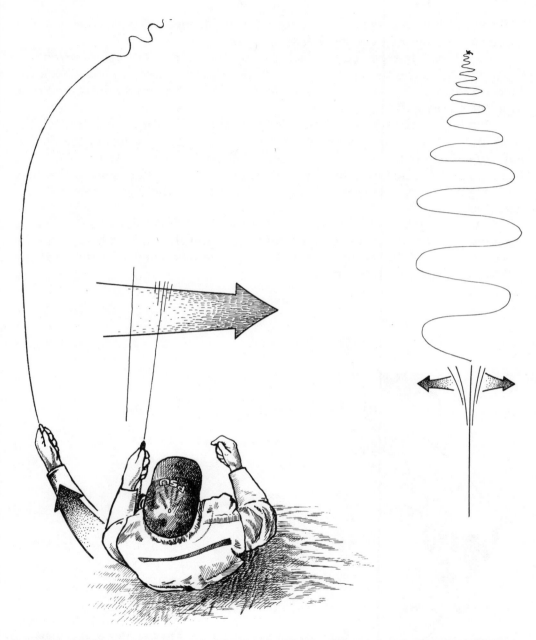

The reach cast (left): Shock the rod, reach by drifting the rod upstream, then drop the elbow and rod tip. The snake cast (right): Shock the rod, shake the rod tip back and forth, then drop the elbow and rod tip.

and rod tip. This cast really stacks both line and leader. With this one, you can smoke a cigar before drag sets in (well, almost).

A hook cast lets you curve slack line upstream, around faster currents in front of you, so the fly has more time in the slower water beyond. Shock the forward cast and throw the hook by rolling your wrist over and upstream, then drop the elbow and then the tip.

Mending on the water is critical for good float time. Often anglers kick the slack out of leaders they worked hard to put in. And they tested the leader, adjusting the tippet to make sure it would collapse properly with that fly. (Here I might point out that each fly has a different density, a different air resistance; you may have three dries on #12 regular-shank hooks that have three different densities.)

So the leader is ready. You shocked the forward stroke, changed the level of the elbow and rod tip, the fly is floating beautifully, and with one mighty sweep of the rod on the upstream mend you've destroyed all your work by pulling the slack out of the leader.

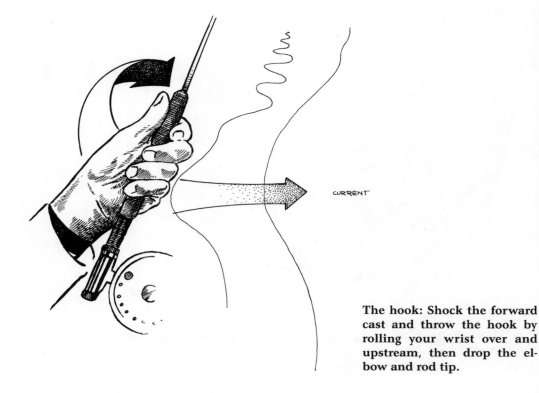

CURRENT

The hook: Shock the forward cast and throw the hook by rolling your wrist over and upstream, then drop the elbow and rod tip.

Instead, make the mends small ones, just off the rod tip. You can roll the rod tip (upstream or down, whatever is needed), kick out slack off the rod tip, and never straighten the leader or tippet.

I may be sounding like the wrestling coach I once was. Then, we worked on doing things properly, perfecting the small things and then drilling until they were second nature: *Shock the forward cast—now mend—drop the elbow— now drop the rod tip—now get it right this time!* And I thought fly fishing was supposed to be fun!

Well, doing it right is. And learning these techniques ended years of frustration for me.

LEADER SELECTION

If you're fishing a dry fly in windy conditions, you probably can't control a long leader and an extended tippet. You might be able to turn the leader over, but even with excellent loop control, it is unlikely you'll get that combination of accuracy and slack—in the leader up to the fly—for that long drift.

When casting in under brush, a long leader and tippet—even a tippet right for the density of the fly—will lift the fly and hang it on the brush you're trying to avoid. And, as shown, leader and tippet adjustment is equally important for a good bottom-roll in nymphing.

George Harvey experimented with a dry-fly leader design for years and eventually came up with one that has been labeled one of the most significant contributions to fly fishing in the past fifty years. The experiment began on Spruce Creek with a jar of Japanese beetles. George chummed a few trout to the top, then inserted a section of leader into a beetle, dropped the beetle and leader section above the trout, and observed. The impaled beetle floated freely, naturally. George graduated the leader diameter up to .015″ and it made no difference; the trout continued to take them.

The experiment proved that as long as the drift was drag-free, one could get away with heavier tippets. A heavier tippet that can fool fish means that fish can be landed more quickly, with less stress for the fish, less lactic acid buildup, and a greater survival rate for released fish. And a heavier tippet can hold bigger fish with fewer breakoffs, especially on hookups. It's a greater challenge to out-slick a sophisticated trout with a heavier tippet. Today George seldom goes below 5X (.006″) for touchy trout in clear water.

Harvey's leader is made of both stiff mono and soft; the stiff to turn it over, the limp, or soft, for an extended float. The first section of soft is a foot of 2X (.009″), which causes the collapse. The tippet should match the density of the

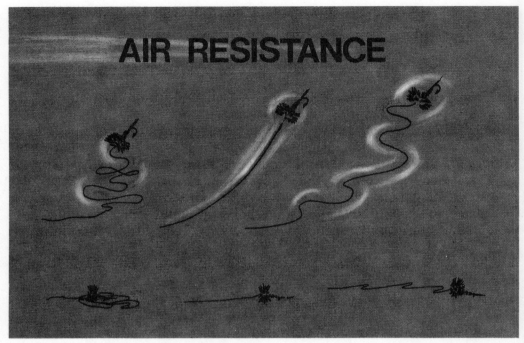

If the fly collapses behind the leader or tippet, then the fly is too dense for the length of the tippet or the tippet diameter is too small. If the tippet straightens, the tippet is too short or the diameter too great. You want those soft curves of leader right up to the fly.

fly. If the fly collapses behind the leader or the tippet, then the fly is too dense for the length of the tippet or for the diameter (or both). If the tippet straightens, even with a good check on the cast and changes in the level of the line, then the tippet is too short or the diameter too thick. Tippet length and diameter are *not* determined by hook size. It's possible to have three flies, all tied on an identical #12 hook, each with a different density and each requiring a different tippet length and diameter.

George would challenge me each time we fished together: "Did you check your leader? Is it constructed properly? Are you getting those soft S-curves of leader right up to the fly?"

It has become a habit with me. I won't fish until I get the desired result. I'll check the cast (stop the forward cast abruptly), then quickly drop my elbow, then the rod tip, to change the levels that collapse the leader, and I'll do this till I get the right slack in the tippet, those soft S-curves to the fly.

Each fly has a different density and therefore needs a different tippet. There is no standard leader for every occasion. I'll adjust both the stiff and soft sections for water or other conditions. It may be a 6-foot leader in tight brush or a 10-footer in open water with a multitude of velocity changes. Remember, different types of water may require a change in leader and tippet length/diameter, too.

One morning on a gem of a limestone stream, the Trico hatch was in gear and trout were sipping everywhere. George Harvey was standing next to me when a trout broke in front of us. Hurriedly I cast over the fish—the fly was refused. Quickly I cast again, before George had a chance to lift his rod. I wanted to take that fish—we always enjoy a little friendly competition. But then George was ready and the competition ended with his first drift. The trout never hesitated; it sucked the fly in as it would a natural. In my haste to take the fish I overpowered the cast and straightened the leader, which instantly resulted in drag.

The action concluded by 11 A.M. "How'd you do?" asked George.

"Pretty good," I replied. "I probably caught a dozen fish."

"I guess it depends on what you consider good," said George.

"Well, how did you do?" I responded.

"Maybe thirty or more," George replied. "They were easy."

Lessons can be difficult, but this is how we learn. You should profit in defeat, by fish or fisherman, but learn from your mistakes and file away the insights from each experience.

With George Harvey's blessings, I'll give you his leader formula—but remember, adjust for the conditions you face.

Often we stumble onto a pattern that produces and simply accept our good fortune. But understanding a few basics of insect identification—size, shape, color, motion, and how they interact—can increase our fishing success and enjoyment.

When working a limestone stream during mayfly time, in the morning before the hatch is under way I'll fish the bottom with a shrimp or cress bug imitation. Mayfly nymph activity can be at a standstill in the cold of a spring

(APPROX.) 9½' LEADER TO .007 (4X)

NAIL KNOT		HARD NYLON				SOFT NYLON	
	.017	.015	.013	.011	.009	.008	.007
LINE	10"	20"	20"	20"	12"	18"	22" to 28"

(APPROX.) 10½' LEADER TO .006 (5X)

NAIL KNOT		HARD NYLON					SOFT NYLON	
	.017	.015	.013	.011	.009	.008	.007	.006
LINE	10"	20"	20"	20"	12"	12"	18"	22" to 30"

The George Harvey leader formula.

morning, but those trout know what a cress bug or a shrimp is—they're there year-round and the trout are conditioned to them. Until air temperatures warm the water and spur the hatch, the trout will move to a cress bug or a shrimp.

The most difficult aspect of fly fishing is recognizing what the fish have been conditioned to. The most visible bugs aren't necessarily what they're taking, especially when hatches are shifting gears. For instance, when the green drake hatch is in its early stages, a drake imitation may appear to be the ticket—flies drift by like sailboats, the trout are surface feeding . . . but not on the drakes. Over the past ten days the sulphur hatch was the dominant show, and the trout were conditioned to its density and the size, color, and movement of sulphurs. They may stay on them till the drake hatch takes over as the feature attraction, in numbers and size, from nymphal activity on the bottom to the adults on top.

On many occasions I've cast my arm off not recognizing or understanding what had taken place before versus what was happening at the moment. I should have worked a #16 Sulphur instead of the Green Drake.

Unless you're on the stream day after day, can read the signs, and know the

Large green drake mayflies drift by like sailboats, but the smaller sulphurs are dominant and the trout are conditioned to them.

stream's hatch calendar, it's damn tough to pinpoint exactly what's going on. On a stream for the first time, even veteran anglers play guessing games, become frustrated, and come up empty. (I speak from experience more than I like to admit.)

I've had my eyes opened many times in disbelief while watching trout lift and sip for tiny midge pupae and no-see-ums, only to have my friend and mentor George Harvey use a #10 deerhair ant to take the same fish—a fish that had frustrated an army of anglers.

Trout become conditioned to terrestrial insects from May to October. They see carpenter ants every day, so even though they may be feeding on the most readily available insect, a fat ant or cricket won't go unnoticed. Often it will out-fish anything else!

George Harvey and I were discussing the number of different dry-fly patterns we had used over the years, and his comment was, "You know, I've used probably less than a dozen patterns consistently in my lifetime—that covers a span of seventy-seven years. An Adams in sizes #12 to #20, Sulphurs from #10 to #20, a Harvey Spruce Fly (black hackle, black quill, wood duck wings) in sizes #16 to #20, a Gordon Quill from #12 to #20, a ginger quill in the same sizes, a deerhair Humpy #12 to #18, a green deerhair inchworm in #12 to #16, a black deerhair ant from a #10 to #18, a green-, yellow-, and black-bodied caddis from #12 to #18, and a Trico from #18 to #24, and that pretty much covers it. Oh, I have dozens of different patterns I carry, but when it comes right down to it, these flies cover most situations." When I thought about it I had to agree. A selection like this one gives you the colors, shades, and sizes to cover most situations.

LIP CURRENTS

It was a summer afternoon on a mountain freestone stream, and I was having my share of problems. The first pool had set the tempo: I could see a trout near the surface where the water left the pool, and my first cast was a direct shot. Too direct—the leader straightened, the fly raced over the current lip, and the fish disappeared. On the next pool my approach was too close, and a wake announced a frightened trout dashing for cover.

On the following pool my approach was better, as I stayed back and lowered my profile. I opened my casting loop, and the leader, designed for a drag-free float, looked as though it would accomplish its purpose. The fly danced toward the brink of the lip, a trout slid under it, but drag set in and the fish pushed water ahead of it as it ran for safety.

What had I done wrong? The cast was too far beyond the lip—it should

The currents that converge at the lip of a pool carry food. This area offers a velocity change for the trout and a vantage point from which to spot danger.

have been directly on it. The currents were too fast and I had allowed time for drift, time that I didn't have.

Dry-fly fishing for mountain trout is challenging, particularly in the low, clear waters of late season. The stream's most challenging obstacles are lip currents, those shooting, funneling flows that drop at the tails of pools. They can be disaster areas for an angler battling drag, and they can be a trout's best friend: The currents that converge at the lip of a pool carry food; the velocity change at the lip enables a fish to hold position without fighting currents; and the lip offers a good vantage point from which to spot danger.

Most of the time an upstream approach and casting position are advisable because fish *do* face into the current—most often that is upstream. But sometimes obstructions make a downstream approach more productive, or you may have to cast from a considerable distance off the bank above the lip.

Suppose you see a trout surface feeding at the edge of a lip, between two boulders where a considerable amount of water and drop increase the current's speed. You're not going to get any drift time, but you *will* get immediate drag—no matter what casting technique you use—if you cast straight into the chute from below.

Position yourself as close to the fish as possible. Being close offers better line control and allows greater accuracy for casting to the trout and over or around obstructions. Close may also mean a better angle to your quarry – off to one side.

To get close to the lip, keep a low profile. Fish against a background and close to the bank, keeping down on one knee or both. A lip with a riffly surface, converging currents, or a considerable drop will help you get close. A shallow, flat lip forces you to keep your distance.

When the water is low and clear and you've got a population of well-worked-over trout, then keeping your distance is imperative. Poke a rod tip over shy trout in low, clear water and wave it around and you'll cause a stampede. That approach may be possible in the spring when the water is up or off-color, but not in the low, clear water of the summer.

Your leader is critical when fishing lip currents. Stop a cast sharply overhead and let the line and leader drop at your feet. See if the tippet lies in S-curves; if it straightens, it is too short. If the tippet falls in a pile and it is difficult to cast the fly, shorten it. The tippet diameter depends on the clarity of the water and the density of the fly, but I never go smaller than 6X, because when I hook a fish, I want to land it quickly, not worry it to death.

Your leader may be 10 feet long when you have casting room, but when you step into a brushpile you can't handle that much. Then, the leader might be 5 or 6 feet long, but the design is basically the same: a combination of stiff and soft monofilament, and a long tippet section that casts the fly accurately and falls in S-curves.

I've always compared casting with shooting pool, particularly when lip currents are involved. You make some straight shots, but a majority of the casts are combinations. The rod is a cue and you put English on your line and leader with your wrist and fingers. Where your thumb, knuckles, and rod tip go, the line and fly go.

A straight cast directly into the lip means trouble. Anytime you straighten the line and leader in fast water, you get drag. If you must cast straight to the lip, check your cast high and drop your elbow and rod tip, then elevate the rod. This will give you a wide, high loop and extra float time – if your cast is not too deep into the lip. When you must work directly below the lip, try to get as close as you can. (In some situations directly below the lip, close may be as far away as 40 feet.)

Another cast that puts slack into the tippet is the drop cast. Push the thumb of the casting hand up and quickly drop the rod tip to collapse the loop. Not only do you get slack in the leader, but the fly plops to the water heavily, an immediate attraction to the trout.

One of the best ways to attack lip currents on an upstream approach is to move off to the side and work at an angle. You won't be casting directly into the current, and from an angle you have different casting options—those combination shots again. Open the loop and simultaneously cut your wrist in the direction of the cast to throw a downstream hook, to make the fly lead the leader and line down to the lip.

Here's another combination shot you can use: As the line straightens on the forward cast, lift it over the bank, rocks, logs, or anything that can hold the line off the water. Shock the line with a quick stop, lift it over the obstruction, and quickly drop your elbow and rod tip as the line falls. The leader drops with soft S-curves to the fly, and the obstruction will prevent line from being swept away with the current.

An underhand lift is another good slack-leader cast: On the power stroke, give your wrist an underhand "kick" to make the tippet and fly rise, then drop.

As the line straightens out on the forward cast, lift it over the bank, a rock, or anything that will hold the line off the water.

I have purposely avoided the term "slack-line cast," because you can have all the slack line in the world and still get drag if your leader isn't right. The line can be perfectly straight, but you must have slack in the leader – right up to the fly.

The flow on a lip is generally faster than the water above it, so you can't cast too far above and expect a drag-free float. When you see a trout on the lip, get the fly in close. Cast too far above and beyond the fish, and you'll watch the fly and leader drag over it.

Casting the fly close to the fish not only means less leader on the water, but it also gives the trout less time to examine the fly and make a choice about whether to attack it or lose it. Your first drift is the one that counts, because each subsequent cast over a fish diminishes your chances. Make each new cast upstream of your previous one – you won't waste time on unwilling fish and you'll cover more water and more fish.

Trout in a mountain-stream pool maintain a pecking order in which the biggest trout is dominant, controlling the best feeding lanes; the other trout line up accordingly. When the pool's lip offers the most food and the most comfortable current, the biggest fish will be there, with the smallest fish at the pool's head. If you can get a good drag-free float on the lip with your first cast and take a good trout, don't bother with a second cast – you took the best fish. Move on and give the other fish a break. If you take a parr-size trout off the lip, punch the next cast well up in the pool, close to cover and the major currents at the top; with luck, the best fish will move to the fly.

Because of the pecking order, when you hook a small trout on the lip of a pool, get it out of there immediately. Control the trout's direction before it realizes what's wrong; the fish will be off balance, allowing you to maneuver it over the lip and around obstacles below it. Of course, you may lose an occasional trout, and there will be times when you have no choice but to play the fish in the pool and put the other fish down. If you can land the fish on the lip without spooking the rest, the pool's sentry is gone and the others can be left unguarded. Whether that sentry fish is big or little, it can spot you from a heck of a distance away, so your approach is critical.

Use as long a rod as you can get away with. In tight brush I prefer a 7- or 7½-foot rod – the longer the rod, the more line you can lift over the currents. As soon as the fly settles on the water, point the rod skyward with your arm fully extended to lift the line over the break of the lip for an extended float.

Lip currents have always been difficult for me; they've helped many fish avoid my hook and have pulled and hung innumerable flies into the rocks and debris at their bases. I've learned to deal with them more effectively, but there will still be times when the lip has the last smile.

Use as long a rod as you can get away with. With your arm and rod held skyward, you can lift more line over the lip and hold the fly in the productive water longer. *Photo by George Lavanish.*

ON-STREAM STRATEGY

Join me while I fish a stretch of water with a dry fly. I'm a lefty most of the time, so walk along or wade and crawl with me, and watch over my right shoulder as I talk you through this venture.

The first pool is a beauty. We'll slip below it to a piece of shallow, flat water, choose the fly, and make sure the leader will work with it. Then we'll fish the pool.

It's August, and there is some mayfly activity, but as we make our way to the stream, I notice Japanese beetles clinging to the wild grape leaves near the water. August is terrestrial time, and there are always ants, crickets, and hoppers available.

I'm going to go with a Humpy, a tailless one with black floss underneath the deerhair body. Beetles don't have tails, nor do other terrestrials. I've done better with no-tail Humpies than with ones having a tail.

The leader we are going to start with is George Harvey's formula, a combo of stiff and soft monofilament: the stiff to turn it over, and the soft to give us

Terrestrials don't have tails, beetles don't have tails. I feel I've done better with no-tail humpies; they give a better silhouette. *Photo by the author.*

Even if the last few inches of tippet straighten, the currents pulling through the segment of straightened tippet mean drag.

float time. The length of the leader is determined by several factors: how tight the stream is, whether you have room to cast a long leader, whether the stream is clear or off-color (if it's off-color you can get away with a shorter leader, while clarity could call for a longer one). Windy conditions can force you to go shorter; you have neither control nor accuracy in heavy wind with a long leader.

The pool we are about to fish has plenty of open space and a lot of casting room, and the water is clear. A 10-foot leader or one a mite longer might work. Let's build a leader: 12 inches of .017 off the fly line, 20 inches of .015, 20 inches of .013, 20 inches of .011 (0X), all stiff mono. Now the soft mono: 12 inches of .009 (2X), 18 inches of .008 (3X). And now the tippet, with a #12 Humpy. I want a tippet with a bit more diameter—.007 (4X) will be my choice.

Let's work with the tippet till we get the result we're after. I'll tie the Humpy onto 30 inches of 4X, strip enough line out to load the rod tip, maybe 30 feet, check the cast high (stopping the rod sharply, overhead), then drop the elbow, then the rod tip to the water. The fly landed behind the leader; it collapsed. We'd better shorten the tippet a few inches, retie the fly, and check the cast again. That's it—now we have the soft curves of leader right up to the fly. The tippet length is 25 inches. We're ready to fish.

This is important—you must adjust the tippet according to the density of the fly. If the fly is a #22 Trico, then the tippet can be longer, maybe 3 feet, and the diameter smaller, .006 (5X) or .005 (6X). If the fly is larger, then the tippet can be shorter, the diameter greater. With a tippet that's too short and has too great a diameter, the tippet will straighten out, and that means drag. Work with the tippet and fly till you get those soft curves of leader right up to the fly. George Harvey feels strongly about this, and I know it will increase the number of fish that you rise.

What will our casting position be for this pool? Being a left-hander, I'll move off to the right side for casting freedom. We need to check for any obstacles we must work around, such as tree limbs or brush. We also must locate the major currents that bring the food to the fish. Trout like cover and often position where the main currents come close to cover. Your best casting approach might not be from behind on an upstream approach; it may be from the top of the pool or off to one side.

The main currents in this pool sweep down through the center, fan, then

What are the obstacles you must work around? Where are the major currents that come close to cover? Where is your best position for casting freedom? The main current in this pool sweeps through the center, fans, and flattens out; trout are sipping at the tail.

flatten out at the tail. Trout are sipping on top at the tail. We come in low, go slowly, and crouch on both knees. We'll get as close as we can without spooking the fish from behind. Close means better line control, less line on the water, and accuracy.

I can see one trout, a nice fish that is just under the surface. This trout is in a specific lie, a velocity change, and unless frightened it can hold in this position for hours. This fish knows exactly how insects drift to it; a fly dragging over or by it would be an alarm that would send the fish racing for the depth of the pool and safety.

I make the first cast behind the fish; if it turns for the fly it will see the fly and not the leader. The trout can feel the vibration as the fly hits the water. The fish turns but doesn't take; the cast was a little too far behind. The second cast is off to the side, at an angle, so if the trout turns it again will see the fly and not the leader. The cast was on target, but the trout was moving to a natural and didn't see the fly. It returns to its former position. The next cast is to the right of the fish and about 4 inches above it – this is where accuracy comes into play. The trout doesn't have a lot of time to make a decision if the fly is presented close to it. Too far above and the trout has too long to look at it, and there is a greater chance for drag to set in. And again the cast was made at an angle to the fish so that it would see the fly first but not the leader. The most common mistake is to cast up over the fish. If you line it you can put it down, but if you don't, the first thing the trout will see is the leader and not the fly. This is one reason some fish grow so large!

The trout lifts, tilts, and sucks the Humpy in. Subduing the fish doesn't take long. Getting an angle – using side pressure – and turning the trout's head first to one side, then the other, keeps the fish off balance and drastically changes its game plan for escape. The trout never really had a chance to get out of the starting blocks; it expends energy quickly and soon succumbs to the pressure of the rod. The trout is not exhausted, there is no great buildup of lactic acid within its system, and with the removal of the barbless hook, the trout slides into the depth of the pool to rest and hopefully live to perpetuate the species and to outslick another angler on another day.

Ahead of us lies broken water, midstream boulders forming a series of pockets that offer ideal holding water for trout. We will stay with the same leader – it's working well. We are wading upstream, and in broken water we can get closer to the fish. The casts are shorter, and the casting mechanics change.

I still shock the cast overhead, with that short, squeezing stroke, but now I drop the elbow and quickly drive the rod tip down to the water. This sudden level change stacks the leader and piles it in soft coils in the pocket. As soon as the leader collapses, I lift the rod tip high, lifting the line off the water, giving the fly and leader all kinds of drift time in the pocket. The fly floats naturally, even moving upstream to the top of the pocket and giving the trout time to find it. A longer rod (9 or 10 feet or even longer) is paramount to drift time. If the line is lifted over the major currents, there will be less line on the water for the currents to pull through—one key to an extended float—and the fly is held in the productive area longer.

The deerhair Humpy floats like a cork in the mixing pocket water, and each pocket produces either a rise or a hooked fish. It's exciting! Our leader is working, we've got a fly that is working, and the first cast in each pocket should rise a fish. We cover the water, but we don't pound it; a good drift in an area, and we move on. The more water covered the more fish we'll catch.

Above the riffs the water flattens, the river's main current swings to the left bank, and the water deepens next to the bank and glides under a canopy of pine and rhododendron boughs. It is here that the trout are rising under the protective cover of the foliage.

The water is clear here, and the depth of the water prevents me from positioning as close as I would like. I can't get as close to the fish as I did in the pocket water, so the casts will have to be longer. Now I must drift the rod tip farther forward, to the level of the boughs I must go under, before I make the casting stroke. It's the same short, squeezing stroke. The fly lifts on the cast and hangs on the limb I'm trying to go under. The leader is too long, and the tippet is too long for the density of the Humpy. I lose the fly, wade ashore, sit down on a log and adjust the leader, cut back the stiff mono sections, and shorten the tippet to 22 inches.

The density of the fly was far too air-resistant with the tippet and leader length. No matter what casting stroke you employ, if the tippet is too long for the density of the fly, it will lift on the cast—every time—and if you want to get back under the overhangs, you will be into everything but the water.

We're faced here with a tough casting challenge; there is but little space between the boughs and the water. No matter how tough a situation you're in, and how difficult the cast, even if it seems impossible, take a shot at it—it's the only way to learn. Sure, you may lose a fly—you should have two flies anyhow—but you may surprise yourself with a great cast; it's a confidence builder.

I get the fly back under the overhang, and it's a decent float, but I'm getting a refusal. Why? The trout are feeding steadily; has there been a change in the food chain? I strain to see what is on the water: blue-winged olives. In my anxiety to take those fish under the brush, I failed to observe what was happening around me, and the fish had changed what they were feeding on. I change to a size #18 Blue-Winged Olive. I also have to lengthen the tippet a couple of inches. I can still get under the brush, but with the density of the smaller fly, I can get longer float time with the adjustment.

Before I cast I'll watch the trout closest to me. The wings of the olives stand high enough for me to follow their drift. I'm watching flies drifting over the fish, and it is accepting them. Had I not seen the fly disappear in the wake of the rise, I would have switched to a nymph and fished it just under the surface. Trout have excellent vision. They see those flies drifting by, and if they are not intercepting them, the trout are telling you to switch to a nymph.

Finally, with nothing more than a squeeze of the rod handle on the forward cast, keeping the rod tip at the level of the limb to go under, not dropping it, I get the fly to the trout. The take is deliberate. I set the hook, and a sizable fish rolls on the surface. With side pressure I take it out from under the limb. The trout turns and bolts downstream, and pulls free.

To catch fish, you've got to be able to cast, and the secret of a good forward cast is a good backcast. One of the best casting tips I've ever received was from Ralph Dougherty, a retired surgeon and an all-American end for the University of Pittsburgh under Jock Sunderland in the late twenties. Ralph was a superb caster. On occasion Ralph and I would fish together. On one such trip I was

I'm watching individual flies. If I see one disappear in a rise, I'll stay with the dry fly. If the trout is rising and refusing floating mayflies, I'll switch to nymphs.

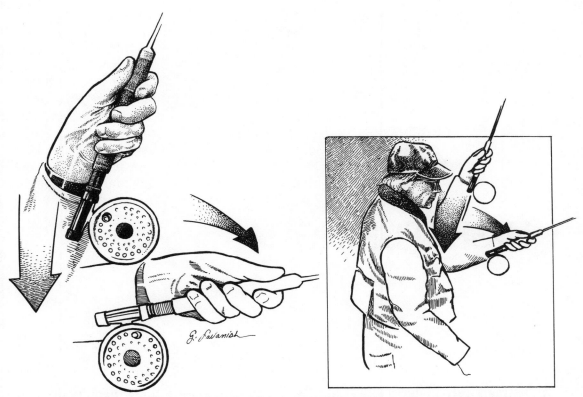

Check the cast—drop the elbow and rod tip—with a leader that will work and a fly that turns 'em on. Your catching is bound to increase.

having trouble distance-casting, holding the line up on the backcast. Ralph saw my problem and said, "Joe, climb the angle of the line with the fly rod. See the angle of the line as you lift it off the water, then take the rod tip right up that angle and stop it overhead." It solved the backcast problem and made me a better caster. It works for all techniques, including the ones used throughout these pages.

To cure tailing loops on the forecast, Ralph said, in his quiet manner, "Joe, just push your thumb down on the forward casting stroke; that takes the line over the rod tip." Bless you Ralph, and thanks.

6

NIGHT FISHING

It was a July night in 1975, and I was fishing a favorite long, deep pool on a Pennsylvania limestone stream, at 2 A.M. in the first phase of the moon. Other than the murmur of the riffle upstream mixed with summer night sounds, it was black and hushed.

Suddenly the tranquility was shattered by a watery explosion. I felt the hair on my neck rise. For a moment I thought a deer had leaped into the water, but when the quiet returned I knew that some hapless trout or sucker had fallen victim to a predatory brown.

I haunted that pool for the next two years, fishing in the late spring and summer, working big wet flies through the dark of the moon. On occasion I'd fish when the moon was full, either between 3 and 5 A.M. (when light is reduced), or when clouds obscured it. Darkness provides cover for big browns, and the food chain moves at night: Crayfish and sculpins are nocturnal, insects hatch at night, and baitfish are easier to trap in the dark.

My quest ended August 7, 1977. The water was at its summer low, but a light rain fell that dark evening, adding extra oxygen to the water, which can stir fish. My spirits were high. I'd taken a big brown of 6 pounds or so the night before. Lefty Kreh had needed some night photography for the *Baltimore Sun,* and the action gave him a story.

Al Haag accompanied me this time. He didn't want to fish, he said, just watch.

A riffle entered the pool at the top, and hemlock boughs on the far side of the stream were only a couple of feet off the water; behind them was an eddy. I worked the top with a pair of wet flies, from the riffle to where the pool flattened and deepened, and returned to the riffs for a second run-through. At night I'll fish a pool four or five times, and I'll cover the water slowly and carefully, giving fish more time to sense and locate the flies.

It behooves you to work a spot in daylight first to get to know the features of the pool and get a feel for the casting stroke – how far to drift the rod forward before the power stroke to get you under the limbs, for instance. In darkness, without this knowledge, you'll be into everything *but* the water.

Knowing your water also gives you confidence; you know where you can expect fish. The head and tail of a pool is usually productive. Trout slide back to the tail to lie in ambush for other fish or move to the riffs at the head of a pool, where crayfish and sculpins are abundant.

Knowing your water might be recognizing the sound of water dropping over a particular boulder, telling you exactly where to put yourself in relation to a hotspot or danger. Even the features of the bottom – gravel bars, ledges, and off-shaped stones – are landmarks you can feel in the dark with your feet as you wade.

I punched a pair of #1/0 wets behind the boughs, then lifted the rod and twitched the tip to set the flies in motion. The first order of business after the cast is to make sure the flies aren't hung up, then get them moving. (Often the disturbance of a fly hitting the water is the attention-getter, and that first twitch spurs the action.) My fly was designed by George Harvey back in the '30s; he showed it to me in the '50s, while I was in college, but swore me to secrecy till he published it in his book, *Techniques of Trout Fishing and Fly Tying.* George's "pusher" pattern has big goose-feather wings, cupped forward, that move back and forth with each lift of the rod tip.

I feel a night pattern should do two things: displace water so a trout can detect movement through its lateral line, and move *in* the water so when the trout does locate it, it's alive. I'm a firm believer in tying motion into a fly.

I go shorter than usual on the leader (6 feet) and heavy on the tippet – in this case, 10-lb. test. A long leader won't turn over a pair of big wet flies, and I want a tippet strong enough to pressure a big fish and land it. And I want a rod stiff enough to turn over a pair of #1/0 wets, too. My choice is a 9-foot rod for a DT6 floating line, unless casting is restricted, in which case I go with an

8-footer. In moving water, sinking lines belly and are impossible to control, and you sacrifice sensitivity — use a floater. Weight-forward lines can be used but are impractical because of the roll-casting that is imperative in many situations.

The cast was straight across the stream. I moved the rod tip with and ahead of the drift to keep the belly out of the line, to be in touch with the flies — too much slack on the water makes it difficult to set the hook, and you can't feel the flies as they drift. I held the rod vertically to allow for enough slack from rod tip to fly so the trout could inhale the fly. Trout don't grab, they inhale.

The drift was short-lived, stopping abruptly. I set the hook hard, and a heavy fish rolled and thrashed atop the water. Though the flies were close to the bottom, big fish, once hooked, tend to roll on top. "Did you hear that?" Al asked excitedly.

"Yeah," I answered. "That's my fish!"

The first run was a sizzler. The trout headed for a fallen tree halfway down the pool, but I applied side pressure and turned the fish's head to keep it off balance. Fish become disoriented at night once you turn them a couple of times, though not so in the daytime. The fish began to tire. It was directly before me when I felt the rod tip poke into the boughs overhead. I snapped on my flashlight to solve the problem, and when the light hit the water the trout dashed headlong downstream. I managed to free the rod, regain line control, and stop the run. I finally slid 34 inches and 16 pounds of brown trout into the shallows, got my arms under the fish and heaved it onto the bank. It was a Pennsylvania record, and remained so for eleven years. It is still a state fly-rod record.

What are the odds of taking a trophy fish at night? I mean a single fish that you spotted or learned of from another angler. I'm not talking about a group of big trout on a spawning run or some western or Alaskan river that has a population of big trout; I'm talking about a single behemoth that might inhabit your local waters.

If you have the time and patience and technique, with luck and persistence you might take him.

Big trout feed whenever light is reduced. During these times a trout may go on a binge and stuff itself in a forty-minute period, devouring a foot-long sucker, three crayfish, and a 6-inch chub; it may not feed again for three days. When the pool is deep and 50 yards long, what are your chances of getting your fly over that fish at the right time? And even if you put the fly over the fish, there's no guarantee it will take.

Add these other variables: A heavy rain that clouds the water and diffuses the light can be a turn-on in daytime but not at night, since off-color water at night inhibits a trout's vision. Heavy fog on the water is a turn-off too. I don't know if it affects the trout's vision or is related to barometric pressure, but I've never done well under such conditions. A sudden drop in water temperature also can quickly turn fish off. Long, hot days, with water temperatures in the 70s, can mean inactivity and migration. Barometric pressure changes from moving fronts can put fish down. And when conditions are perfect and your trophy is on the prowl, you can't always be there – your significant other might say, "No fishing tonight!"

One system has worked well for me many years at night: big wet flies.

Big fish don't expend that much energy – they usually trap their food rather than chase it. When fishing big wets, I ask myself one question: Am I getting my flies down to the fish? It has been my experience that the real heavyweights seldom cruise the top for food. They will lift off the bottom, where they spend 90 percent of their time, to intercept food, but for the most part they don't feed on top.

OK, you've made the cast, you've lifted the tip and twitched the flies, and now you're leading the flies through the drift. Slowly you retrieve, with a hand-twist. One, two, three, thumb and fingers slowly pick up the line, now twitch the rod and repeat. One, two, three, slowly gather line, twitch. The line straightens out below. Keep the rod tip up. Continue the three count and twitch the tip again. The line stops, you set the hook and for a brief moment don't know if the fish is 14 inches or a 34-inch leviathan. This thrill, this uncertainty is what keeps me coming back. *Is this one a trophy?*

A trout's night vision in waters with clarity has drastically changed my thinking, approach, and techniques when night fishing. Water temperatures and seasons also affect my night ventures.

Relative to trout and night vision, an early experience comes to mind. It was mid-May 1946, and I was seventeen. A sulphur hatch was in progress on Spring Creek in central Pennsylvania, and fish were rising everywhere. I managed to take only a couple of small fish, but I doggedly hung on till after dark, well after the surface activity ceased. The pool was at the railroad trestle at Oak Hall, a deep one with sunken logs on the bottom – great cover for trout. Because of the lack of surface-feeding trout, I had changed from a dry fly to a #12 Dark Cahill wet fly.

I positioned myself at the head of the pool and let my fly swing down and across the pool, then retrieved it slowly with a hand-twist retrieve. I was a persistent kid, and even though I had little hope or expectation of catching a fish, I fished on, until I was finally rewarded – the line became taut, a fish had hooked itself, and I landed a foot-long brown trout. A fitting reward for patience. On the bicycle trip home that night I couldn't help but wonder how the trout could see that fly, as dark as it was.

Years later, in the summer of 1957, a happening on Penns Creek reinforced my belief that trout have excellent vision in darkness.

I was fishing for trout using big wet flies, with marginal success. I was positioned below an eel wall that ran across the stream. These walls were stones piled upon each other forming a V, with the water funneled to the apex of the V. In the days before the construction of the hydro dam on the Susquehanna River, eels and migratory fish worked their way from the Chesapeake Bay into the Susquehanna River and its tributaries, including Penns Creek. The eel walls had been built by the early settlers to trap fish.

The water behind me and above the wall was higher, being dammed by the stonework, and was nearly at eye level. I had been concentrating on the pockets below the wall, but the sound of splashing fish directed my attention to activity behind me. Faintly in the night light I could catch the flecks of broken water from a rise. These fish were feeding steadily, but on what? Using a fine mesh net, I trapped tiny insects from the flow. They were Tricorythodes duns. It wasn't until years later that I learned that the duns of the Trico basically hatched at night, but what I learned that night was that trout, in total darkness, can spot minute insects — insects that can be imitated on size #22 and #24 hooks.

I firmly believe that though a trout does not have the range of vision at night it has in daylight, it has excellent vision in a restricted area — a distinct window.

This understanding ties directly to tactics and catching fish. Hence my early successes with wet flies at night, particularly when there was hatching activity. Matching the basic size of the nymph has enabled me to catch more and larger fish than I could on top with a dry fly. With wet flies you can cover more water, and wet flies twitched or drifted over surface feeders can be quite effective.

When fishing the green drake hatch, for example, use a pair of #8 wet flies tied on 2X long hooks constructed with duck quill wings, a dark tan head hackle, a straw-colored body, palmered with a dark tan hackle. The technique is a down-and-across stream presentation, pulsating the rod tip to give the flies action. Don't look only for surface-feeding fish, but cover the water. When fishing a sulphur hatch, use a pair of Dark Cahill wets, with the same technique, and cover the water.

A pair of wet flies during a stonefly hatch can be big-time producers. Tie the fly on a #6 or #8 2X long or 3X long shank hook with either tan or olive kip tail wings, a dark-brown hen hackle for the head, an orange or yellow chenille body, palmered with a dark-brown hackle. These big, meaty wets imitate the nymphs as they crawl and undulate toward the shoreline or crawl up on logs and midstream boulders.

Use a down-and-across stream drift, leading the flies with the rod tip, and bouncing the rod tip. This well imitates the movement of these big nymphs, and because they migrate to shore, I work the flies along and near the bank, as well as around in-stream boulders, logs, and debris. These nymphs crawl up on objects as they leave the water to hatch into terrestrial insects.

Wet flies in sizes #14, #12, #10, and #8 are producers at night. In most streams there is some kind of hatching activity during the summer. I'll fish wet flies in the above sizes as long as I can still wade a stream, but in the late spring and summer months when the water temperatures can hold in the mid and high 60s, trout can be more active. The big fish chase more—they move for food—and at this time I work bigger flies: #4, #2, #1, #1/0, #2/0. When their metabolism is in gear and their body tissues need nourishment, big fish go for a mouthful. They can kill and devour a foot-long sucker and a 9-inch trout, with a side order of three crayfish. It is amazing how much they can inhale, and they may not feed again for three days. If you can locate a big fish and stay with it long enough, sooner or later you should raise it, so be persistent.

Back in 1954, I was in George Harvey's angling class at Penn State University. One evening while visiting him, he asked me if I wanted to see some big fish. I agreed, and he took me to a butcher shop located on the banks of Spring Creek and with his flashlight pointed out a line of brown trout in the 18- to 24-inch class, all lined up at the discharge pipe that entered the stream. The butcher shop was illegally dumping the refuse from the shop at night by simply pushing the blood, innards, and meat scraps into the stream, and those big browns were lined up for the smorgasbord. The butcher shop no longer exists—something about a run-in with the authorities!

Then George said to me, "I'll show you a fly that will catch those fish, but only if you promise not to show it to anyone." I promised and was sworn to secrecy. Then in his book *Techniques of Trout Fishing and Fly Tying*, published in 1985 by Metz Hatchery in Belleville, Pennsylvania, George told how to tie and fish the fly. It's called the Harvey Pusher fly. This fly pushes water and has great movement.

I only ever took one of those trout below that pipe on that fly, but I've taken hundreds of trout with it since—including the Pennsylvania state record trout in 1977. That record has since been broken, but it is still the largest fly-caught trout in open waters in Pennsylvania.

Okay then, for the most part, big flies for big trout, but not always! Seasons, water temperatures, and conditioning can also dictate the size of the fly.

In December 1990, Michigander Tom Johnson and I, along with Reid

Once their metabolism is in gear at optimum temperatures and they need nourishment, big fish go for a mouthful, like a #1/0 or #2/0 fly. *Photo by Paul Blankenhorn.*

Sigety, another fine Michigan angler, headed for the White River in Arkansas. Tom had fished the river before under the same conditions and had a handle on the technique. We were after big browns on the spawning run, strictly catch and release, with barbless hooks. I wanted photographs, and I had a preconceived notion that a pair of size 1/0 Harvey Pusher flies would be just the ticket for those big fish. But nothing could have been farther from the truth.

By the end of the second unsuccessful night, I was asking Tom the secret of his success. Fly size was the answer. Those fish were not chasing; water temperatures below the tailrace in that cold December night air were down, and those fish had other things on their mind: the reproduction of the species. They were spawning and they were not about to chase anything. They would move over to pick up a fly but not chase. Second, the food chain to which they were conditioned in that environment consisted of sculpins, shrimp, and cress bugs, and the bulk of the sculpin population was smaller sculpins. These trout in the 3- to 12-pound class wanted small flies and became downright finicky. On our

With level line of small diameter—running line—you can cover a greater area, roll the bottom in deep, fast water, and reach fish you've never reached before. Such as this one. *Photo by Tom Johnson.*

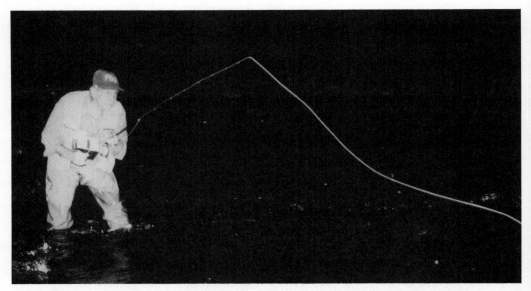

A short tuck or a down and upper cast is used to get the nymph on the bottom right off the cast.

last night they refused a #8 pattern, and it wasn't until we geared down to a #10 regular shank pattern that we began to catch fish. This was a conditioned response: We had hooked and released many fish on #8 patterns, and they began to back off from #8s.

The night technique we employed was the Dai-Riki Sci-Angler Slime Line system using caterpillars (slinkies) for the weight. This technique is one of touch and feel; you adjust the weight by its feel on the bottom. You can feel the weight slowly tic-tic-ticking along the bottom. That is the drift you are striving for—a slow, natural roll. And the take! You can, if you are in touch, feel the trout mouth the fly; the drift may stop, or you may feel the heavy tug of a deliberate take, but at times it's a subtle take—you just sense it.

Night fishing the bottom employs two basic approaches: the system just described, which is based on feel, or one that is a combination of sight and feel. Yes, sight at night! At night you can get closer to the fish, and when nymphing with a conventional fly line, you stay with a short line, covering a distance no longer than 20 feet, preferably shorter, from the rod tip to the nymph. You can't control more line than that. Even in total darkness, if your fly line is light in color or has a fluorescent glow, as most fly lines do today, you will be able to see the line.

Keep the rod high off the cast; elevate the rod tip as the line comes back to you–this keeps you in touch with the nymph on the bottom, and with the rod tip elevated you have better visibility. If you are using two nymphs, the top nymph off the dropper rides high, and if the trout are moving up this doubles your chances. Lead the nymph through the drift with the rod tip. In most cases the fly line and a portion of the leader is showing, depending on the length of leader and the depth of the water. In deeper water, the front portion of the fly line can be immersed.

Use a tuck cast or a down-and-upper, keep your elbow in along your side, and use your wrist. This prevents you from pushing with the arm on the cast and taking the energy from the rod tip. It's the wrist that makes these casts work.

The rod tip is high on the execution of the cast (eleven o'clock) *and remains up* upon the completion of the cast. Now you have an angle from rod tip to nymph and are in touch with the nymph practically off the cast. Quickly pick

The rod tip stays up and I have visibility of the line and line control from rod tip to nymph.

up the slack line until you feel the nymph on the bottom. Lead the nymph through the drift slowly elevating the rod, and at the same time use either a strip or a hand-twist retrieve to keep the line taut. The retrieve you should use depends on the speed of the water. If the water is fast, stripping is better; if there is not a lot of current, a hand-twist retrieve is the most effective. You are not using much line, so the line intake is limited.

The weight adjustment for the depth and speed of the water is a combination of weight tied within the nymph or nymphs plus weight added on the leader. The result of the proper balance is a slow, rolling, bouncing, natural drift.

In most cases, trout are more deliberate when they are feeding at night, and the take can be easy to detect. The line may abruptly stop, but that is not always the case; sometimes the drift of the line simply slows, or there is a slight hesitation, or you sense the take. If the take is solid, you may feel the fish, but

And after a short drift, I'm into a trout. *Photos by Katharine Holsworth.*

A most enjoyable and productive night venture is nymphing the riffs and pockets when there is hatching activity. *Photo by Katharine Holsworth.*

this type of fishing takes the ultimate in concentration, sight and feel working together in unison.

One of the most enjoyable and productive night ventures is nymphing the riffs and pockets when there is good hatching activity. The food chain is moving, and so are the trout. While many trout are surface feeding, some of the best fish are on the bottom.

So many times when the surface activity stops there is an exodus of fly fishers leaving the waters. But in actuality the fishing is not over, it's prime time. Nymphs continue to move, the trout have been conditioned to the nymphal activity, and the food chain in part is nocturnal. Sculpins, crayfish, and nymphs all move at night.

If the stream is fertile, there is nymphal movement throughout the year. Various mayflies hatch throughout the summer months, and in most limestone waters there are either cress bugs or shrimp or both year-round. I've had some enjoyable fishing at night on limestone waters even in the winter in Pennsylvania.

My first night nymphing began in the early fifties with the green drake hatch on Penns Creek. An army of anglers had fished into the darkness, but once the hatching ceased and the flies left the water, the fly fishers left.

I was convinced that I could take a fish after the hatch ended, but I worked wet flies for an hour without success, and my enthusiasm waned. *Why not drift a nymph on the bottom? What do I have to lose?* I thought. I rigged a pair of Green Drake nymphs 2 feet apart with enough split-shot between them to get the flies to the bottom, and used the mono system for the line. There wasn't any guess-work when the trout took, and I landed a fine 16-inch brown trout. Two others followed, and I was beside myself with excitement. It was a major break-through in my angling tuition.

After that experience, I began working over trout during the hatches from mid-May and on into the summer nights. I used nymphs as small as #16 and #14, but for the most part #12s worked the best.

A #12 pattern tied with a partridge tail, tan fur dubbing, ribbed with brass wire, loosely dubbed dark-brown fur for the wing case, and partridge fibers tied in on either side for the wings and flattened makes for a nymph that has good movement in the water. The flattened nymph rocks back and forth as the currents interplay across it. This sulphur nymph imitation has been effective from mid-May to early fall.

When night nymphing I alternate between two systems. If I'm working riffs, pockets, or glides that have limited depth (say 3 feet or less), I go with a fly line—a light color or fluorescent double taper 6-weight, which has a diameter heavy enough for visibility, yet a taper light enough to handle the casting and control of the nymph. In pools or deep glides I'll switch to a running line, be it Slime Line, monofilament, or a 1- or 2-weight level fly line, and either weight it with a slinky (caterpillar) or add split-shot between the nymphs.

THE TOP

Other than fishing the major hatches on top, I've commented little about fishing the surface at night.

The bulk of the food chain is down on the bottom—suckers, trout, crayfish, sculpins, and nymphs give fish a variety of choices. Big trout may cruise and pick off what is in front of them—on the bottom. The greatest percentage of big trout I've taken have been under the surface, so for the most part I've stayed with that.

Sure I've tried deerhair frogs, deerhair bugs, and mouse patterns but have had limited success, raising only a few leviathans at night.

One top-water technique that does produce and has merit in the summer months is to drag, down and across or across and down, an Ed Shenk cricket pattern. Ed Shenk uses this tactic very effectively. Live crickets take trout and have long been used by the bait fishermen, who even rigged a harness for them, made a double hook system, and worked them on top and under.

Cast out and across, lift the rod tip, and drag and skitter the cricket. The wake of the dragging fly is an attention-getter, and I've had trout hit behind the fly, missing it. At times I've held the cricket in one spot to give trout a chance to find it. Work the fly slowly across the currents and be ready when it straightens below you; trout sometimes follow the fly and pounce on it when it stops. I've also taken trout on it on a dead drift.

It's a fun way to fish. The rise can be explosive or subtle. As with hunting rabbits, you never know when you're going to jump one.

ONE NIGHT'S STRATEGY

Okay, now for some night-fishing strategy—the thought process during a night's fishing.

At the edge of darkness, work wet flies. Earlier in the evening a few flies are still airborne—a few *Potamanthus* (a big sulphur), a couple of large *Hexagenia,* and some small sulphurs. Enough activity to let you know there is sufficient nymphal activity on the bottom and emerging to the top to stir trout.

Put on a brace of wet flies, a Sulphur wet pattern, and a darker tail fly, a Dark Cahill, #12 patterns first. Into darkness change to dark flies in larger sizes, #8s.

If the wets are not producing, and it won't take you long to realize, switch to a pair of nymphs, both Sulphurs, a #12, on a dropper 2 feet and the bottom nymph a #10 30 inches up from the tail fly. Work a short line and concentrate on the riffs, or where a riff enters a deep hole.

Near midnight the big fish begin to cruise in the cover of darkness, their security blanket. Now work a pair of Harvey Pusher flies, 2 feet apart, #4 at first and later a pair of #1s or #1/0s.

The action slows. Now use a rod previously rigged with the long line, the level line, be it a Slime Line or a 1-weight level fly line. Adjust the weight of the slinky or caterpillar and roll a pair of black nymphs on the bottom, woollybuggers or wigglers; you are prospecting and covering more water, a greater area.

As daylight is just beginning to break, perhaps you can catch a big fish out before it returns to hiding. Using a single Shenk Sculpin, a shot on its nose, on either the long line or a double-taper fly line, work the guts, tails of pools, and around cover.

Then it's ham, eggs, toast, and coffee.

INDEX

American River, South Fork, 35
approaches, brush fishing, 146, 148–49; dry-fly fishing, 122; night fishing, 171–73, 180–84
Arawjo, Daryl, 23, 79, 83, 100
Armstrong Spring Creek (Montana), 25
Au Sable River (Michigan), 47
Avalanche Lake (Glacier National Park), 24

backcasting, brush fishing, 156, 239
Bergman, Ray, 93
Betsey River (Michigan), 47
big-river systems, nymphing, 202–3
Black Gnat, fly, 101
Blankenhorn, Paul, 91, 198
Blue Quill patterns, 134
bottom fishing, wet flies, 96–99
bottom streamers, 107
brook trout, effect of oxygen loss on, 23; feeding temperatures, 21, 23–24
Brown, Bob, 24
Brown Drake hatches, 171, 173
brown trout, effect of oxygen loss on, 23; feeding temperatures, 21
brushy streams: casting strategy for, 207–8; nymphing, 206–8

Cahill hatches, 171; Dark Cahill fly, 101
casting and approach, brush fishing, 146–62
casting, dry flies, 122–24, 126–27, 133–34, 219–23; drop, 229; tips for, 239
casting techniques: for brushy streams, 207–8; for lip currents, 228–31; for night fishing, 248–50; for pocket water, 194–98; for sight fishing, 200–2

casting, tuck, 50–54, 191–92; downer-and-upper, 54–56, 58; rolling tuck, 57, 60–62; tuck and mend, 57–58, 63
casting, wet flies, 86
casts: down-and-upper, 249; drop, 229; hook, 222; parachute, 220–22; reach, 220; snake, 220; straight, 229; tuck, 191–92, 249; underhand lift, 230
Chavez, Tim, 205, 206
check cast, dry flies, 127–28
circle cast, brush fishing, 152–56
circle push cast, brush fishing, 158
circle roll cast, brush fishing, 157
Clarks Creek (Pennsylvania), 24
Close, George, 93
conditioning, 188–90; effect on trout, 23; effect on hatchery trout, 24
Cortland's Nymph Tip, 58; Cobra monofilament, 59
count-and-retrieve system, with wet flies, 98
cress-bug fly, 67
current velocities, 71–72
curve cast, brush fishing, 154–56; open loop, 160
cutoff point, in trout migration, 33–34

Dai-Riki Sci-Angler Slime Line system, 248
Dark Cahill fly, 101
Delaware River, East Branch, 34–35; West Branch, 34–35
Dougherty, Ralph, 143, 162, 238, 239
down-and-across cast, night fishing, 174
down-and-upper cast, 249
downer-and-upper tuck cast, nymph fishing, 54–56, 175
downstream-and-across casting, for wet flies, 89
downstream cast, short-line, pocket-water, for wet flies, 97; straight, for wet flies, 95–96
downstream drift cast, for wet flies, 94–95

downstream riff technique, 177
drag, prevention of, 123, 153
drifts, natural, 91–92, 94–95; speed of, 107
drop-and-drift cast, brush fishing, 159
drop cast, for dry flies, 129–30, 229
droppers, tying, 102–3
dry flies, leaders for, 140–42, 223–27; lip currents and, 227–31; on-stream strategy for, 232–39; patterns, 227; selection of, 134–38; tippets for, 141–42, 234–35; tying, 138–40
dry-fly fishing, 119; casting, 122–23, 127–30, 219–23, 239; fly selection, 134–38; mapping the stream, 119–20; on-the-bank approach, 122

Experti, Bob, 216

feeding activity of trout, effect of water-temperature fluctuation on, 25
feeding habits of trout, 168
feeding temperatures for trout, 23–24, 187, 189
flat-bodied nymph, 73
flies, adding movement to, 178–79
float time, 219
fly casting, brush fishing, 152
fly selection, 205–6
forecast, tailing loops on, 239
freestone streams, arrangement of fish in, 144–46; length of leader for, 124; mountain, 46; profile of, 38; types of baitfish in, 106

Green Drake hatches, 22–23, 170–74
Green Drake nymph, fly, 70

hackles, oversize, 136–38; three-hackle fly, 138–39, 141
Haag, Al, 137–38, 241
hand-twist retrieves, for nymphing, 64–65; for streamers, 109–10
HANNA Instrument Co., 190
Hartswick, Max, 217
Hartswick, Tom, 217
Harvey, George, 17, 21, 48–49, 54, 104, 121, 140–42, 162, 210, 223, 225, 227, 235, 241, 245
Harvey Pusher fly, 245
Harvey's Stonefly nymph, 69
hatchery trout, 190
hatches, 134–38; Green Drake, 22–23, 170–74; Hexagenia, 171, 173; White Fly, 171
hatching patterns, 173–74
heavyweight nymph, 76–77
Hendrickson patterns, 134
Hexagenia hatches, 171, 173
hook cast, 222
hooks, for night fishing, 179
Humpies, no-tail, 232

imitation, wet-fly, 99–102
insects, terrestrial, 135–37

Johnson, Tom, 245, 247

Kennedy, William, 189
Kerstetter, Butch, 202
Kettle Creek (Pennsylvania), 19
Kreh, Bernard "Lefty," 17, 241
Krumrine, Don, 99

leaders, for brush fishing, 158, 160; for dry flies, 124, 126, 140–42, 151, 223–27; George Harvey's formula for, 104, 225, 232–34; for night fishing, 161, 170, 175, 241; for nymphing, 62; for use in pocket water, 194; for wet flies, 103–4
Letort Creek (Pennsylvania), 25
lightweight nymph, 76–77
limestone streams, 39–44; types of baitfish in, 106
lines, for nymphing, 58–59; for wet flies, 103–4
lip currents, 227–31; casting techniques for, 228–31
lip-hooking minnows with natural drift, 107–8
live-minnow technique, 112
locating trout, for night fishing, 165–67, 170
low-profile approach, brush fishing, 146
Loyalsock Creek (Pennsylvania), 30, 33

McCullough, Vance, 204
Manistee River (Michigan), 47
mapping the stream, for dry-fly fishing, 119–20
Matthews, Larry, 202
mending, 219, 222–23
middle-weight nymph, 76–77
migration of trout, 32–33; cutoff point, 33–34
Miller, Tom, 34, 44, 89, 105, 163
Milliron, Miles, 98
minnows, lip-hooking, 107–8; live-minnow technique, 112; "strung" minnow technique, 110–11
monofilament, advantages of, 112–13; casting, 59

night fishing: casting techniques, 248–50; deep glides, 252; leaders for, 241; nymphing the riffs and pockets, 251–52; pools, 252; rods for, 241; strategy, 253; surface, 252; tippets for, 241; wet flies for, 243, 244–45
night-nymphing leader, 174
night pattern, 241
no-weight nymph, 75, 77
nymph and crustacean designs, 65–70
nymph fly, emerging, 68
nymphing, in big waters, 202–3; a brushy stream, 206–8; fly selection, 205–6; hooks for, 74; leader-and-weight system for, 59; leaders for, 62; leaders for night fishing, 175; lines for, 58–59; in pockets, 191–98, 251–52; riffs, 251–52; short-line, for night fishing, 176; by sight, 198–202; upstream casting, 56–57; weight selection, 204–5
nymphs, effect of current velocities on, 71–72; for night fishing, 174–76; weighting, 71, 74–83

on-the-bank approach, with dry flies, 122
open-loop cast, dry flies, 129, 131
open-loop curve cast, brush fishing, 154–56, 160
oxygen, effect on trout, 23, 187–88

parachute cast, 220–22
Parmachene Belle, 101
Penns Creek (Pennsylvania), 24, 44, 202, 244, 252
Pennsylvania Fish Commission, 189
Pere Marquette River (Michigan), 22, 47
pH, 190; levels, 189–90
pocket water, 191–98; casting strategy for, 194–98; leaders for use in, 194; nymphing, 251–52; weights for use in, 192–94
push cast, dry flies, 127, 129

Quill Gordon patterns, 134

rainbow trout, effect of oxygen loss on, 23; feeding
    temperatures, 21
Rajeff, Steve, 202
reach cast, 220
red-fin streamer, 115
retrieves, 64–65; hand-twist, 64–65, 109–10; streamers,
    109; strip-line, 64–65, 110
riffs, nymphing, 251–52
rod-line angle, with wet flies, 87–88
rods, for night fishing, 241
roll cast, brush fishing, 157
rolling tuck cast, nymph fishing, 57, 60–62
Rote, Les, 107, 112, 202
round-bodied nymphs, 75
Royal Coachman, fly, 96

Sacramento River (California), 35
San Juan River (New Mexico), 189, 205, 206
Scheffler, Jack, 89
Schreffler, Clyde, 84–85, 210
sculpin imitations, 107–9, 174, 176–77; weighting, 109
S-curve leaders, 125
Shenk, Ed, 109, 111, 252
short-line casting, wet flies, 90
short-line nymphing, night fishing, 176
Sigety, Reid, 245–47
sight fishing, 198–202; casting strategies for, 200–2
Silver Doctor; fly, 96
sink holes, 42–43
sinking and lifting, 99
sinking lines, for nymphing, 59
sinking-tip lines, for nymphing, 59
skittering technique, for wet flies, 92–93
Smith, Buff, 22
snake cast, 220
Snake River (Wyoming), 119
Spring Creek (Pennsylvania), 84–85, 87, 92, 187, 209, 243
spring holes, locations of, 39, 41–42
Spruce Creek, 223
straight cast, for dry flies, 229
straight downstream cast, for wet flies, 95–96
straight leaders, 125
streamers, floating line, 114; night fishing, 174; red-fin,
    115; techniques for, 214–16; working upstream, 109
streams, coastal, types of baitfish in, 106
strip-line retrieve, nymphing, 64–65; streamers, 110
"strung" minnow technique, 110–11
sulphurs, hatches, 171; types of, 134
super-heavyweight nymph, 76–77
surface fishing, night, 252
surface nymph, 75
Swarts, Dunson, and Wright, 189
switch casting, brush fishing, 156, 158

tackle, for brush fishing, 158, 160–61; for night fishing,
    165, 170–71
Techniques of Fly Tying and Trout Fishing (Harvey), 241,
    245
thermometers, importance of, 19–20, 22, 26, 119
Thompson Run (Pennsylvania), 198
three-hackle fly, 138–39, 141, 149
three-fly system, 102–3
tight-loop cast, for night fishing, 166
tip-action approach, downstream, for wet flies, 88–89
tippets, 234–35; for dry flies, 126, 141–42; for night
    fishing, 241
tributaries, locating, 25–26
Tricorythodes duns, 244
trophy fish, 242–43
trout, effect of conditioning on, 23–24, 188–90; effect of
    oxygen on, 23, 187–88; effect of water-temperature
    fluctuation on, 20–23, 25, 187–89; feeding habits,
    168; feeding temperatures, 23–24, 187, 189; hatchery,
    190; locating for night fishing, 165–67, 170;
    migrations, 32–34; night vision, 243–44; pecking
    order, 231; positions in pool, 165–67; water chemistry
    effects on, 189–90
tuck cast, 50–54, 63, 191–92, 249; downer-and-upper,
    54–56, 58; rolling, 57, 60–62; for streamers, 108;
    tuck-and-mend, 57–58, 63

underhand lift cast, with dry flies, 130, 132, 230
upstream approach, brush fishing, 148–49
upstream casting with natural drift, for wet flies, 89–91,
    96; straight, for wet flies, 97

water chemistry, effect on trout, 189–90
water clarity, importance of, 121
water temperature, effect on trout, 20–23, 187–89; in
    freestone streams, 38; for night fishing, 167–68;
    patterns of, 35–37; fluctuation in early season, 25–29;
    fluctuation in mid- and late season, 30–32
weather conditions, for night fishing, 168–69
Weaver, Lewie, 17, 107, 112, 116–17, 202, 216
weighted flies on droppers, 80
weight-forward lines, 103–4
weights, selecting, 204–5; for use in pocket water, 192–94
wet flies, night fishing, 174, 177–83, 243, 244–45; reasons
    for using, 211–12; sizes, 245–48; techniques for, 211
White Fly hatches, 171
White River (Arkansas), 189, 247
Wise River (Montana), 66
Woods, Craig, 66
Woolly Worm, fly, 175
Wright, Phil, Jr., 66

Yellow Breeches (Pennsylvania), 163–64, 188
Youngman, John, 48
Young Woman's Creek (Pennsylvania), 121